FROM *Sugar* CAMPS TO *Star* BARNS

FROM *Sugar* CAMPS TO *Star* BARNS

Rural Life and Landscape in a Western Pennsylvania Community

Sally McMurry

THE PENNSYLVANIA STATE UNIVERSITY PRESS ★ UNIVERSITY PARK, PENNSYLVANIA

This book has been aided by a grant from Furthermore, the publication program of The J. M. Kaplan Fund.

Library of Congress Cataloging-in-Publication Data

McMurry, Sally Ann, 1954–
    From sugar camps to star barns : rural life and landscape in a
western Pennsylvania community / Sally McMurry.
        p.   cm.
    Includes bibliographical references.
    ISBN 0-271-02107-1 (alk. paper)—ISBN 0-271-02108-x
        (pbk. : alk. paper)
    1. Somerset County (Pa.)—Social life and customs. 2. Country
life—Pennsylvania—Somerset County. 3. Somerset County
(Pa.)—Rural conditions. 4. Landscape—Social aspects—
Pennsylvania—Somerset County—History. 5. Vernacular
architecture—Pennsylvania—Somerset County—History.
6. Somerset County (Pa.)—Economic conditions. I. Title.

F157.S6 M38 2001
974.8'79—dc21

                                        00-140099

for my mother

Margaret Gifford McMurry

★

★ *contents*

★ list of illustrations

★ acknowledgments

This book originated as a narrative report for a local architectural survey, a piece of "gray literature," as it's known in preservationists' language. In the early 1990s, the Somerset Historical Center undertook a Vernacular Architecture Survey. After a "windshield" survey of the county, teams of workers carefully recorded the entire building complex for several dozen farmsteads—measuring buildings; conducting deed searches and oral histories and seeking other forms of documentation; dating where possible; and making extensive notes on construction techniques, building sequence, and the like. The result was a rich mine of data on local farm buildings—not only barns and houses, but also seldom-considered outbuildings, such as springhouses and sugar camps. The original narrative combined this remarkable data with primary and secondary material on the county's agricultural history in order to fashion an interpretation of the county's vernacular architecture. It attracted state and national attention and was awarded several honors. Thinking that this worthy venture, a collaboration between academia and a local historical organization, ought to receive still wider exposure in a more accessible published form, I proposed to turn the narrative into a well-illustrated book. The Somerset Historical Center warmly endorsed the project, and this volume is the result.

I would above all like to point out that this book has been made possible by the assiduous data gathering and survey work of Somerset Historical Center staff, of consultants, and of summer interns. It builds on work done by Barbara Budde, Lynn David, David Dunn, Pamela Hickey, Beth Holler, Cynthia Mason, Frank McKelvey, Sanford Rikoon, Chris Schrock, Mark Ware, Langdon Wright, and Emily Wright. Without their help I could not have completed this narrative, and I thank them. I would also like to thank the current Somerset Historical Center staff—especially Sue Seese, Bernice Sarver, Barbara Black, and Charlie Fox—for their help and hospitality while I worked on this project. My own role has been to conduct further research in both primary and secondary materials, to attempt to place the buildings into an appropriate context, and to locate more illustrative material. The interpretations presented here are my own. Bernard Herman and Gabrielle Lanier furnished helpful contextual and conceptual material in a one-day workshop in Lancaster County in 1994. Penetrating comments from Bernie and from Dan Freas (in the capacity of manuscript readers) pushed me to think even more carefully about the wider implications of this research, and I appreciate their rigor. Peter Potter and Laura Reed-Morrisson have been encouraging and thoughtful editors, and working with them has been an immense pleasure. Whatever faults remain in the book surely are my responsibility and not theirs.

Many people, some of whom I have never actually met, also helped me as I tried to track down materials. I would like to thank Charlotte Tancin of the Hunt Institute for Botanical Documentation in Pittsburgh and Jacqueline Bonnemains of the Charles Alexandre Lesueur collection in Le Havre, France. I spent a delightful day roaming the Somerset hills with Lu Donnelly and David Brumble of the Heinz Architectural Center. Robert Ensminger alerted me to an important published diary, and through that, I was fortunate enough to make contact with Kay Rhoads. The staff of the Penn State libraries, especially Sandy Stelts, rendered cheerful assistance at a most difficult time in the life of the libraries. The Penn State College of the Liberal Arts, through a research grant, funded some of the costs of reproducing illustrations. I also benefited from using the latter part of a sabbatical in 1992–93 to get the project under way. Gregg Roeber furnished valuable bibliographical assistance along the way, and Mike Sherbon of the Pennsylvania State Archives provided admirably efficient and timely help in getting images from those collections.

As always, my family—Barry, Paul, and Eric—supported the project with a bountiful supply of cheery patience, and I thank them.

★ *introduction*

Pennsylvania is one of the most rural states in the nation; 31 percent (or 3,658,000) of its 11.8 million people live in rural places.[1] Two of the state's two major economic enterprises, tourism and agriculture, both rely directly on the rural environment for their continued sustenance. Thousands of visitors come to Pennsylvania each year not only to visit the great cities of Philadelphia and Pittsburgh but also to get a taste of the state's rich farming country, immortalized—or perhaps caricatured—in countless tea-towel and calendar images of "hex" barns, solid farmhouses, and covered bridges. Rural Pennsylvania exerts an enduring attraction partly because it seems exotic to a citizenry now remote from any sort of everyday knowledge about how food is produced. But the rural landscape's visual appearance, too, has a powerful appeal. Myth-making nostalgia and overt distortion surely play a role in making the countryside scenery so attractive, but there are also deeper reasons for its charm. The landscapes of rural Pennsylvania possess qualities we often miss in today's standardized, disposable architecture: human scale, careful craftsmanship, harmony with fields and plantings, and locally distinctive forms. In short, historic rural landscapes are evocative, richly textured testimonies to the lives and skills of generations of vernacular builders. The term "vernacular" here refers to buildings and other landscape elements (such as field patterns and fencing) constructed not by professional architects but by local builders, craft workers, and users in accordance with accumulated, shared cultural knowledge. Vernacular building tends toward refinement of proven solutions; vernacular construction tends toward materials that age gracefully. The result is that, very often, vernacular buildings come to be cherished.[2] Over time, vernacular builders evolve spaces and landscapes that are comfortable, harmonious, adaptable, and aesthetically of a piece with the cultures they express. In short, they produce well-defined and easily recognizable places. A true sense of place—an increasingly elusive concept in our Internet age—marks vernacular landscapes.

This book is the story of one such place, a landscape that evolved in a corner of southwestern Pennsylvania known as Somerset County. The book grew out of an award-winning Vernacular Architecture Survey conducted by staff at the Somerset Historical Center (a site of the Pennsylvania Historical and Museum Commission). The fruitful collaboration that ensued between local initiatives and academic participants can be a model for others seeking to document their own local landscapes. I hope that this book will prove helpful to preservationists, planners, local historical organizations, and indeed to any citizens who are interested in stewardship of our historical resources. I have tried to keep this audience in mind as I have told this story: it is framed in a narrative fashion, informed by scholarly debates—but, I hope, not obtrusively so.

This is a local story, concerned with the particulars of landscape evolution in a specific geographic location. Yet on another level, the story is not local at all, for the same basic elements shaped rural landscapes all over America, with variations in geography, soils, climates, and peoples. While Somerset's people developed a predominantly Pennsylvania German building vocabulary, Hudson Valley farm families created a Dutch-American landscape and New Englanders invented the connected farm complex. All were local responses to larger forces. This book explores how the men and women of Somerset County confronted the challenges of establishing settlements in the eighteenth century, the "market revolution" that transformed the economy in the nineteenth century, and industrialization in the twentieth. A forest people in the early days of the republic, Somerset folk soon became a farming people and created a rich agricultural landscape; then, with the rise of coal mining, the county's rural landscape showed industrial influences. Throughout, vernacular designers continually adapted buildings, fields, and forests in a continually unfolding dialogue. The voices in this conversation were not always in harmony; conflict, as well as cooperation, shaped the land. Nevertheless, the outcome—more often than not— has been an enduring sense of place.

I ⋆ *A Forest People, 1780–1820*

In 1795, just as the new American republic began its struggle to assert itself, Somerset County, Pennsylvania, was formally established. In retrospect, the decades from 1790 to about 1820 seem full of promise and vitality. American manufacturing, still in its early stages, was gathering momentum. Overseas markets for grain were gaining strength. An expanding population portended a vigorous domestic market. Despite the nation's embarrassing lack of international credibility and the worrisome tendency toward partisanship in domestic politics, most citizens were optimistic about the new nation's prospects. The American elite was eagerly pursuing gentility and sophistication. Urbanites on the eastern seaboard retained their cultural orientation across the Atlantic, and prosperous merchants reshaped their lives, emulating cosmopolitan ideals of refinement. They began to shape landscapes that reflected their participation in this Atlantic world—but in very localistic ways.

In Charleston, South Carolina, for example, a new vernacular type emerged, one that has since become famous as the "single house." The single house developed as a transparent expression of social status and hierarchy: in such spaces as expensively finished parlors, members of the mercantile elite engaged in competitive status display. The single house also reinforced the oppressive social hierarchy of African-American slavery. In Federal-era rural Massachusetts, middling farmers began to erect two-story houses that featured complex workspaces and reflected republican ideas of beauty and convenience. In post–Revolutionary War Virginia, a "housing revolution" took place: middling landowners built small houses, which in quality rivaled that of the big plantation houses of the first families.

Not everyone participated fully in these developments, however. Vast distances separated settlements, especially in the trans-Allegheny west. Most people lived intensely local, rural lives, defined foremost by kinship and community; their contact with the wider culture, though consistent enough, was thin, and often failed to resonate with their everyday preoccupations. The landscapes these people fashioned reflected their tenuous relationship to the metropolitan center. The proclamation of hierarchy and refinement was much more fitful, and in some ways the landscape actually seemed to express distrust of cosmopolitan values.

Somerset County in the late eighteenth and early nineteenth centuries was just such a society. Its residents were preeminently a forest people. The label "forest society" is certainly apt for this era, since the forest and its products played such an important part in everyday life. But we should take care not to confuse the idea of the forest society with stereotypes arising from schoolbook notions of the "frontier." Most famously stated by Frederick Jackson Turner, of course, the "frontier thesis" often implicitly equated the frontier with a forest environment. Turner attributed to the forest environment the atavistic power to erase culture, to take people back to a primitive state. His argument has been vigorously debated since its appearance in 1893, but it has come under particularly intense scrutiny in the last few decades. Scholars have completely discredited Turner's notion of a frontier—that it draws a line between savagery and civilization—and its corollary—that the West was essentially empty territory. They point out that if frontiers exist at all, they consist of fluid boundaries between human cultures. Moreover, the notion of the West as a place of relative social equality where capitalism arrived late has come under attack, along with the assumption of frontier isolation. It is now accepted that consumer goods, for example, penetrated quite early (and to a surprising extent) every remote corner of the nation. Contemporary analysts argue that people in the backcountry may have led more rudimentary lives than their counterparts on the eastern seaboard, but they nonetheless shared fundamental aspirations and values held by the wider metropolitan culture, especially the yearning for sophistication and refinement.[1]

Yet in reinterpreting the idea of the frontier, we need not discard entirely the idea that newly settled areas could also have had distinctive experiences because of their position vis-à-vis the metropolitan center. Bernard Bailyn, for example, characterizes all of colonial America as a margin or periphery in which social controls were weak, allowing the bizarre tendencies latent in human societies to be magnified. This concept has some validity for the post-colonial period as well. A recent sensitive portrait of Daniel Boone shows convincingly that he and his compatriots headed west to "escape hierarchy and control" and that they cherished "radical notions of independent action." William Cooper, the upstate New York magnate of the early nineteenth century, spent his entire life seeking to achieve gentility and refinement, but he was never able to escape his provincial origins.[2]

What clues does the early Somerset County landscape offer in sorting out this complex relationship? What did everyday landscapes communicate about the local people's relationship to the wider culture—and, indeed, about their own conceptualization of their place in that culture? What we seem to see in the landscape is a backcountry culture that embraced some tokens of metropolitan sophistication, yet rejected others. Its relationship to the larger world was, in a word, ambivalent; this ambivalence shows not only in the documentary record but also in the landscape.

As the people began to carve a built landscape from their wooded environment, they quickly created powerfully symbolic expressions of the dominant values of a settled society. The rapid enclosure of the land is a case in point. Fences communicated messages of regularity and control as well as neighborly responsibility and respect for others' property. In addition, the numerous architectural references to older landscapes represented the people's identification with the settled societies they had left. Almost any banked building, for example, evoked an entire set of spatial and landscape values from areas further east, especially Germanic areas. Similarly, complexes of main buildings and ancillary buildings—though simpler than those found elsewhere—adopted the familiar principal features of farmstead organization found in places like Berks County's Oley Valley and Lancaster, Lebanon, and York Counties. Even the dominant log construction was a way of participating in a much larger national (perhaps even international) landscape formation. A visitor could encounter well-built and permanent log structures anywhere in the young nation; thus, even recently settled areas like Somerset County could immediately participate in a national building culture.

However, even if we accept that the traditional label of "frontier," with all its connotations, does not apply to early Somerset County, we must take into account the inescapable evidence of a conflict that, to a large extent, can be read as a clash between local values and those of outsiders. Residents put up fencing, yes; their worm fences and brush fences were crude and sloppy, though, compared with more refined versions. The decision to create a farm landscape with only a tiny proportion of land in field crops bespoke not simply an early stage of development but also values of subsistence—and even, perhaps, a determined effort to hold "civilized" society at bay. Local elites pointedly did *not* embrace a culture of refinement in their building practices. Within the typical early Somerset County house, spatial organization conflicted with more sophisticated visitors' expectations for social separation, for rituals of politeness, for individual separation and recognition. A closer look at Somerset County will help expose the ambivalence of early landscape formation.

Somerset County, Pennsylvania (Fig. 1), is bounded on the east by the Allegheny Mountain and on the west by Laurel Hill. Part of the Allegheny Mountain section of the Allegheny Plateau, the county's topography has had a profound effect on its history. The two ridges historically have hemmed in the valleys between, fending off outside influences and creating an isolated area in which an insular local culture could develop. Altitude, too, has shaped the county's past. The state's highest peak is in Somerset County, and the mountain climate is unusually cool, allowing only short growing seasons. Indeed, Somerset County's climate matches those of New York State and Pennsylvania's Northern Tier more than those of counties immediately to the east and west; in parts of Somerset, there are fewer than one hundred frost-free days each year. Nevertheless, soils between the ridges have been characterized as well suited to agriculture, and the native vegetation was luxurious when Euro-Americans first encountered it. Fine stands of hardwoods and pines covered the region. A thick understory of shrubs such as mountain laurel (Fig. 2) grew in abundance beneath the tulip trees, spruces, sugar maples, oaks, and chestnuts. Beneath the surface, too, lay extensive deposits of bituminous coal. These basic geological and biological realities have mightily influenced the cultural landscapes of Somerset County.[3]

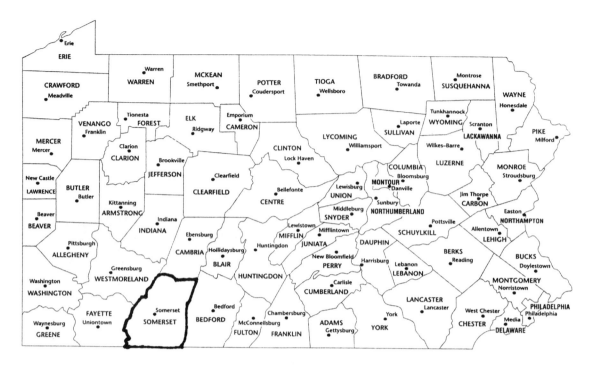

FIG. I
Map of Pennsylvania, showing Somerset County. From E. Willard Miller, ed., A *Geography of Pennsylvania* (University Park: The Pennsylvania State University Press, 1995), frontispiece. By permission.

The future Somerset County lay athwart important routes to the Ohio Valley, so it was traversed by Europeans and Native Americans early on. Most early European visitors to the region were traders, missionaries, military men, and hunters. The ill-fated Braddock expedition came through here, as did the future General Washington. But for the first three-quarters of the eighteenth century, the area was essentially a place to get *through* on the way to somewhere else. Moravian missionary John Heckewelder, for example, who logged thirty thousand miles in a lifetime of ministry to the Indians, made excursions that took him across the Allegheny Mountain, through the "Glades," and on across Laurel Mountain to the Ohio Valley. In March of 1762, coming from Bethlehem in the east, he ascended the Allegheny Mountain through a chilling snow: he and his companions had "a most painful ride" up, and "were reminded of our possible fate by a large number of carcasses of horses, which were scattered along the entire path." They began the descent, only to "soon [find] ourselves in the midst of a thick and dark forest of hemlock trees." After slogging through miles of uninhabited territory, they finally reached a hunter's cabin in a place called Edmond's Swamp (see Fig. 3): "Scarcely had we entered, when the wolves began their dismal howl; the hunter's night music all the year round. . . . Jack [the hunter] had no stable; but our horses found tolerable pasture on a piece of land of about three acres, which had been cleared and fenced in by the hunter and his sons." All night the travelers were kept awake by the howling wolves, clanking horses' bells, and guards shouting to each other in the darkness. The next day at Stoney Creek the water was too high to ford, so they were ferried across on a sugar trough, a crude, shallow, hand-gouged container for maple sugar.[4]

FIG. 2

Kalmia latifolia (mountain laurel) grew thickly on the Somerset County mountain slopes. Illustration from Jacob Bigelow, *American Medical Botany*, vol. 1, pt. 2 (Boston: Cummings and Hilliard, 1817–1820), plate 13. Courtesy of Hunt Institute for Botanical Documentation, Carnegie Mellon University, Pittsburgh, Pennsylvania.

Heckewelder's account captures the rudimentary nature of economic life in Bedford County in those uncertain days when the Great War for Empire was coming to a climax. The few European residents of the area that would become Somerset County lived by hunting, sheltering travelers, and making maple sugar. The landscape was dominated by dense forest cover. The valleys between the ridges, which would later become the agriculturally rich Glades, offered still another kind of obstacle during the eighteenth century: miry swamp. Here and there, a tiny fenced clearing like "Jack's" kept the forest and the wolves at bay.

This daunting landscape confronted people who intended to start homes and farms when they began to make their way to what is now Somerset County in the late 1760s. Germans and Pennsylvania Germans from the eastern counties moved to Brothersvalley Township.[5] By 1795 there were enough residents to warrant splitting off Somerset County from Bedford County. We do not know much about the specific geographic origins of these early inhabitants, but we do know that many came from eastern Pennsylvania counties that were predominantly Pennsylvania German (such as Berks and Lancaster), others came from the south, and still others immigrated directly from Europe. Scholars disagree on what proportion of Somerset County residents represent what ethnic groups, but regardless of how the numbers are calculated, Pennsylvania Germans have

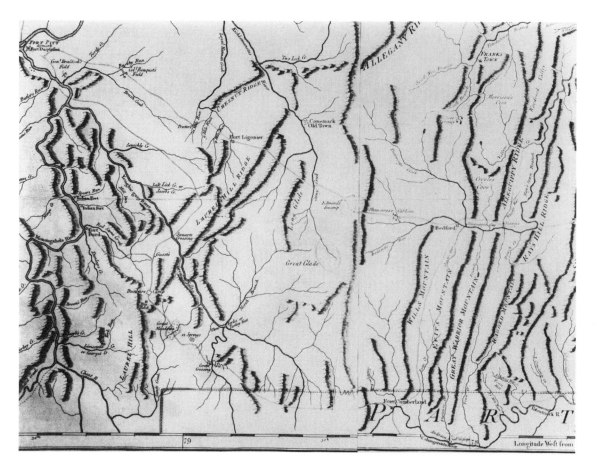

FIG. 3

Streams and mountain topography dominate this 1775 manuscript map. Places like Edmond's Swamp and the "Glades" were notable for their openness. From *A map of Pennsylvania: exhibiting not only the improved parts of the province, but alfo its extensive frontiers: laid down from actual surveys and chiefly from the late map of W. Scull . . . ,* c. 1775. Facsimile, Historical Collections and Labor Archives, The Pennsylvania State University Libraries.

historically made up a significant percentage of the county's population.[6] People of Scots-Irish and English extraction also were well represented at first; Anglo-American migrants from New Jersey, for example, moved into Lower Turkeyfoot Township.

Just getting to Somerset County remained a challenge well into the nineteenth century. Henry Adams observed in his classic *History of the United States of America* that in 1800 the young nation was more closely connected across the Atlantic to Europe than to its own interior, and other historians of the early republic have usually felt obligated to make clichéd mention of the rudimentary state of the transportation system. Yet any sampling of travel narratives from the period will convey afresh how intimidating and exhausting the journey was. Typically, journal writers waxed enthusiastic in the first days westward from Philadelphia, describing prosperous country towns and fat farms. But once they hit the hills, "hear [*sic*]," lamented one emigrant, "began sorrow." Travelers struggled to the top of the first ridge, only to see ridge after ridge stretching out in waves before them. Even the main thoroughfare over the Allegheny Mountain was "execrable," reported an irritated John Palmer in 1818: "it is impossible for an Englishman to conceive how bad. Pieces of rock, great stones, stumps, logs, and whole trees, besides continual acclivities, rendered our journey very perilous. We saw several loaded wagons upset." The slopes were so steep that the coach's riders, like sailors, found themselves scrambling to heed the driver's instruction that they shift the load: "To the right, gentlemen! To the left!"[7]

EARLY CROPS, TOOLS, AND METHODS

In 1771, traveler Harmon Husband came upon Philip Wagerline's clearing in "Brothers Valley." Wagerline had lived there three years and was raising grain and potatoes. By the time of the 1783–84 tax assessment, more than 1,500 souls inhabited the townships of Brothersvalley, Quemahoning, Milford, and Turkeyfoot, dwelling in more than three hundred houses. By 1795 (see Fig. 4), the county's six original townships had 868 farms, and nearly a thousand houses; the essential early mills for processing lumber, grain, and flaxseed had begun to appear. Residents had laboriously cleared 22,000 acres, an average of 25 per farm. Five years later, the county's population stood at about 9,000.[8]

By 1810, the process of settlement and clearing had gathered momentum. The county's 11,000 residents lived in sixteen hundred dwellings. Gristmills, sawmills, fulling mills, and oil

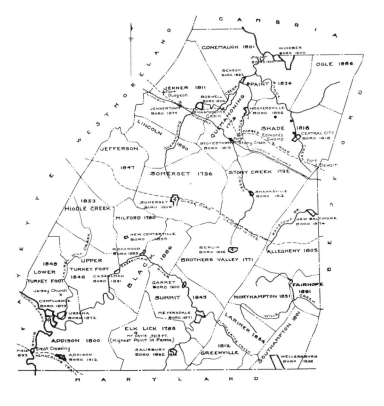

FIG. 4
"Historical Map of Somerset County Showing
Formation of Townships," *Laurel Messenger*
(August 1978), 3. By permission. By 1795,
when the county was formed, it had six
townships; more were added later.

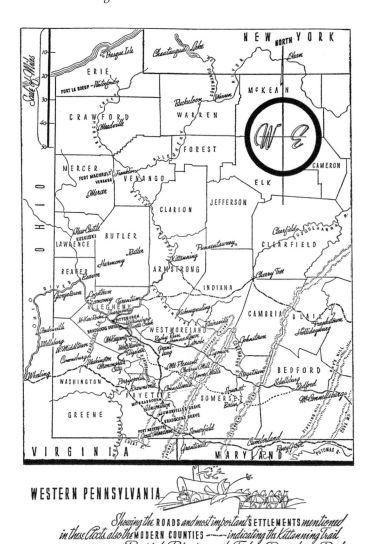

FIG. 5
Three important roads traversed Somerset
County around 1790. From John W. Harpster,
ed., *Pen Pictures of Early Western Pennsylvania*
(Pittsburgh: University of Pittsburgh Press,
1938), frontispiece.

mills processed grain, logs, woven cloth, and flaxseed, respectively. A whopping ninety-two stills
furnished whiskey for local consumption and for trade. Nearly five hundred looms clacked away
in private homes, producing well over a hundred thousand yards of cloth. Cleared land was estimated at nearly 50,000 acres, but even so, at least 90 percent of the county's land area still lay
under forest. Blacksmiths, carpenters, coopers, and other artisans plied their trades.[9] Though many
of these people doubtless worked at their trades full-time, a number were also involved in farmwork; conversely, most farmers possessed some sort of artisanal skill as well. In short, this society
was the epitome of the young republic: an overwhelmingly agrarian society. Even the small-scale
manufacturing activity arose in response to the needs of farmers. Several important roads—the
National Road, the Glade Road, and the Forbes or Pennsylvania Road—traversed the county
roughly from southeast to northwest. The roads cut through the southwestern, middle, and northern portions of the county, respectively (see Fig. 5).[10] These trails served migrants and packhorses

laden with imported goods (coffee, glassware, and the like) destined for local households; later, the horses would carry out whiskey, maple sugar, and perhaps potash or butter to markets in the East or down the Ohio and Mississippi river systems.

If we move away from statistics and focus instead upon the characteristics of the preindustrial farmstead and farming community, we can begin to sketch a portrait of early life in Somerset County. It is important to remember that by the time that this part of western Pennsylvania was settled, migrants were coming out of a well-established society and culture on the eastern seaboard. Whether German, Scots-Irish, or Anglo-American, they brought with them ideas, customs, values, and techniques from the settled rural life they had left behind. They were not totally isolated: they maintained contact with the seaboard and beyond through transportation, trade, mail, and personal connections. At the same time, they sought to create a measure of self-sufficiency, forging a considerable degree of community autonomy. This selective blend of customs and practices, of outward- and inward-looking ways, would characterize Somerset County agriculture—and its vernacular building—into the twentieth century.[11]

In the first years of settling and establishing themselves on the land, the new residents tackled tasks that confronted all settlers then moving westward across the Allegheny Ridge. Clearing, of course, was a first priority. Practicing a technique that colonial-era settlers farther east had learned from Native Americans, people girdled trees, leaving them to die and fall. Stump fields became prominent features of the human landscape. John Heckewelder wrote in 1797 that "much dead timber is to be seen standing upon the fields." A decade later, Philadelphia merchant Joshua Gilpin noted "a great deal of girdled timber yet remaining in the fields" off the beaten track.[12]

Gilpin gave a compelling impression of farms at this stage: "the farm houses fields & meadows peeping out from among the trees give a pleasing idea of the progress of improvement—in the forests." In the little clearings, families busied themselves planting, tending, and harvesting crops among the stumps. In addition to the harvest of cultivated crops, families gathered and preserved hay from the woodlands and "glades," clearings that probably had begun as small cleared areas and possibly had been extended (through burning, for example) by the previous Native American inhabitants.[13] With the onset of winter, settlers worked at clearing, burning logs for potash, and collecting wood for fencing and building purposes. Butchering occurred in the cold-weather months. Early spring was the time to tap trees and make maple sugar.

A closer look at these elements in the early agrarian economy helps us form a picture of how people worked, traded, and interacted with each other. Grain and garden crops were certainly not dominant items in this rural forest economy, but they symbolized the transformation of the forest into cultivated farmland. Eighteenth-century inventories mention wheat, oats, peas, buckwheat, rye, flax, barley, cabbage, turnips, and potatoes. Some early Somerset County residents grew corn successfully, but the county's cool climate made this a chancy proposition. After his sojourn in the area (1797–99), Horatio Gates wrote, "Maize has not an opportunity of ripening once, perhaps in ten years." Oats, by contrast, thrived in the cool hills; Gates and others remarked its high quality and copious yields.[14] Grain provided the raw material for distilling whiskey, a major "cash crop"

FIG. 6
Heavy wooden plows, occasionally drawn by oxen, limited the amount of land that could be farmed by a single family. Illustration for September from *Baer's Agricultural Almanac* (Lancaster, Pa.: John Baer, 1832). Rare Books and Manuscripts, The Pennsylvania State University Libraries.

and ingredient of social life. All of these grains provided animal and human food, and the rye and oats also furnished straw for bedding.

These field crops were planted, tended, harvested, and processed largely by hand. Heavy wooden plows (see Fig. 6) and harrows prepared the ground.[15] Seed was sown broadcast. After seedlings emerged, simple hoes for grubbing, sprouting, and cultivating kept weeds at bay. The sickle, a tool employed since ancient times, was used to cut the grain at harvesttime (see Fig. 7). Buckwheat and oats were sometimes cut with a hand cradle.[16] After being cured in shocks, grain was threshed with a flail or by a horse treading.

Farming with hand tools demanded intensive labor—and cooperation. Grain harvesting, for example, had to be done speedily, and the help of neighbors was essential. In 1899, Samuel Philson (who had been a young teenager in the 1820s) remembered that in early Somerset County, "The reaping party was generally composed of the farmer himself and his neighbors, and the apprentice boys, who were allowed ten to fifteen days of each harvest season in which to earn pocket money for the year. . . . [Reapers were] followed by boys to gather and old men to shock the reaped grain neatly to protect it while seasoning before being stored."[17] Somerset County women, too, participated in the grain harvest. Indeed, when his daughters married, Peter Leibundgutt (Livengood) gave them "corn hoes" and sickles. This tradition of fieldwork for women reached back to European antecedents and (more recently) to colonial days. Contemporary observers such as Benjamin Rush thought that Pennsylvania German women did more outdoor work than other women, but actually all women worked in the fields throughout the mid-Atlantic region.[18]

Haymaking was another critical task. Hay furnished crucial winter rations for livestock in this harsh climate. The very first supplies of hay were gathered from the natural grasses growing

FIG. 7
The sickle had been in use since ancient times. Illustration for July from *Baer's Agricultural Almanac*, 1832. Rare Books and Manuscripts, The Pennsylvania State University Libraries.

luxuriantly in the Glades. John Heckewelder noted "fine meadows" in the Glades in 1797. Anna Maust Bender remembered that her grandfather had harvested "wild" hay early in the nineteenth century: "I remember Grandpa calling the wild hay they harvested *shinamon* grass hay. It was very fine and soft." All across the American colonies, livestock had foraged on this native vegetation. But nowhere could these fragile plants withstand the impact of grazing, and they were rapidly replaced by the more aggressive European grasses. Somerset County was no exception.[19]

As the "wild" hay gave out, the pioneers continued to gather hay from the meadows (increasingly made up of "volunteer," aggressive European species), but they also began to raise "tame" hay—that is, hay deliberately grown from selected seed. It is hard to know just how widespread this practice was, but again we can turn to inventories for some indications of what wealthier farmers were doing. John Black's 1803 inventory listed "12 Tun of Glade Hay," appraised at $54, "14 Tun of Timothy hay," worth $140, and another "22 Tun of Glade Hay," worth only $11. Timothy (see Fig. 8) was the highly regarded "English hay," adopted as the standard by progressive farmers all over the East.[20]

By the early nineteenth century, these cultivated meadows formed part of a developing landscape of rural labor at haymaking time. Philson recalled:

Very frequently, in passing through the country, you could see twelve to sixteen mowers working abreast, each one cutting about four feet wide. . . . All the grass was cut for hay with German scythes, which were sharpened upon a small "dengel stuck" [see Fig. 9] almost daily, and sharpened by a peculiarly shaped—I think imported—whetstone which each mower carried in a pouch at his waist. Also on his waist strap was carried a cow's horn with water. We boys of 10 to 13 years of age followed the mowers to scatter the grass and to keep them supplied with water and liquor.

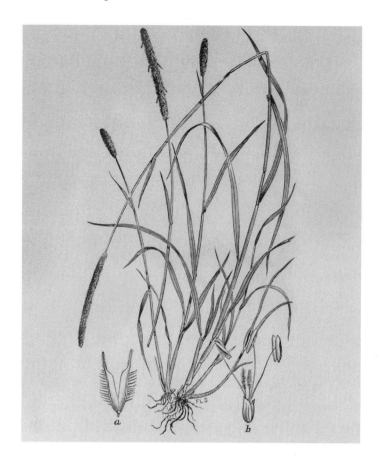

FIG. 8
Timothy (*Phleum pratense*) was a "tame" grass that farmers began to cultivate systematically for its superior hay. Frank Lamson-Scribner, *American Grasses* (Washington: Government Printing Office, 1897), 132.

As soon as the hay was seasoned a number of hands, mostly females, with hand rakes formed the winrows [*sic*], while the men and boys loaded the wagons and stored away in barns.[21]

Flax raising and processing, too, called forth coordinated effort. When the flax (see Fig. 10) was ready for pulling—i. e., uprooting—men and women did this work together. Then followed the arduous and time-consuming tasks of retting, braking (Fig. 11), heckling, scutching, combing, and spinning, tasks often done in "bees." (Two New England girls traveling in Pennsylvania in 1788 thought it so odd to see women scutching that they could not control their laughter; the German women rebuked the girls, saying that if they lived in the backwoods they would learn to scutch soon enough.) Eighteenth-century inventories regularly listed flax brakes, hetchels, spinning wheels, tow linen, linen cloth, and occasionally looms and loom tacklings.[22]

Maple sugar was a key element in the frontier-era economy, as it was easy to produce under frontier conditions. Sugaring—a skill originally passed from Native Americans to the French in the seventeenth century and then to other Europeans—took place in early spring, when work was comparatively slack and when scarcity of food and trade items was greatest. It took no preparation, in terms of planting, plowing, and so on; one simply went into the forest (see Fig. 12). When the sap was running, people tapped the sugar maple (Fig. 13). Sugaring required relatively few

Pennsylvania German harvesters commonly carried a *dengel stuck*, which was used for sharpening tools. Early nineteenth-century example, Somerset Historical Center. Photograph by the author.

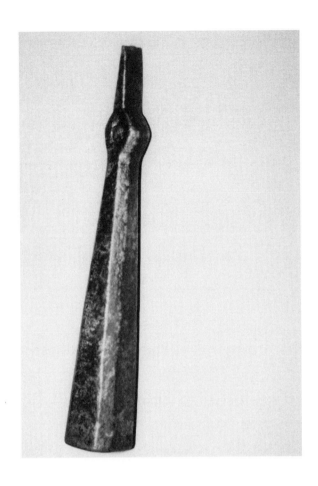

The blue flowers of the flax plant, *Linum usitatissimum*, made a lovely show in early summer. Flax was grown for fiber and seed. Agricultural botanist William Darlington lamented the disappearance of this plant from the rural repertoire, but in Somerset County it still flourished in his day. William Darlington, *American Weeds and Useful Plants* (New York: A. O. Moore and Co., 1859), 70. Rare Books and Manuscripts, The Pennsylvania State University Libraries.

1. LI'NUM, *L.* FLAX.
[The classical name for the plant.]

Capsule of 5 united carpels, each 2-seeded, but divided into 2 single-seeded cells by a false partition, projecting from the back of the carpels.

1. L. USITATIS'SIMUM, L. Leaves alternate, lance-linear, very acute; flowers on long pedicels; capsules globose, mucronate.

MOST USEFUL (OR COMMON) LINUM. Flax.

Fr. Lin. *Germ.* Gemeiner Flachs. *Span.* Lino.

Root annual. *Stem* 2–3 feet high, slender, terete, smooth, corymbosely branched at summit. *Leaves* an inch to an inch and a half long. *Petals* rather large, blue, often with a tinge of purple, very caducous. *Seeds* lance-ovate, smooth and shining.

Cultivated, and occasionally spontaneous in cultivated grounds. Native of Europe. *Fl.* June. *Fr.* July.

Obs. This valuable plant—once considered so indispensable among the crops of our farmers—is now but little cultivated. I have not seen a flax-patch for a number of years: whereas, in the "good old times"—before *Spinning-wheels* were superseded by *Pianos*—every rural family cultivated and manufactured as much flax as was required for domestic purposes. But now, the Cotton-plant of the South has nearly banished the Flax-plant from the Middle and Northern States. Nor is the revolution thus effected a subject of regret, with the farmer.

48

FIG. 11
Flax culture was shared by men and women. Here, a man is shown using the flax brake. Illustration for March from *Baer's Agricultural Almanac*, 1832. Rare Books and Manuscripts, The Pennsylvania State University Libraries.

tools: kettles, a sled and horse, and homemade wooden "keelers" (troughs) and spiles (taps). The sugar camp usually consisted of a kettle suspended between forked posts. The finished product, in the form of cakes or crumbled, found a number of uses: it became the family's sweetener, a raw material essential in curing, and a compact item to trade. Men, women, and children attended the slow, protracted process of boiling, thickening, pouring, and stirring.[23]

Domesticated livestock and their products formed another key component of the frontier agrarian economy. By 1810, there were over five thousand horses, fifteen thousand cattle, and thirteen thousand sheep in Somerset County—more beasts, by far, than humans! Indeed, early tax assessments show that most taxable households (and probably most households overall) possessed a few cattle, sheep, and horses. Herds were small: the most anyone was taxed for was five horses and six horned cattle.[24] Swine were not recorded in the assessments, but they surely roamed the woods foraging for acorns and other nuts; of forty eighteenth-century Somerset County estate inventories, fully half listed swine. From these animals, the pioneer families obtained meat, milk, butter, and cheese (during the spring and summer months); labor power; transportation; and wool and woolen goods.

Again, men's work and women's work were intertwined in turning these raw livestock materials into useful household items. Dairying was traditionally women's concern, and many inventories show milk crocks, butter churns, the occasional cheese press, and butter tubs. Milking apparently was a shared task; some, but not all, regarded it strictly as women's work.[25] Women sheared sheep, spun yarn, and wove cloth. Neighbors took turns going from house to house, butchering and turning hogs into hams, bacon, sausage, scrapple, and other preserved meats.

Hunting and gathering occupied an important place in early Somerset County culture. Game was plentiful—almost too much so, in some instances, as local authorities placed bounties on such nuisances as wolves. For some households, hunting supplied meat for the family table and skins to trade or process into needed equipment. Emigrant travelers often mentioned venison as part of the fare at local inns.[26] All family members made forays into the woods and meadows to gather nuts, berries, and probably medicinal plants for family use. The nuts and dried berries would provide welcome variety and nutrients in the monotonous winter diet.

The farmstead garden—tended mostly by women—furnished essential dietary staples: potatoes, cabbages, turnips, radishes, and other items such as beans, pumpkins, and cucumbers. Carefully preserved dried beans, root crops stored in cellars, sauerkraut, and pickles afforded variety in the wintertime. Many inventories mention cabbage tubs, cabbage and cucumber cutters, and pickling crocks. As orchards reached bearing age, the family's diet diversified, and women worked to dry fruits, especially apples.[27]

Once local gristmills (or in some spots, treadmills) were available, families could enjoy bread and buckwheat cakes instead of having to grind grain with a pestle or consume it boiled or in the form of hominy; dough trays turn up frequently in inventories of the 1790s. Women eventually also added the poultry yard to their domain, raising not only hens but also geese.[28] (Feathers were in high demand for home use and for market trade.)

FIG. 12
Maple sugaring. This early-nineteenth-century drawing depicts sugaring farther west (in Indiana territory), but the essentials were the same in Pennsylvania. Charles Alexandre Lesueur Collection, Muséum d'Histoire Naturelle, Le Havre, N° 62001-1.

FIG. 13
Leaf and fruit of *Acer saccharum*, the sugar
maple. This lovely tree was the source of maple
sugar, a major food and form of cash in
Somerset County. François André Michaux,
*The North American sylva, or, A description of
the forest trees of the United States, Canada, and
Nova Scotia . . .* , vol. 1 (Philadelphia: R. P.
Smith, 1853), plate 42. Rare Books and
Manuscripts, The Pennsylvania State
University Libraries.

People were perhaps the most important "product" of the farm. Women, of course, bore and raised children, the farm's future labor force. Though we do not have specific documentation for western Pennsylvania in this period, frontier population data for other areas are well studied; it is likely that in Somerset, as in those places, birth rates were high and families large. A sample of households from Brothersvalley Township shows that the average household contained over seven people in 1800. To be sure, household members were not always related, but this is a rough index of family size. America was a young republic in more than one sense. John Mack Faragher reminds us that in pioneer Illinois, women's health was often overtaxed by the combined stresses of farm-making and childbearing, not to mention performing the daily tasks (such as cooking, laundering, and soapmaking) that maintained the family.[29]

Early residents of Somerset County also focused on seasonality. Eighteenth-century farmers' almanacs emphasized the rhythm of the seasons and reflected people's vision of what historian Carolyn Merchant has called an "animate cosmos," in which people encountered the natural world as a living, dynamic being. Premodern farm people saw humans as part of nature, so their intellectual, religious, and natural worlds were seamlessly joined. It made sense to them to relate signs of the zodiac to the human body and to beliefs about the weather, soils, and crops.[30]

PREINDUSTRIAL CULTURE AND VALUES

A distinctive set of values and customs held this agrarian society together. Community effort was essential if the work was to be done, but it was hardly an egalitarian society. Disparities of wealth and social status marked rural life. Especially up on the mountain ridges, travelers encountered poverty and even destitution. Jean-Louis (John) Badollet, a Swiss-born surveyor journeying to Fayette County in 1793–94, traversed Laurel Hill and stopped at a lodging there. He wrote, "I never saw such wretchedness since I was in this country. Of all the members of the family, not one had any shirt or shift on, and the woman happening to stand before the fire I saw her nakedness through a thin petticoat. . . . My first reflection was a jovial one at such a sight, but soon . . . [I] checked that ill natured disposition to evoke merriment out of the distresses of another."[31]

By contrast, in the more fertile valleys, Badollet saw neither "self-denials of wretchedness" nor "excess of luxury," but rather a place in which "constant industry is attended . . . with wealth and happiness." Some, like F. A. Michaux, thought that wealth tended to have an ethnic dimension; the Germans, he declared, "live much better than the Americans." But he also noted that everyone has "milk, butter, smoked or salt meat, and maize," and "even the poorest man has one or more horses, and it is very seldom that a person visits his neighbor on foot."[32]

Tenancy was common. Direct Tax manuscripts, for example, show that at least fifty men occupied land owned by someone else. Formal tenancy agreements also survive for the era. An 1812 indenture between Thomas Vickroy of Bedford County and Andrew Specht of Somerset County specified that Specht would "deliver unto the said Thomas the one third part of all grain Viz the Wheat, Rie & Oats in the Stack at the Barn, Buckwheat & Corn in the Bushel, the one third of all the Potatoes in good order in the hole, and the one half of all the Hay in the Stack or mow, said Andrew to be allowed the priviledge to Sow one half acre of Flax, and the Garden for his own use all other Crop he shall give a shear thereof, and the said Thomas shall repay unto the said Andrew the one third of the Taxes." The tenant was also expected to maintain an orchard, and was prohibited from cutting green timber "except for repairs." Agreements sometimes specified that the tenant must build a house or barn, and sometimes both; some stipulated that the tenant must plant an orchard, or fence so many acres of land. It is impossible to tell without a more detailed study what this all meant in social terms, but other work has shown that while tenancy certainly indicated a social hierarchy, it did not always imply extreme poverty or social stress; in a developing area, it offered a practical means by which landlords could improve their property and allowed young men without a lot of capital to get a start in farming.[33]

Wealth created social hierarchies, then, but groups were also subordinated on the basis of sex or age. Adult men organized and controlled work and property. They determined when women and boys would work "for themselves"—a significant phrase in itself, since it implies that only on special occasions would they do so, and then only by permission. At all other times they would serve the household. Women were deeply involved in what we would call "productive" work, but this work did not garner them much in the way of legal recognition or social status. Under the law in colonial and early national Pennsylvania, married women had virtually no legal right to the property and wealth that they helped create.[34] The hierarchy of age, gender, and skill is also apparent in the assignment of the skilled but light work of shocking to "old men."

From top to bottom, all were enmeshed in a network of mutual dependency. Little cash changed hands in these early years, but rigorously kept "book accounts" show exchanges of goods, labor, and services among neighbors rich and poor. Sometimes years would pass before accounts were "settled," and debts could carry on almost indefinitely. Prices were not always fixed by an abstract "market" but by particular circumstances—storekeepers might charge a widow less than a male landowner, for instance. This interdependency helped offset some of the authoritarian aspects of the social hierarchy. People who depended so much on each other couldn't afford to antagonize their neighbors.[35]

An intense sociability also helped the frontier community to thrive. People continually circulated and socialized, usually in the context of work. Men, women, and children traveled to other farms to visit with neighbors and kinfolk while they husked, threshed, raised barns, spun, butchered, and so on. A notable indicator of this everyday movement turns up again in inventories, many of which list a sidesaddle or "woman's saddle." Though women were subordinated legally, socially, and culturally, they also enjoyed a considerable degree of geographic mobility. Englishman John Palmer noticed that "the women all travel on horse-back in these mountainous regions. It would be next to impossible for them to travel any other way." Upper-class women would have had greater access to horses and sidesaddles than poorer women would, but even so, the dictates of neighborliness made it essential for all to travel.[36]

Taken as a whole, farming neighborhoods in early Somerset County followed strategies that placed a high value upon community self-sufficiency and upon establishing offspring in farming. The phrase "community self-sufficiency" is appropriate here, because it is likely that only the very largest farms approached literal self-sufficiency; most farm families, working a small cleared area, probably produced only part of what they needed and traded or bartered for the rest in local and wider markets. By this means they achieved a high degree of *local* self-sufficiency.[37]

Margaret Dwight's account of her journey to the Ohio country in 1810 offers evidence for how much local self-sufficiency was, in fact, achieved. Around Allegheny Mountain, she wrote, "the children and girls, are all very much attracted by my little black buttons, and the manner in which my frock is made, and the wagoneers by the colour of it—there will be little of it left by the time I get to Warren."[38] Clearly, the local people had had limited exposure to the cloth and buttons that originated in New England, partly due to their sheer isolation but also because so many made their own cloth and clothing.

Families accumulated property, but these accumulations were not necessarily seen as "profits"; rather, they tended to take the form of land and equipment to set up sons and daughters.[39] This was especially true among Pennsylvania Germans, whose gifts to young couples tended to follow formulaic "recipes" for sons and daughters. The key gift to a son (besides land) would be a desk—a private place in which a household head would keep accounts and documents. Daughters, by contrast, received a chest or cupboard to house linens and housewares. Somerset County's Peter

Livengood followed these conventions faithfully. He carefully recorded each child's marriage portion in the front of his diary. In 1786 his son Peter married Anna Butschuschin (Beachy); Peter Sr. "started them with" a bed, a mare and a horse, two cows, two sheep, a saddle and bridle, a horse collar, two axes, a grubbing hoe, a Testament and prayer book, "two screws to a plough," two sacks, six milk pigs [small pigs], forty feet of boards for a chest, one bell, two "cow straners," one Bible, six pounds owed to Peter Jr., land, and eighty small apple trees. The next year, when daughter Marrey married, she received a bed, iron pot and pan, tinware dish, platter, plate, and spoon, mare and sidesaddle, two cows and calves and another cow, one walnut chest, a spinning wheel, four small pigs, one corn hoe, two sheep, one sickle, two cowbells, two sacks, books, money to the son-in-law, a belly tub and krout steamer, pewter dish, and two iron spoons. Most families could not have afforded such generosity, but this was the ideal.[40]

Preindustrial work patterns and values operated on a plane unfamiliar to most people today. Work was seasonal, often intermittent, and uneven in pace. Labor was task-oriented—that is, focused on accomplishing a specific job (such as threshing or buttermaking)—rather than run according to the clock. Whiskey was integral to social life and to farmwork, with both men and women imbibing freely. Margaret Dwight wrote in 1810 to her cousin in New England that "I have learned Elizabeth to eat raw *pork* & drink whiskey." Local residents' fondness for strong drink was a recurring theme in period travel narratives. In remembering his journey through southwestern Pennsylvania in 1802, Frenchman F. A. Michaux concluded, contemptuously, that "a passion for spirituous liquors is one of the traits which characterize the peasantry of the interior of the United States." Henry Fearon, author of a popular emigrant's guide published in 1818, could not contain his disgust at the conditions he found on Allegheny Mountain:

> [The inn was] a miserable log-house, or what you would call a dog-hole; it was crowded with emigrants. I asked for something to eat, but could only obtain for an answer, "I guess whiskey is all the feed we have on sale." I have met with several similar instances, when I have asked, "Have you any meat?" "No." "Either hot or cold will make no difference to me." "I guess I don't know." "Have you any fowls?" "No." "Fish?" "No." . . . "I will pay you any price you please." "I guess we have only rum and whiskey feed."

Indignant travelers complained of "scenes of the most turbulent Merriment," lubricated of course by liquor.[41] But a common belief of the day was that spirits imparted strength for work, and as a practical matter, the alternatives were few. Not surprisingly, levels of violence could be high in such a climate.

Indeed, the early republic has been called the "Alcoholic Republic," as annual per capita consumption reached four gallons of pure alcohol per year. During these years, whiskey replaced rum as the major form of distilled drink. Backcountry farmers, who could transport their grain to market most easily in this liquid form, played important roles as producers and as consumers. They cherished their drinking culture and, when the occasion demanded, they acted to protect it. It was no coincidence that the 1794 Whiskey Rebellion's epicenter was located in Western Pennsylvania.

Yet though the drinking culture remained strong in the backcountry, the older view of alcohol as a "good creature" was confronted by a developing critique, one driven by capitalism and its accompanying demand for productivity, discipline, and sobriety. The harsh comments by outsiders such as Fearon and Michaux testified to this cultural conflict.[42]

To visitors, frontier residents often seemed not only too attached to drink but also slothful and unambitious to boot. Johann David Schoepf, a Swiss citizen traveling near Laurel Hill in the 1780s, criticized local residents

> who from a preference for doing nothing, and an old indifference to many conveniences, neglect and dread the quieter and more certain pursuits of agriculture. . . . They shun everything which appears to demand of them law and order, dread anything which breathes constraint. They hate the name of a Justice, and yet they are not transgressors. Their object is merely wild, altogether natural freedom, and hunting is what pleases them. An insignificant cabin of unhewn logs; corn and a little wheat, a few cows and pigs, this is all their riches but they need no more. They get game from the woods; skins bring them in whiskey and clothes.[43]

Schoepf was evaluating local life from the perspective of his own more cosmopolitan European background. His subjects did not necessarily represent typical residents, but this flavor of independence and self-sufficiency would persist in Somerset County.

It may seem illogical that markets had great importance in this context, especially since very little cash changed hands. But markets were actually crucial to ensure a well-rounded "competency." Even the simple life that Schoepf so trenchantly criticized relied on exchange. For more ambitious families, home-produced items such as linen cloth or maple sugar could both serve family subsistence needs and be traded in distant markets. Since the county was traversed by three major roads, travelers and their animals constituted an important market for locally produced goods. And as in other backcountry areas, Somerset Countians were connected to national and international trade networks. Though they invested primarily in land and bonds, they acquired consumer goods too. Such items as pewterware, found frequently in Somerset County inventories, reflected their owners' aspirations to gentility. Late-eighteenth-century store accounts from Bedford County list "Queen ware," "China plates," and "teapots" among the store's wares; this particular store is known to have been patronized by customers from Somerset County.[44]

Thus, preindustrial rural life in Somerset County was conducted in a cultural context dominated by the values of sociability, shared work, and community self-sufficiency. These values were realized, in turn, in early Somerset County vernacular buildings.

EXPRESSIONS IN BUILDINGS AND SPACE: AN ARCHITECTURE OF SOCIABILITY AND WORK

Only a few buildings remain from this formative period, but fortunately, a rich trove of archival sources can offer a glimpse of how the characteristic landscape of the region appeared at the turn of the century. One of the core sources is the manuscript schedule for the 1798 Direct Tax. In the summer of 1798, when diplomatic crises seemed likely to culminate in war, the Congress—intending to levy a progressive tax—passed a law mandating a nationwide valuation of all dwelling houses. Though the unpopular act was soon repealed and the tax never actually collected, a vast amount of information on the nation's building stock was gathered, and most of the original manuscripts survive for Pennsylvania. Assessors recorded dwellings in two basic categories: those valued over and those valued under $100. For dwellings worth under $100, assessors noted dimensions, value, and whether other buildings stood on the property; for dwellings worth more than $100, they also indicated building materials, the number of stories, the number of window openings and "lights" (glass panes), and outbuildings. This fund of information, along with extant buildings, tax records, census records, travelers' descriptions, and maps, can be used to build a picture of the landscape at the turn of the century.

It comes as no surprise that the dominant building materials in this forest society were logs. The Direct Tax schedule listed 1,235 dwellings in Somerset County.[45] Only five stone dwellings (and just two frame dwellings) existed in the entire county. Everything else was made of logs: "hued log," "round logs," "half round logs," or just plain "logs." John Heckewelder, traveling near Stoystown in 1797, noted ten or twelve buildings there, "built as usual of logs."[46]

The early dwellings that Somerset County residents erected certainly matched the schoolbook stereotype of the log cabin. Joshua Gilpin described them in this way: "In general any person who chuses goes upon the lands he finds vacant, & there begins an improvement, by building a house where every thing is of logs the chimney not excepted & the roof formed of split pieces of staves—kept down by logs placed on the outside—this rude shelter from the weather which has frequently not a particle of iron in its whole composition."[47] Englishman Henry Fearon left an equally colorful—if less flattering—picture:

> The character of the mountain inhabitants appears cold, friendless, unfeeling, callous, and selfish. . . . Log-houses are the only habitations for many miles. They are formed of the trunks of trees; about twenty feet in length, and six inches in diameter, cut at the ends, and placed upon each other. The roof is framed in a similar manner. In some houses there are windows; in others the door performs a double office. The chimney is erected outside, and in a similar manner to the body of the house. Some have clay in their chimneys, which is a precaution very necessary in these western palaces. In some the space between the logs remains open; in others it is filled with clay. The hinges are generally wood. Locks are not used. In some there are two apartments; in others but one, for all the various operations of cooking, eating, sleeping, and, upon great occasions, washing. The pigs also come in for their due share of the log residence.[48]

As these observers noted, the simplest of these rude dwellings consisted of a single room, or "single pen." One surviving house, the Jonas and Christina Shultz farm (Fig. 14) in Shade Township, measured only 19' × 15', with one and one-half stories. Just two window openings, asymmetrically

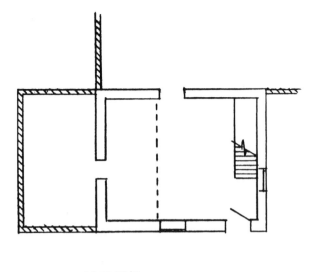

FIG. 14
The Jonas and Christina Shultz house (c.
1800–1820) typified the single-pen log house.
Somerset Historical Center. This and all other
Somerset Historical Center drawings are by
Barbara Budde.

HOUSE

placed, provided scant light. A few single-pen log structures still exist in the county; the Emert house
in Lincoln Township (Fig. 15) is an example.

More than these early single-pen structures were later enlarged, as was the case with the two
examples just discussed. These buildings were larger, but spatially they were close relatives to the
one-room structures. Many of the area's early log houses typically had a first floor divided into two
unequally sized rooms, entered directly through an off-center doorway. Narrow, enclosed stairways
provided access to the sleeping area. Asymmetrical window, door, and chimney placement indicated the internal organization.[49]

More spacious (and spatially complex) were houses with three- or four-room floor plans that
derived loosely from eastern Pennsylvania traditions. In German-settled areas of eastern Pennsylvania in the eighteenth century, the "Continental" house consisted of three or four rooms (*küche,
kammer, stube,* and sometimes a small fourth room; see Fig. 16). The rooms, usually of unequal size,
ranged around an interior chimney stack that usually accommodated both a fireplace and heating
stove. Visitors entered directly into the kitchen (*küche*) area. The *stube,* or stove room, served as
social and family space; the *kammer* was the main bedchamber.[50] Often this house would be
banked over a spring or root cellar area. By the late eighteenth century, just at the moment when
Somerset County was being settled, this archetypal colonial *flurküchenhaus* in other areas was giving way to different patterns. The kitchen was no longer always the principal entry space, and
instead was often moved to a basement location. Exteriors became more symmetrical.

Early Somerset County houses reflect this transitional, unstable phase. Some had three- or four-
room plans, but hardly any of these extant buildings have the classic *küche, stube,* and *kammer* in
their traditional places. Rather, most houses with three or four rooms assembled some key elements
of the form, more or less freely combined. For example, the John and Catherine Schneider house,
31' × 25' (see Fig. 17), has four interconnected asymmetrical rooms. Its main living spaces are

entered directly from the main door. A large exterior cooking fireplace was located on a gable end rather than centrally. Other homes might have two (rather than one) off-center interior chimneys.

Regardless of the floor plan, many of these buildings were banked. Banked construction had ample precedent in the Pennsylvania German east (though it was not limited exclusively to people of Germanic background). Often a spring ran right through the cellar area. Colonial-era "Swiss" houses had their gabled ends built into the bank, with facilities for heavy cooking, distilling, and dairying in the basement. Germanic banked structures often had a partial cellar for root storage and located the cooking fireplace on the main level, where the rooms were arranged with direct external and internal access. Similarly arranged sleeping rooms sometimes made up a third level.[51] In Somerset County, early banked structures (see Fig. 18) served similar functions. On some farms, for example, the cellar had no water or fireplace and so probably provided storage space for roots. In other cases, houses had water in the basement, but no fireplace, suggesting storage and dairying functions. The most comprehensive banked houses boasted the entire basement complement of fireplace, root cellar, and dairy.[52]

FIG. 15
The Emert house (c. 1830) is another survival of a simple early house type. Lincoln Township, south view. Somerset Historical Center.

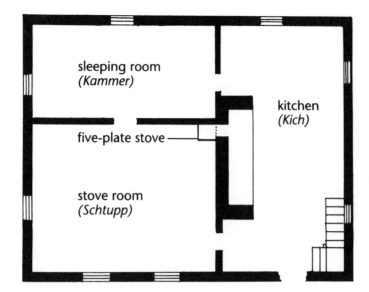

FIG. 16
Pennsylvania German "Continental" plan.
From "Springhouse Dwelling," in *The
Visual Dictionary of American Domestic
Architecture*, by Rachel Carley, with
illustrations by Ray Skibinski and Ed Lam.
© 1994 Ray Skibinski and Roundtable
Press. Reprinted by permission of Henry
Holt and Company, LLC.

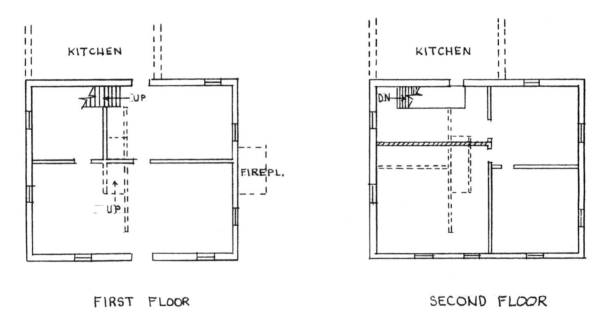

FIG. 17
The John and Catherine Schneider house (c. 1818), in Quemahoning Township, had asymmetrical, directly
connected rooms that fostered the sociable culture of the early nineteenth century. Somerset Historical Center.

These standing buildings faithfully depict the range of dwelling types that made up the domestic landscape at the turn of the century. The 1798 Direct Tax allows us to take a closer look at
interiors across this range, from the smallest to the more expensive and roomier dwellings. We
find spaces filled to the rafters with people working, cooking, and sleeping, all the while in intimate social contact.

FIG. 18
Settlers from eastern Pennsylvania brought with them traditions of banked construction. This is an early banked one-room log cabin (c. 1830), Lincoln Township. Somerset Historical Center.

At the lower end of the socioeconomic scale, people crammed themselves into small, dark houses. Houses worth less than $100 averaged just 15' × 19'—exactly the dimensions of the Jonas Shultz house—and had an average value of just $22. Most probably had just one story, or perhaps a story and a half. Windows were few. Within these small spaces, life went on cheek by jowl. When we link up information from the Direct Tax with the Heads of Household census of 1800, we can find concrete details about just how intimately people lived. In Brothersvalley, these tiny structures sheltered an average of 8.76 people! In 1798, for example, Ernest Deetz lived in an 18' × 18' house worth $35. The 1800 population census shows that he lived with his wife and 8 children under 10. Michael Kurtz owned an 18' × 24' "Cabin" valued at $40; in 1800 he is listed with 4 young children and 2 women.[53]

Even among the better houses (worth more than $100), most were valued under $800. These dwellings averaged 26' × 31'; two-thirds had two stories. In 1800, the households in these buildings averaged 6.7 people, and while there were still plenty of little children underfoot, the general pattern shows that these families were a bit further along in the life cycle. The household of Jacob Gibler Sr., for example, consisted of 2 children under 10, 2 between 10 and 15, 3 young men between 16 and 25, and 2 adults over 45. They occupied a two-story house—36' × 28', with seven windows—valued at $300. These slightly more elaborate houses were not really different in kind from their smaller neighbors. To be sure, they had more light, but still not much. Commonly, they could boast three windows; three-quarters of these better-quality dwellings had six or fewer windows.[54]

This brief overview points up one clear characteristic of the early Somerset County built landscape: it was dominated by modest housing, even for families who could afford fancier homes.[55] These people may have owned valuable goods, but still chose to live in unremarkable dwellings. Conrad Beamer's will, for example, was probated in 1801. Among many other luxury items, the inventory mentions a clock and case, worth $20; a mahogany desk, valued at $15; six Windsor chairs; a "Dinning table" [*sic*]; and a "large walnut table." A few items hinted that perhaps the vaunted "consumer revolution" of the eighteenth century was reaching the Somerset ridges. A ten-plate stove, pewterware, iron pots and kettles, stew kettle, teakettle, and coffeepot are just a few of the utensils that filled his well-stocked kitchen. Several feather beds were listed, valuable items in those days. Finally, among Beamer's possessions, the estate assessors listed a "Negro girl." Conrad Beamer was one of only three people in Brothersvalley to own human chattel. Clearly, Beamer chose to display his personal wealth in ways that would have been very obvious to his neighbors.[56]

One might expect Beamer to also show off his wealth in an ostentatious house, but we find from the 1798 Direct Tax that in fact Conrad Beamer was not even a homeowner: he occupied a log house owned by John Colpenning. It was 25' × 30', with two stories, five windows, and sixty lights, worth $200. This is interesting on several levels. First, evidently Beamer was a tenant, perhaps preferring to invest his assets in land (he owned 337 acres), consumer goods, human chattel, and livestock. Second, while his dwelling definitely falls on the higher end, with its sixty lights and $200 valuation, it was only of average size, and built of log.[57]

Of course, as a tenant Beamer may not have chosen the design of his house. But the pattern holds in other cases. Take John Brubaker, a yeoman whose inventory listed (among other things) a writing desk, looking glass, and windmill, but whose one-and-a-half story log house measured 27' × 30', had only two windows, and was valued at $150. David Ream, of Turkeyfoot Township, left many valuable goods (including several guns), but his house was only 17' × 25', with eight windows, valued at $150.

Travelers' comments reinforce this pattern. F. A. Michaux visited a well-to-do mill owner, just west of Laurel Hill, "who might easily procure himself better accommodation; he lives, however, in a common log-house, with only one room, 24 to 30 feet long, and on all sides exposed to the weather. Four large beds . . . are drawn into the middle of the chamber at night, receive the whole family, consisting of six persons, and sometimes of strangers who come to obtain a night's lodging." From Michaux's European perspective, this state of things would be considered incongruous with the miller's relatively high social status, but not, he stressed, in western Pennsylvania. Other travelers' sense of status was assaulted when they had to share sleeping quarters. Itinerant minister Robert Boyd, traveling the Somerset circuit in 1808, "passed dreary nights" in the homes of his coreligionists. There were seldom enough beds to go around, so Boyd was forced to share, much to his distaste. "Such was the filthy condition of the beds, that I had to use my pocket handkerchief to prevent the clothes from touching my face."[58]

Just as the exteriors of Somerset County housing shared a common visual vocabulary, so the interiors also had a common spatial language. Their spatial layout—whether a "Continental" plan, hall-and-parlor plan, single-pen plan, or two-room plan—*all* encouraged people to come into contact with each other. The asymmetrical external facade conveyed a message: an approaching visitor would enter directly into one of the family's main living rooms. Inhabitants of the house would have direct access to other rooms, and hence to each other; for example, the main bedroom opened directly onto the parlor or *stube* space. Indeed, the parlor was often the master bedroom.

The *stube*, or stove room, was a distinctively Pennsylvania German social space. Early eastern Pennsylvania Germans even had a saying: "no stove, no *stube*; no *stube*, no home." As the household's central hearth room, the *stube* represented Pennsylvania German culture and values with special resonance. The patriarch, for example, claimed the best chair in the well-lit corner diagonally opposite the stove, while traditionally the woman of the house could not expect a seat at all. In Somerset County, the *stube* tradition continued. Brothersvalley's "wealthy Dutch farmers" came in for especially lavish praise from Jean-Louis Badollet, who approvingly described their "tight houses [and] warm stove-rooms." Clearly, westering Pennsylvania Germans clung to the traditional stove room even if they truncated some of the formulaic aspects of the "Continental" house. Even animals, Badollet observed, gravitated to the *stube:* "My Bitch, is remaining behind wherever she finds a stove room and children to feed her." The quality of these houses set a high standard that was difficult to match, though; Badollet criticized a "middling Dutch farmer" named Hoover for his "abominable stove room" whose air "had not been changed perhaps for six months and stunk in a very disgusting degree. My bitch there fared but poorly."[59]

All in all, the architectural repertoire put to use by the local elite was quite limited. In Somerset County, the well-to-do families proclaimed their social status in measured tones, only slightly modifying the external appearance, scale, and materials of their homes. They almost never deviated from the norm of log construction. They might set themselves apart from their less prosperous neighbors by building bigger houses with two stories and more than the ordinary number of glass windows, but they did not elect to build huge, ostentatious mansions.

The Somerset County elite took this path at a time when well-to-do people in other parts of the country were experimenting with more ostentatious architectural forms. Nationally, the 1798 Direct Tax reveals extreme inequality in housing—indeed, some scholars have argued that housing inequality was greater in 1798 than it was in the late twentieth century. Social display and competition for status often found their expression in architecture. In cities of the eastern seaboard, merchants and traders fashioned lavish city houses that looked outward to a cosmopolitan, competitive Atlantic world. Nor was architectural pretension confined to urban areas. The Connecticut Valley's "River Gods" erected impressive hilltop mansions. The longer-settled plantation regions of the South—the Carolina lowcountry, for example—also are famous for their extensive and loudly hierarchical plantation complexes, dominated by a "big house." Closer to Somerset County, fully 42 percent of Lancaster County's better houses were constructed of stone, frame, or brick. Even near the confluence of rivers in Pittsburgh, some merchants, tavern keepers, ironmasters, and mill owners lived in substantial stone houses averaging over $300 in value.[60]

In Somerset County, though, several factors converged to ensure that this type of landscape did not emerge. First, the undeveloped state of the local economy meant that skilled artisans and building supply sources such as brickyards were scarce. People invested their resources first in land, livestock, and even tools and consumer goods before thinking about new buildings.

Second, while inequality surely existed in Somerset County, the disparities within the local hierarchy weren't as marked as they were elsewhere in the young nation. In Philadelphia or South Carolina, a tiny percentage of the population controlled a huge portion of the total wealth. In the Somerset County backcountry, by contrast, the top 10 percent of the taxables owned 30 percent of the wealth—a large portion, but not as lopsided as in Charleston or Virginia. In 1800, at least three-quarters of the males sixteen years of age and over were taxable—that is, they owned some real or personal property. Of the remaining quarter, a substantial fraction was composed of teenage boys who weren't likely to own property yet. The point is that in Somerset County there were fewer social distinctions that could be manifested in architecture.[61]

Third, the dominance of Germanic culture ensured that wealth was accumulated less in the form of houses than in land, animals, and bonds. This was a continuation of Pennsylvania German custom in southeastern Pennsylvania. In eastern Pennsylvania, Germans—in comparison with "the English"—tended to underfurnish their homes, even when their means permitted more lavishly decorated interiors. Somerset County's German emigrants seem to have perpetuated these patterns.[62]

There is one more important reason that people in this backcountry region muted their architectural expression. Local cultural and social conditions virtually guaranteed that sociability would be highly valued, no matter what place a person occupied on the social ladder. Hierarchy was important and all-pervasive, but life could not go on without relying on others. To set oneself apart—whether through symbolic statements expressed in architectural ornament or through spatial means, such as hallways and walls—would be to invite trouble. In this society, status was made clear in nonarchitectural ways, and each resident depended upon the others; continual social interaction helped sustain that interdependence and make it successful. People nourished identities forged in relation to social ties rather than to ideals of personal independence and ostentatious display. They worked, played, ate, and slept together out of necessity—but also in keeping with social values. Everywhere, social contact prevailed over individual privacy. The arrangement that best served this culture was "open."[63]

The preindustrial Somerset County farmstead buildings thus were not "domestic" in the same way that modern residences are; the latter emphasize private, mostly leisure activity for nuclear family members, but in early housing, almost every space was a workspace. Basement and kitchen areas were the most constantly busy worksites, but other rooms and even the upper floors were often given over to productive labor. It was not uncommon for families to extend productive activity even to the attic spaces, by smoking meats in the upper chimney area or by storing foodstuffs there. Thus, understanding how work and space interacted is central to understanding the preindustrial house.

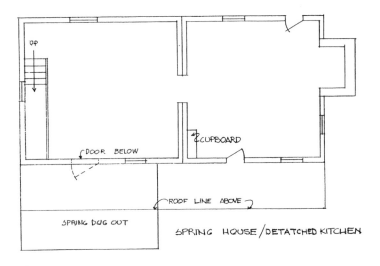

FIG. 19
Somerset County's early detached kitchens were not built to remove heavy work from the main house but to augment working space for artisans and tavern keepers. This detached kitchen on the Fritz family farm in Brothersvalley Township dates to the first quarter of the nineteenth century. Somerset Historical Center.

In simple one- or two-room houses, the main rooms were simultaneously kitchen, living area, and sleeping quarters. The kitchen function predominated, since food processing work took up so much time and space. In more complex structures, this work took place in the basements of banked dwellings or in detached kitchens.

In a period when the overall built landscape was thin, detached kitchens stood out. Detached kitchens were often as large as the dwelling itself and were well equipped. An early-nineteenth-century example, measuring 16' square, had a large fireplace (55" across) and a floor-to-ceiling cupboard (see Fig. 19). A contemporaneous 32' × 16' structure incorporated not just a cooking fireplace but also a bake oven. A third was built over a spring, creating a comprehensive structure that could be used for heavy cooking (rendering lard, making soap, boiling apple butter, and so on), laundering, and dairying.[64]

Why did vernacular builders erect detached kitchens? Some scholars have interpreted eighteenth-century German-American detached kitchens in North Carolina and Virginia as evidence of the minority group's "acculturation" to the Anglo-American values of refinement. The appearance of detached kitchens in Delaware, where they were built by members of all nationalities, has been interpreted more in functional terms—as part of a trend toward differentiation and specialization of space.[65] But in Somerset County, none of these explanations apply.

The Direct Tax of 1798 offers some tantalizing clues about the function of buildings called "kitchens" in Somerset County. Fifty-nine kitchens appeared in the Somerset County inventory, averaging 15' × 20'—as large as many a dwelling. If we look at kitchen owners' occupations, a pattern emerges: a disproportionate number of kitchens were erected by artisans or tradespeople.[66] Hatters, masons, joiners, a tanner, a "taylor," and a weaver had kitchens, as did a number of people who kept taverns or stores. Here is an interesting pattern indeed. What might it mean? One possibility that comes to mind immediately is that, in crowded artisan dwellings, there simply wasn't enough space for food processing and artisan work—hence a separate kitchen. Artisans' dwellings, as primary worksites, must have been strained to accommodate tools and workers for rural cottage industries producing hats, cloth, furniture, shoes, and other space-consuming products. Artisans tended to devote most of their time and resources to their craft, so their investment in buildings reflects this. Apprentices, too, took up space. Tavern owners would need a large kitchen to cook for guests. For those who were "in trade," as the expression went, perhaps the house was where goods were kept and customers entertained.

All this information prompts a rethinking of the early "kitchen" as an outbuilding. Much later, the term "summer kitchen" would appear, referring to a place that clearly facilitated farmwork. But it appears that in the late eighteenth and early nineteenth centuries, the "kitchen" functioned as an adjunct to trade as much as to farming. No store buildings appear in the Direct Tax, yet a number of taxables are listed as "[in] trade" or as having a "store." For them, kitchen work would be easier to carry on in separate quarters. In this light, then, theories of "acculturation" and hypotheses about social distancing or heat do not seem very pertinent. Rather, particular occupations created practical needs that were served by separate kitchens.[67]

As we move outward from the house we encounter the dooryard space, called the *vorhof* by Pennsylvania Germans. Work activities—especially in warm weather—would have spilled over to occupy the area immediately surrounding the house on the kitchen-door side. It is likely that this space would have been the location for the many ephemeral workplaces—those erected for a specific task, then dismantled. The very earliest settlers might grind grain here, chop wood, dry beans and pumpkins, and so on. Many inventories mention bee swarms that were housed in hives; these probably wouldn't have been located very close to the house but would have been found in the vicinity.[68]

Beyond the dooryard, the preindustrial farmstead itself was still not highly defined spatially. The cleared area was very small, about 20 acres—a small fraction of the average landholding, which was around 225 acres.[69] On this tiny acreage, farmsteads often lacked even shelter for livestock; the 1798 Direct Tax listed 1,235 dwellings but only 472 barns and 227 stables. To be sure, a few minor structures escaped the notice of the assessors. One estate inventory listed "Hoggs in the Pen," for example, referring to a rudimentary shelter for bad weather and fattening up. But in general, Somerset County farmers butchered livestock rather than carry it through the winter, letting a few survivors huddle miserably against a haystack through the cold weather. Frequently, animals simply foraged for themselves. Anne Royall found sheep roaming through the woods in 1829: "Sheep run at large on the mountains, look very white and clean, and are larger than those farther east." We have already seen that cattle decimated the native grasses as they searched for forage in the Glades. Inventories mention "Hoggs in the Woods." Crops, too, often were left in the field. Inventories mention grain "in the sheaf" and stacks of hay, implying limited barn space. Henry Beam, for example, left several stacks of hay, oats, rye, and wheat in 1802.[70]

Because animal shelter was limited, fences took on great importance (Fig. 20). Erecting fences was a high-priority task and occupied much of the settlers' time. In this period, fencing had many complex functions, both social and practical. Customary practice and law dictated that wandering beasts must be fenced out of gardens and orchards, so often these spaces would be enclosed

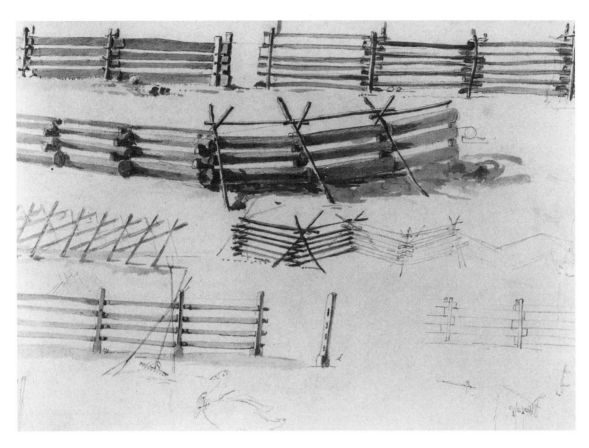

FIG. 20
French naturalist Charles Alexandre Lesueur sketched these types of fencing in western Pennsylvania about 1820. Fences served to keep animals out of the fields and to mark property boundaries. Charles Alexandre Lesueur Collection, Muséum d'Histoire Naturelle, Le Havre, N° 39075.

first. As more acreage was cleared, fencing indicated property boundaries (division fences) and subdivisions within properties (field fences)—along with garden, house, and orchard enclosures.

Common fencing types fell into a hierarchy, in practical and symbolic terms. In some areas, agricultural reformer John Lorain observed that fences were simply "formed by falling the timber in the line where the fences are designed to be run, and by supplying the deficiencies which will afterwards appear, with the limbs and tops of the trees which happen to have taken too great a spread, from the center of the line of the fence." The most frequently seen fence type was the "worm" or "stake-and-rider" fence. This zigzag affair was constructed of sawn, split, or round rails set in panels at 120 degrees; earth-fast stakes anchored the angles, and "riders" were then placed in the "X" for added stability and height. These fences were generally between five and eight rails high. Observers in Somerset County noted eight-rail-high stake-and-rider fences, and farming contracts often stipulated that the tenant erect such fencing. Post-and-rail fences, however, required more labor. One early resident of western Pennsylvania noted that building these fences occasioned "extra whiskey, and other good cheer . . . [and] labor they are bound to return, when their neighbors have to encounter the same work." Post-and-rail fences made up for the extra expense, because they took up less room and were more secure, especially if palings (vertical members) were attached to them for added sturdiness. These tended to set off house, garden, or orchard. Sometimes, fences were made of palings set close together, sometimes interwoven with wattles (supple young twigs, interlaced horizontally). Thomas Vickroy's accounts with Jacob Mock refer to "Pailings" made by Mock for one of Vickroy's properties.[71]

Fencing had important symbolic connotations. Even in the earliest colonial days, fences marked out the boundaries of private property and communicated "improvement," forming part of the justification for displacing Native Americans all over the eastern seaboard. (Settlers often denied the Indians' claim to the land by arguing that the Indians lacked fixed, private property in land, and moreover that they had not made "improvements." Fences symbolized both the private-property system and the ideology of "improvement.") In the new nation, fencing came to be associated with a republican virtue that equated profit and productivity with good citizenship: orderly fences indicated systematic agriculture. They also encoded social distinctions of wealth. But in more recently settled and less developed regions like Somerset County, notions of "common" land persisted, especially where animal owners continued to let their stock roam free to forage. In this forest society, an average farm had less than 10 percent of its acreage cleared, and fences mainly fended off wild and domesticated creatures. Thomas Vickroy's contracts with tenants imply that fences functioned as barriers that protected croplands and meadows. Frederick Cobaugh, for example, agreed "to clear Thirty acres of ground & put it under good staked & ridered fence." William Hand agreed to "sprout the fields and fence corners that he may put in and farm." Joseph McVicker was directed to "grub clear and fence five acres of upland . . . to extend from the Meadow up to adjoin the Road, . . . to leave the whole under good and lawful staked and ridered fence separate from the Meadow fence."[72]

Of course, fences could simultaneously communicate the impulse to set boundaries to private property, to mark off one's own holdings. Early Somerset County fences, then, like so many other aspects of the preindustrial material culture, contained ambiguous messages. Barriers expressed mutuality, because they were erected by neighbors working together to make sure everyone's crops were protected. Boundaries expressed hierarchy because they visibly set off one person's real estate holdings from another's.[73]

After fences, outbuildings for the crops and animals took up the time and attention of the early Somerset County residents. Early on, the farmstead complex consisted of a few basic structures. The most important buildings, of course, were the barns and stables. The 1798 Direct Tax shows that Somerset County barns were typically built of log, with average dimensions of 23' by 52'. We do not know how many levels these barns had, but they could have been either English three-bay barns or Germanic *grundscheier* barns (see Fig. 21). Tenancy agreements specify log barns with two cribs (enclosed interior spaces, usually square) and a central mow (an open, floor-to-ceiling space where hay was stored), without mention of multiple levels. Harmon Husband's estate inventory (1795), for instance, mentions three mows "full hay," suggesting either a large

FIG. 21

This log three-bay barn in Lincoln Township is of uncertain date, but it represents the relatively simple early unbanked barns of the county. Most early farms lacked barns altogether, though. Somerset Historical Center.

barn or more than one barn. Other inventories, such as John Markley's (1796), also mention substantial amounts of "hay in the barn," implying large structures. Jacob Kooser kept rye "on the loft threshed."[74] Stables tended to be smaller—an average of 18' × 22'—and were probably used more for housing livestock and equipment than for storing crops. Some farms had both a barn and a stable; others just had a stable for one or two animals.

Smaller structures mentioned in the archival record include chicken coops, hog houses, and "caves" for root crops. Only twenty-nine springhouses were mentioned in the Direct Tax; some banked houses were built over springs, but in general the springhouse was a rarity. The relative insignificance of springhouses on the landscape testifies to the marginal place that dairying occupied in the developing economy.

All in all, the early Somerset County landscape was but lightly built. As much activity took place outdoors as within—and perhaps more. The people's workplaces were, more often than not, under the open sky. If barns were small or nonexistent, such farm tasks as threshing and husking would have taken place somewhere other than the barn floor (perhaps in the dooryard). Milking almost certainly was performed outside the barn, either in the field or the yard. When we think of this period, we should imagine people outdoors—scutching, hackling, churning, chopping, sawing, boiling.

Property boundaries were well established, but not confining. Farmsteads quickly became connected to each other and to commercial and religious places. Buildings for manufacturing and cottage industry quickly became focal points in road and path networks. Gristmills, sawmills, fulling mills, and oil mills (for linseed oil) provided essential processing services; in 1798, twenty-three gristmills and sixteen sawmills were listed in the county. These were situated where adequate waterpower could be found, but they usually were not self-contained units. Rather, they stood on farmsteads, and their owners usually both farmed and ran the mills. Smith shops, hatter shops, tan houses, potter shops, weave houses, cooper shops, and saddler shops were located at crossroads villages, such as Berlin (in Brothersvalley Township) or Somerset Town.

Finally, there was a sacred dimension to the landscape. The "Calvanist Congragation" [*sic*] had a meetinghouse and schoolhouse listed in the 1798 Direct Tax, and the "Pine Ridge Congragation" had a "church" and schoolhouse. Services were frequently held in people's homes or at inns. Mennonite Bishop Christian Newcomer visited Berlin in 1799; at Seiler's and at John Zuck's, "a numerous congregation had assembled, more than the house could contain. In the evening, the people assembled again; and we had a melting time."[75] Though the formal, built dimension of religion was limited in this period, the church community still formed the core of at least some people's spiritual and social lives. But despite the ever powerful retrospective historical memory that gives a prominent place to pioneering religious groups in the county (especially the Brethren, the Lutheran and Reformed congregations, and the Jersey Baptists), it is not at all clear that religion played a dominant role in the early culture. There is no way to know for sure whether most people attended church regularly, but historical documentation from other areas suggests that though church attendance was on the rise during this period, it started from a very low level—sometimes as low as 10 percent of the adult population. There is little reason to believe that religious matters in Somerset County were very different from those in other parts of the young nation.[76]

When we consider the range of activities in which people engaged and the geographic settings for those activities, the picture that emerges is one of a landscape in which the woodlands, roads and footpaths, glades, stump fields, cleared fields, meadows, gardens, and dooryards were integral parts of people's homes. Just as houses were not "private" in the modern sense of the word, so too were the country spaces "open." Children chased the livestock and ran errands; men hunted in the woods; all traveled constantly between farmsteads to help one another. Women were not excluded from this life of constant motion. They, too, crisscrossed the countryside. Midwives, especially, could be called on at any time, but their efforts were just extreme examples of the kind of helping activity that went on every day. The entire landscape became a collective workplace for this self-sufficient community.

Somerset County residents, then, most likely did not think of their domestic realms as tightly bounded "private" space. A house might serve as workplace, hostelry, or place of worship, but whatever its use, it was invariably a social place. Sugarmaking, hunting, gathering, clearing— almost every activity required collective effort spread across many property boundaries. The whole landscape took primacy over the individual farmstead in shaping people's lives and consciousness. Fields were tiny. The visual and spatial impact of fencing within this woodland society must have been limited, since the forest (and the public roads that wended through it) essentially constituted "common" land, regardless of whether hogs or humans used it. People lived their everyday lives as much away from the farmstead as within its borders. Our contemporary preoccupation with the buildings in isolation is ahistorical: in the end, it does not capture the essence of people's spatial experience in the settlement era.

★   ★   ★

To sum up, the agrarian landscape of preindustrial Somerset County gave shape to the values of the community. Paths bound neighbors together; people hunted and gathered over everyone's woods and clearings; animals, too, benefited as they foraged across property boundaries, oblivious to the niceties of human legal abstractions. On individual farmsteads, the houses, fields, outbuildings, and barns provided settings for much communal activity. Individualism was not prominent, but as a group, the people cherished a pronounced spirit of local independence. This community was not without hierarchy; on the contrary, distinctions of wealth, sex, and age divided people. Neither was the community free of conflict. Personal violence was probably quite as common in Somerset County as it was on other sections of the frontier (as numerous stories of notorious local murders would amply attest). But the society achieved some coherence and some success at meeting the standards it set for itself.

The built landscape that came out of this society reflected its intensely local focus and its ambivalent relationship to the world beyond. While vernacular builders shared a vocabulary of construction techniques and spatial forms with designers across the region, this vocabulary was expressed only in tentative and limited ways. (There were few signs that local residents would follow the East's embrace of refinement, for example.) Social hierarchies were proclaimed not through architecture but through other means. All in all, the woodland landscape of early Somerset County communicated a distrust of outsiders and of their building idioms. In the nineteenth century, though, local residents would shed some of this distrust and embark on a remarkably creative blending process that would reconcile localism with the more widely dispersed architectural vocabulary.

2 ★ A Farming Country, 1820–1880

The nineteenth century was the "Farmer's Age" in America. Throughout the thriving, confident republic, the number of farms, the acreage of cleared land, and the population all increased dramatically. Agrarian expansion was fueled by a dramatic "market revolution": transportation and communications improvements and innovations in production transformed the ways in which people thought and worked. The market revolution brought new opportunities and challenges to American farm families, whether they worked the black Illinois loam or tended dairy cows in upstate New York. The transition to more market-oriented, capitalist agriculture created new class relationships, encouraged more systematic work processes, and affected concepts of gender. In complex and still mysterious ways, the market revolution was also intertwined with such disparate events as the rise of antislavery movements, the efflorescence of evangelical religion, and even new attitudes to child rearing. Americans' responses to these far-reaching forces were shaped by a variety of factors, including (but not limited to) personal experience, class background, gender, and ethnic heritage. Urban workers dismayed by the de-skilling of artisan trades responded with a critique of capitalism and a call for working-class political solidarity. Middle-class spokespeople created a new concept of labor that depended on gender; they transformed a gendered *division* of labor into a gendered *definition* of labor, one that devalued many kinds of women's work—especially housework. Agricultural reformers and elite farmers called for a more rigorous, scientific, and systematic approach to farming, giving their notions of order a moral tinge.[1]

The nineteenth-century landscape evolved within this context. Across the country, a massive process of reorganization was transforming the look of rural America. This reorganization can be interpreted in many ways. An older, conventional view holds that the reorganization was part of an essentially additive process of economic development, one in which changes took place predictably as a result of progress. That view is problematic because it minimizes the tremendous ambiguity and conflict of the period. Another way of looking at these changes is to cast them as a shift from "folk" to "popular" forms. In hindsight, this model has a satisfying analytical appeal. It observes that "folk" building—which was characteristically regional or local, traditional, homemade, and ethnic—gave way over time to "popular" building, which was characteristically national in distribution, innovative, machine-made or mass-produced, mainstream, and print-oriented. However, even this model doesn't apply neatly, because in most places, the process was protracted and uneven. Most nineteenth-century buildings possessed an admixture of characteristics. (Indeed, even politically, the nation-state wasn't at the center of all citizens' loyalties during most of the century; it would be surprising if their cultural and spatial vocabularies were fully nationalized.[2])

In short, any explanation of landscape change in this period will recognize the complexity of the process. A subtle dynamic was at work—and a central feature of this dynamic was that people reacted to large forces in very localistic ways. Rather than exerting a homogenizing influence, nineteenth-century capitalism actually helped make the landscape more varied. All over the countryside, in places both nearby and remote, rural people created locally distinctive landscapes in response to the forces of market capitalism and cultural change. New England farmers were assembling the connected farm complex while eastern Pennsylvania farmers were making the "Pennsylvania barn" a standard landscape feature. In the Valley of Virginia, yeomen were erecting "I" houses. Farmers in Sugar Creek, Illinois, were fashioning a "landscape of class," putting up stylish farmhouses that contrasted with the housing stock of their poorer neighbors. In Pennsylvania's Cumberland Valley, rural residents set about encasing their log houses with brick. In the Delaware countryside, new, oversized barns exceeded the productive capacities of the farms. In upstate New York, the "Northern basement barn" appeared to accommodate specialized dairying, and a distinctively Dutch American landscape emerged in the Hudson Valley. In widely separated places, country people added pattern-book style to their house exteriors, thus signaling their knowledge of national taste—but they frequently retained older spatial organization behind the facades. And in each of these instances locally distinctive landscapes took shape, formed by local history and culture and by the available repertoire of architectural ideas.

These architectural adaptations represented an accommodation of capitalism and technological change. They were aimed, first and foremost, at enabling people to work more efficiently and productively: they embodied the ideals of rationalism, science, regularity, system, and order. But these spaces also imparted the new social values that were coming to dominate the mainstream culture. They reinforced prevalent forms of social hierarchy (especially class hierarchy). They afforded more options for individuality and privacy. And they communicated aspirations to refinement and gentility. Shifts in patterns of gender relationships, too, found their expression in the landscape. Each particular adaptation was voiced in the terms given by a local repertoire of ideas—a vocabulary the people could command—that helped them express their relationship to the wider world.

In Somerset County, we have an opportunity to observe this process closely. A distinctive ensemble of landscape features came to epitomize well-to-do Somerset County farmsteads: a banked, two-story farmhouse (with a double-decker porch) almost always combined with a Pennsylvania barn. Together with ancillary buildings, this complex of organized farm spaces helped Somerset County residents accommodate the new order by creating efficient workspaces, private spaces, and spaces that told of shifting patterns of gender. Yet like their counterparts in other parts of rural America, Somerset Countians built their farmsteads in a way that actually resulted in a landscape that was arguably more locally "marked" than its settlement-era predecessor.

Massive reorganization took place not only on the scale of the farmstead but also on the scale of the neighborhood. In Somerset County, it translated into regular patterns on the land: political boundaries, property lines, roadway systems, and a countywide system of public schools. So, too, the neighborhood was subjected to a rationalized, rigorous spatial reordering. At the same time, the local landscape was undergoing sacralization in a burst of church and cemetery building. This heightened sacred order reinforced the trend to rationalism in some ways—but in other ways, it implicitly resisted the direction in which the secular society was heading. In short, the attentive observer would see, inscribed in the landscape, signs that the transitions of the nineteenth century were not inevitably smooth ones. The story of Somerset County's transformation is a window onto one community's bumpy road to modernity.

A settled rural culture helped negotiate the fitful confrontation with modernity. In Somerset County, rural people showed a strong tendency to continue the patterns of local self-sufficiency forged in the preindustrial era. The core of the county's industry still catered to agriculture: grain milling and wool processing dominated, even though manufacturing had expanded to include such ventures as stove making. In general, heavy industry made few inroads locally. Coal mining, charcoal production, and iron and steel production were emerging nearby, but not in Somerset itself. Rural Somerset County residents responded to economic change in a highly selective way. During this period, they developed an agrarian economy and culture that blended preindustrial values and customs with more modern ones: consumerism, mechanization, cash orientation, and standardization. Sometimes the blending went smoothly, but at other times, it resulted in conflict and tension.

By this point, many local families had several generations' worth of experience in the county and had developed extensive kin networks. These "persisters," predominantly Germanic in background, had a greater, more lasting impact than the more restless folk who stayed only a short while. A decidedly Pennsylvania German flavor permeated social life. Pennsylvania German foodways, religious institutions, and folkways flourished between the ridges, and the Pennsylvania German dialect was heard everywhere. An isolated "linguistic island" slowly formed; the local dialect related more closely to the dialects of Lebanon, Mifflin, and York Counties than to those further east, but it added a few distinctive expressions as well.[3] In the most heavily Germanic neighborhoods, "sharpers" skulked about, taking advantage of farmers who didn't understand English. Evidently the language was pervasive enough that many could get along well without English—at least most of the time!

Social ties, so important in the frontier period, continued to have a prominent place in people's lives. If anything, the number and variety of people's social contacts increased with better transportation, higher population densities, elaborated kin networks, continued traditions of shared work, and the rise of social and political organizations. Rural people's diaries and accounts show constant visiting of friends and relatives. Rare was the night when the farm family didn't host a guest or two or themselves visit someone.

Cooperative work and the communal web of exchanges persisted, along with the values of local self-sufficiency. Yet at the same time Somerset County rural people strove to integrate new values of consumerism, profit, individualism, and "progress" or "improvement." Discipline, time-orientation, system, and order challenged older work habits oriented toward task work and sociability. Cash exchanges allowed individuals greater autonomy. The story of this period revolves around how rural people navigated this ambiguous cultural terrain.

THE MARKET REVOLUTION AND NEW FARMING PATTERNS

First, some background will help establish the scene. Starting in the 1820–40 period, a number of turnpikes eventually linked the county with Greensburg to the west, Bedford to the east, Johnstown to the northwest, and Cumberland, Maryland, to the south (see Fig. 22). Rail access was possible by the 1850s via Cumberland or by the Pennsylvania Railroad to the north of the county (see Fig. 23), though it was limited until the Connellsville and Somerset & Mineral Point Railroads were completed in 1874. Only this latter route actually penetrated the county.

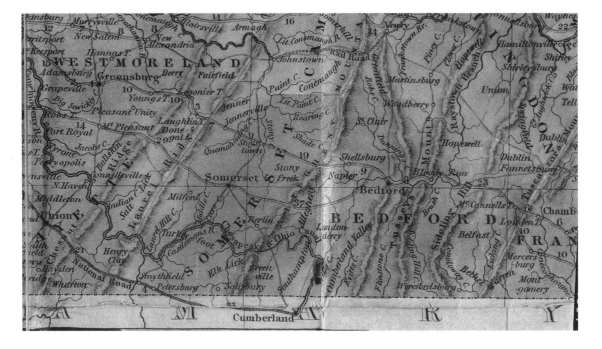

FIG. 22
Mitchell's Pocket Map of Pennsylvania, 1835, showed Somerset County's acquisition of roads. Historical Collections and Labor Archives, The Pennsylvania State University Libraries.

FIG. 23

By midcentury, farmers in the county could get their produce to the Baltimore & Ohio railhead in Cumberland, Maryland, but there were still no railroads in the county itself. *Colton's Map of Pennsylvania* (New York: G. W. and C. B. Colton, 1855). Historical Collections and Labor Archives, The Pennsylvania State University Libraries.

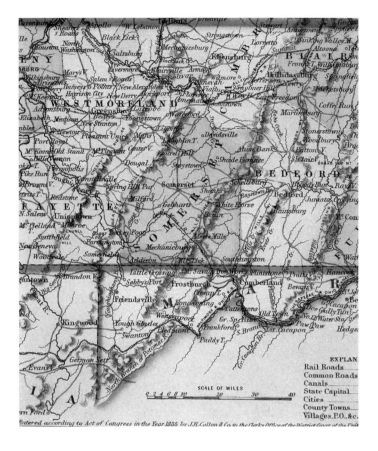

The county's population rose (Fig. 24) and the agrarian economy expanded. Small hamlets, villages, and crossroads grew up, and the population density in rural neighborhoods increased, creating local markets for farm produce. By 1830, the population had reached nearly eighteen thousand, and the cleared acreage approached eighty thousand. Houses outnumbered "cabins." Water-powered mills, situated along streams and runs, performed essential services: cutting lumber, carding wool, fulling cloth, grinding flour, and pressing oil.[4]

The first year for which extensive agricultural statistics are available is 1850. In that year, the county boasted 1,613 farms averaging about 230 acres each, with 100 acres improved. Virtually all of the farms enumerated listed horses, milch cows, and other cattle, sheep, and swine; nearly all listed home manufactures. Two-thirds made maple sugar. A little over half produced flax. Buckwheat was commonly grown, but less than a fifth of the farm families raised Indian corn, and only a very few listed grass or clover seed, hops, or barley. To raise and process these items, Somerset County farms used implements whose per-farm value was estimated at $113, right at the statewide average.[5]

In 1850, Somerset County fully represented statewide and regional trends in some respects, while following a distinctively local path in others. The county occupied an average position where hay, hogs, and minor grains were concerned. As in the pioneer period, Somerset County ranked very low in the state in corn and wheat production. Conversely (again continuing patterns

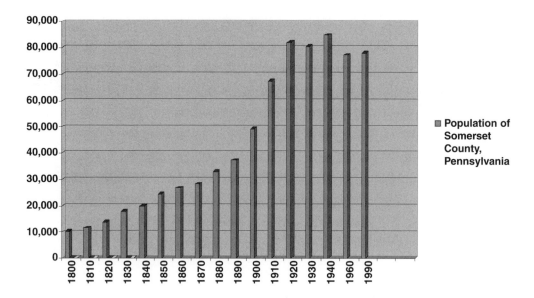

FIG. 24

Population of Somerset County, 1800–1990. Data from U.S. Census statistics.

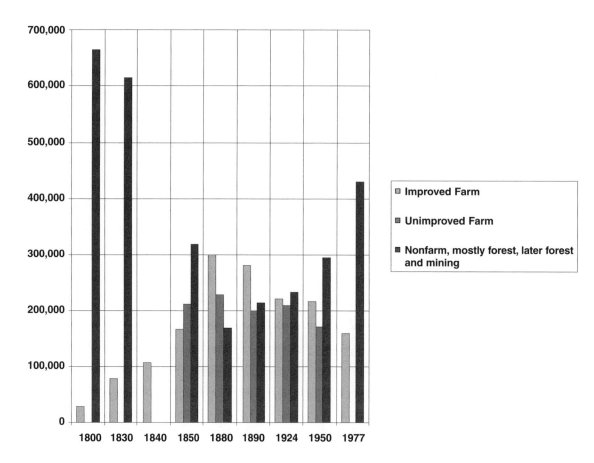

FIG. 25

Farm and nonfarm acreage, Somerset County. The improved farm acreage in Somerset County increased over time, but not until 1880 did the balance tip so that improved acres made up the majority of farm acreage. Data from the U.S. Census of Agriculture.

set earlier), Somerset ranked high in total and per-farm amounts of oats, milch cows, and maple sugar. The county also reported higher than average wool production and home manufactures.[6]

In order to understand patterns of rural landscape formation in this period, we must take into account that the pace of agricultural change quickened significantly. The agricultural statistics for 1880 suggest the broad outlines of change (see Figs. 25, 26, and 28). The number of farms had more than doubled—to 3,393; the average farm size correspondingly diminished to 155 acres, 87 of those improved. Numbers of livestock decreased, as did most crop quantities. Per-farm wheat and buckwheat production, however, remained steady, and other activities actually increased despite the drop in farm size. Indian corn acreage and per-farm production numbers rose dramatically, for example, and maple sugar production also climbed sharply. The average farm quadrupled its harvest of potatoes. Poultry was counted for the first time, and these figures showed 26 hens and 106 dozen eggs on average. The value of farm implements likewise increased (to $134), but not as quickly as it did in other counties: the statewide average was $166.[7]

An examination of individual crops should help explain the new farming patterns that developed over the course of the century. The case of corn, for instance, is intriguing. It suggests that over the generations, local farmers selected hardy strains or strains that would mature quickly. Evidence for this hypothesis comes from the Pennsylvania State College Agricultural Extension reports from the early twentieth century. In 1917, extension agents tried to get Somerset County farmers to raise varieties then favored by the agricultural establishment, but these initiatives were coolly received. The agent's annual report hints at why: "[T]he results of these tests were rather indefinite, due to the fact that we had an early frost which froze the corn before it reached

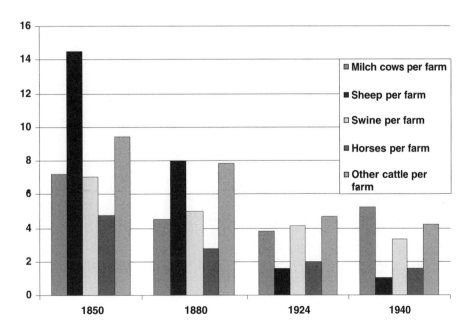

FIG. 26
As farms grew more numerous but smaller, so the numbers of animals on each farm diminished. Data from the U.S. Census of Agriculture.

maturity. . . . The home grown corn did not grow as large but matured earlier than any other corn in the test." The agent was writing in 1917, but the local "home grown" corn to which he referred had likely been raised for some time.[8]

It is fairly easy to explain why wheat production declined in importance (though countywide totals increased, because there were more farms). Wheat had never been of paramount significance in the county—the county's remoteness from markets had prompted farmers to raise other grains and convert them to whiskey—and with the opening of vast wheat fields in the West, it became even less significant. Reasons for the decline of rye are a bit more speculative. Consumption of hard liquor and rye flour products (both, of course, produced from rye grain) dropped steeply during this period, so perhaps we need look no further for an explanation.[9]

A smaller proportion of farms raised buckwheat, but they raised more of it; the peak of buckwheat production in the county wouldn't be reached until 1910, and there were several reasons for the steady interest in it. By the late nineteenth century and early into the twentieth, buckwheat was becoming popular at the "breakfast-table of the city resident," as Cornell University

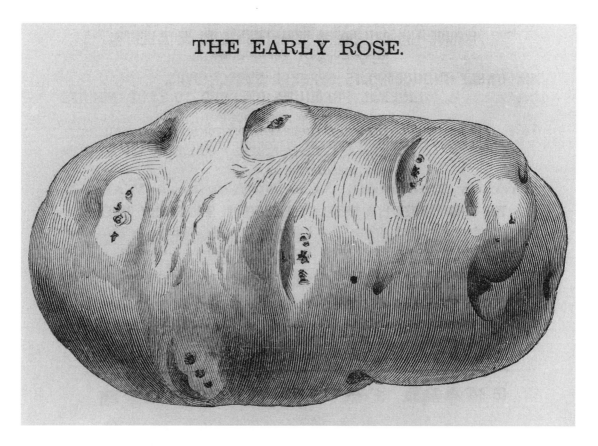

FIG. 27
The "Early Rose" potato was one of the first varieties grown in North American latitudes that responded to changing day length. It was popularized by Chauncey Goodrich, an upstate New York minister. From George W. Best, *Best's Potato Book* (Utica, N.Y.: G. W. Best, 1870), 25.

professor Liberty Hyde Bailey noted. And as new markets for the grain were developing, buckwheat also continued to hold a special place in the local diet. In addition, buckwheat was a highly versatile crop. It flourished in the very type of cool climate that characterized (and still characterizes) the county. It matured quickly, and so was frequently raised when another crop had failed. Its care could be fitted easily into any farm labor routine. It did not need to be machine threshed. Finally, buckwheat, as Bailey observed, "leaves the soil in a peculiarly mellow, ashy condition"—ideal for planting potatoes, another crop of increasing importance.[10]

The quadrupling of potato output reveals the blended forces of tradition, market, and modernization. Potatoes had multiple uses: they were consumed by humans, of course, but also by livestock, so they could function as a component within the old-style "low input" agriculture by helping provide for family subsistence and allowing families to avoid purchasing animal feed and even laundry starch. They were still harvested in the old way, by men and women digging together in the potato patch. At the same time, the tubers found a ready market in the towns. The Somerset *Herald and Whig* ran an urgent appeal in 1864 for "POTATOES! POTATOES! A lot of good potatoes are wanted for which the highest cash prices will be paid." By the 1880s they were shipped out in railroad carloads. Somerset County farmers showed their modernizing tendencies in their willingness to grow varieties that were relatively new, such as "Early Rose" (Fig. 27)—first made available in the late 1860s—and "Red Garnet." Again exemplifying new ways of farming, these varieties originated in the work of a minister in Utica, New York, work that was continued by a farmer in Vermont. Information about these strains would very likely have reached Pennsylvania farmers through the agricultural press. Farmers were beginning to seek information not just from their parents but also from nationally distributed print sources. Of course, they had strong incentive to avoid the disastrous blights of the period as well.[11]

Data about individual farms were captured in the manuscript census of agriculture for 1880. This shows that virtually all farms produced the same mix of agricultural products, differing only in scale. In other words, there was only one basic type of farm in Somerset County—a highly diversified general-farming mix with an important role for forest products and livestock. Differences do emerge in other practices, such as whether farmers paid wages for farm labor (only about half did so) and whether they reported purchasing fertilizer (a small minority did). Here, perhaps, we can see the faint beginnings of a gap between farms that relied on traditional non-cash inputs (family labor, home-produced manure or lime) and those that ventured into a more capital-intensive, modern agriculture. We do know that by the 1870s, a seasonal wage labor force was forming: some local young men became itinerant farm laborers, moving to Franklin County to work in the harvest and then following the climate patterns to return to Somerset in time to obtain work there.[12]

The census statistics do not account for other important farm products and activities. Information on these must come from a range of sources, such as travelers' accounts, estate inventories, local newspapers, and manuscript diaries and account books. A sense of the trade in livestock, for example, is elusive, but can be glimpsed. Droves were reported coming through Somerset in the 1870s, and occasionally the papers advertised livestock fairs. The gossip columns also mentioned

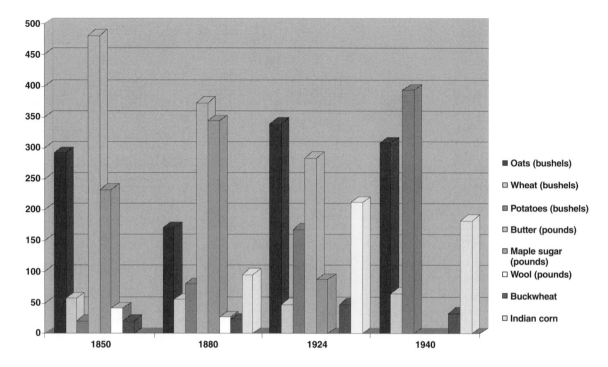

FIG. 28
Over the course of the nineteenth century, Somerset County farm households increased their maple sugar, maize, and potato production, while cutting back on other grains and wool. Data from the U.S. Census of Agriculture.

blooded cattle in various contexts; readers would find out about it, for instance, when a valuable Alderney/Short Horn animal was killed by a locomotive. Locally, there seems to have been a modest trade in blooded stock by the end of this transitional period; the 1876 Beers Atlas directory listed several growers of improved stock, and papers published notices about the horse market, where Eastern drovers bought locally raised animals. In general, though, the importance of beef cattle in the East was diminishing with the expansion of the railroad network and the rise of packinghouses in the West.[13]

The farm garden's importance was much enhanced. These gardens, as before, were worked primarily (but not exclusively) by women. Cabbages and turnips were staple crops throughout the period, especially in German families. Most people probably saved most of their seed, but mail-order seed companies (Fig. 29) also advertised in the local papers—well-known houses, including the famous Rochester (New York) firms like James Vick's, among them. The *Herald* delighted in announcing in the spring of 1871 that bushels of onion sets and hundreds of "papers of lettuce seed" had been planted. By 1876, local newspaper prize lists from the county fair give a sense of a wide range of garden crops. Women claimed premiums for radishes, kohlrabi, lima beans, white beans, cucumbers, peppers, red peppers, beets, rutabaga, watermelon, "cantelope" (the latter two a real accomplishment in this area), squash, "5 varieties pumpkins," celery, onions, yellow beans, parsnips, cauliflower, tomatoes (only just coming into wide favor), peas, rhubarb, and carrots.[14]

Orchards certainly were more extensive and more productive than in the pioneer period. Apple trees were clearly the most numerous. At the fair, men and women entered no fewer than

FIG. 29
Hovey's seedling strawberry, depicted in a
nineteenth-century peddler's plate from a
Rochester, New York, seed house. Hovey and
other Rochester companies advertised liberally
in Somerset County papers, and itinerant
peddlers sold their wares with the help of
enticing illustrations like this one. For local
farm families, purchasing seeds and plants
augmented traditional seed saving and was a
means of introducing new crops—and perhaps
new ideas as well. From D. M. Dewey, *Colored
Fruit Book for the Use of Nurserymen* (Rochester,
N.Y.: n.p., 1859); reprinted in Charles van
Ravenswaay, *A Nineteenth-Century Garden*
(New York: Universe Books, ©1977), 45.

Hovey's Seedling Strawberry

twenty-six varieties, including those with picturesque names such as "Seek No Further" and "Maiden Blush" (Fig. 30), as well as the more familiar "Rambo" and "Baldwin"—types with a variety of characteristics for keeping, flavor, harvesting time, cooking quality, and the like. But families diversified their fruit raising: local and regional nurseries advertised a wide variety of fruit, and real estate advertisements mentioned cherry and peach orchards in addition to the standard apple orchard. The 1876 county fair also exhibited samples of pears, grapes, and cherries.

Local farm women grew or gathered other fruits as well, for they prepared such delicacies as plum butter, dried blackberries and elderberries, and jellies of blackberry, mulberry, elderberry, currant, wild plum, mayapple, raspberry, crab apple, chokecherry, ground-cherry (a relative of the tomato, favored by Pennsylvania Germans for pies and preserves), strawberry, gooseberry, quince, grape, and Siberian crab apple (a small apple described as "good for culinary uses"). These activities extended and elaborated the earlier practices of gathering from the woods and fields, probably supplementing wild fruits with homegrown ones. Not only foodstuffs but also medicines were gathered; a Johnstown druggist solicited ginseng in the local papers in the 1870s.[15]

In this survey of farm "products" we must surely mention lime, coal, and timber. From the 1840s, real estate advertisements in the local newspapers often mentioned coal and limestone deposits on farms as a drawing card. Farmers dug lime, burned it (see Fig. 31), and spread it on

FIG. 30
"Maiden Blush" apple. This variety was one of
dozens that were cultivated for various qualities.
From S. A. Beach, *Apples of New York,* vol. 2
(Albany, N.Y.: J. B. Lyon Co., 1905), 140. The
Pennsylvania State University Libraries.

MAIDEN BLUSH

their own fields or sold it to neighbors; in Brothersvalley, Samuel Boger had a limekiln on his farm in 1847. The widespread presence of coal seams and outcrops in the county had been known since settlement and mined on a small scale for the local market. In his account book from 1861, John King (a Somerset Countian) recorded payments for digging coal. By the centennial year, 1.3 million bushels of coal were excavated around the county, mostly in small amounts and often from farms. On the landscape, these must have appeared as small pits located haphazardly—as geology dictated—on the farmstead.[16]

Every farm had a woodlot. A growing number of sawmills received logs from the woods and turned them into building materials as the landscape of settlement gave way to a much more densely and elaborately built environment of fences and framed buildings. Again, farmers had logs sawn for their own use but also used them as a source of income. Local manufactories, for example, made "shook" (bundles of staves) for the "foreign trade"—the bundles were shipped to the West Indies and Cuba for barrel making—and surely procured their supplies locally. Late in the period, the railroads became another major market for local timber. The Connellsville Railroad demanded supplies for the actual railroad building (for cross-ties, bridges, tunnels, and so on), and when the railway was completed (1874), it provided transportation for exporting timber.[17]

If we look back over this list of nineteenth-century farm products for Somerset County, it is apparent that the standard of living had improved considerably. The rural family enjoyed a more varied diet and had fair prospects for many market crops. Prosperity ruled, especially before the 1870s. People used their newfound wealth to acquire mass-produced, nationally (or internationally) distributed consumer goods. Along with these goods, rural people were exposed to new ideas and values. Somerset County inventories began to show evidence of better-furnished, more

FIG. 31
This farm limekiln in Addison Township dates from about 1880, but similar structures appeared in the 1840s. Farmers not only burned lime for their own farms but also sold lime fertilizer to their neighbors, evidence that local farmers were interested in agricultural improvement. Somerset Historical Center.

comfortable domestic interiors, crowded with such items as "falling leaf tables," "fancy chairs," and rocking chairs. An 1844 ad for a real estate sale gave prominence to a "PIANO" among the items for sale. Few families would have owned pianos, but all recognized that they symbolized the new age; they were mass-produced, imported, and used for leisure-time enjoyment. Some people thought of ingenious ways to acquire these instruments. In 1876, someone placed an ad in the Somerset *Democrat* wanting to trade maple sugar for a piano or parlor organ.[18]

The wider culture confronted rural people at every turn. News coming in through various media gave people a sense of the outside world. With the expanding railway system, people could go see that world for themselves; special centennial trains and even discount accommodations in Philadelphia beckoned.[19] At the Centennial Exposition, fairgoers were exposed to the magnificent Corliss steam engine and to all manner of industrial and commercial goods.

This prosperity was purchased with intensified labor: the farm family was working harder and longer than families had in the frontier period. Numerous tasks took up more time and effort. As orchards matured, family members (men, women, and children) busied themselves picking. The crop was then put to various uses. Some apples were dried for "schnitz"; family members spent many autumn evenings peeling and cutting. Part of the crop was pressed for cider, which in turn was processed into vinegar and apple butter—the latter involving long boiling and stirring over an open kettle. When it was finished, the apple butter was carefully stored in crocks for sale or for home use.

Though it still functioned as an item in local bartering trade with neighbors—and of course as an important component of the family's diet—butter was clearly one of the farm's major commercial products, and buttermaking demanded far more work than it had in the early period. The scale of commercial buttermaking was nowhere near what it was in eastern Pennsylvania or upstate New York, but it was clearly much greater than in the pioneer era. Thomas Gordon's *Pennsylvania Gazetteer* of 1832 observed that in Somerset County, "The chief rural business is grazing. The breed of cattle is somewhat peculiar, being very small horned, and is much esteemed. The butter is of excellent quality, and exported in large quantities." "Glade" butter from the county fetched good prices in Baltimore, Pittsburgh, and Philadelphia—markets serving the expanding urban and nonagricultural population. The butter could be packed in tubs and shipped out via the turnpikes or (after midcentury, in the case of the Baltimore market) from Cumberland on the railroad. Local merchants also took butter "in trade," and continued to do so throughout the period. In 1876, for instance, J. W. Patton published a notice in the Somerset *Democrat* that he needed 10,000 pounds immediately: "I will pay for choice Roll Butter half Cash."[20]

The tools used for buttermaking did not change much throughout the century; neither did the gender division of dairying labor. As before, inventories mention milk crocks, churns, milk pans, and butter tubs. Some listed newer patent devices such as the barrel churn, and local papers advertised dog-powered churns, but few patent devices worked well enough to challenge the older dash-style churn (see Fig. 32). Kegs for storage and shipping were locally made. Buttermaking was still women's

FIG. 32
This dash churn probably dates from the early twentieth century. Despite many attempts to find a better way to churn butter, the dash churn remained the dominant tool for buttermaking. Farm wives (and sometimes husbands too) spent many an hour of brisk, rhythmic plunging in order to "bring the butter." Somerset Historical Center.

work: young women continued to receive milch cows in their inheritances or marriage portions, just as they had in Peter Livengood's day. In 1835, for example, the Wilhelm daughters each received money plus three good milch cows. Throughout the period, both women and men milked the cows; on 8 September 1883, for example, Francis Cable noted that "Lizzie Yoder done the milking" while he and Maria were gone over the weekend. Buttermaking was still a seasonal activity, accomplished when cows were in milk, but the milking season was probably longer than before, as the cows were better fed and sheltered. Overall, buttermaking represented a great deal more work for women in this period than in the early days—not only in the actual churning, patting, salting, and so on but also in cleaning tools and spaces and in readying the butter for market.[21]

LOCAL RESPONSES TO MECHANIZATION AND THE CASH ECONOMY

To some extent, labor was eased by mechanization. Horse-powered and hand-powered implements were brought in from afar on the developing transportation network. There were manufacturers in Pittsburgh and areas farther west, as well as in New York State. But other implements were locally supplied. Lists of locally made agricultural tools show that cast-iron point and share plows were used in midcentury and that horsepower threshers appeared around 1840. According to county historian and entrepreneur Samuel Philson, the Woodcock plow with "wooden beams and handles, and balance of cast-iron, was considered a great improvement" in the 1830s. From the 1840s on, advertisements in the local paper promoted these patent plows, locally manufactured.[22] Horse-powered hay rakes were introduced around 1858 and were soon seen on "good" farms. By 1880, the manufacturing census manuscript listed a few small firms producing cultivators, hay rakes, fanning mills, hay tedders, and horse rakes. Horse-powered mowers made their appearance in the county during the labor-short Civil War years, but they were by no means universal.[23]

Though it attracted attention, mechanized farming had only a limited reach. Most farm labor was still hand work—and hard work. Inventories contain the familiar scythe, cradle, hoes, mattocks, dung forks, and so on. The manufacturing census manuscripts for 1870 show small-scale local manufacture of cradles; George Hay, for example, produced 150 cradles and seven sleighs, all made by hand with "common tools." In 1880, local producers still made more hand rakes than horse rakes.[24] Clearly, Somerset County farming mechanized more slowly than farming in the rest of the state. Indeed, a gap appeared between the county and statewide average value of farm implements. A telling piece appeared in the Somerset *Democrat* for 25 July 1883: "Mr. Peter Brugh [of Bakersville] is taking [his wheat crop] in a new way." The paper reported that he had purchased a share in a "Little Buckeye Binder." A crowd of three dozen people watched as he made his maiden voyage: "[A]ll were surprised to see how nice and fast grain could be taken off." Clearly, the "Little Buckeye" was a novelty that attracted curious onlookers—it was certainly not a commonplace sight. Only the simpler machines were familiar to local rural folk.[25]

There are probably several reasons that county farmers were relatively late adopters of mechanized implements. The hilly terrain probably discouraged Somerset County farmers from trying the relatively new harvesting machines (and still less the ones equipped with touchy and complicated automatic binders). By contrast, farmers who raised wheat on comparatively level ground—in eastern Pennsylvania, for example, or on the midwestern prairies—would have more incentive to buy the latest, expensive new equipment. But beyond these very practical realities, we can point to a certain conservatism, a selectivity, that led Somerset County farm people to adopt some aspects of industrialized and capitalized agriculture while holding fast to their traditional methods in other ways.

This conservative turn of mind was evident in virtually every facet of Somerset County rural life. The persistence of clothmaking at home is one example. This ancient craft continued in Somerset County well after it had disappeared from other areas of the East. Overall, by 1820 the United States was already importing more linen than was homemade here. By 1860, most flax raised in America was used for seed (for the oil used in making paint, or for livestock feed, or for export to—interestingly enough—Irish linen makers). But in pockets of Somerset County, traditionalists kept on pulling flax, spinning, and weaving linens and woolens even until after the Civil War. A county history stated that "[a]t a very late date throughout the region, every farmer had a

FIG. 33
This weaving house on the Wagerline farm was built in 1824, just at the moment when homemade cloth was in decline in most areas. Yet it was used for weaving for several decades—a reminder that many local people refused to give up their cherished homespuns. Somerset Historical Center.

patch of from a quarter to a half acre of flax." The manuscript census shows that the habit wasn't actually universal, but it was quite common. Casselman Valley resident Sarah King picked until 1868; W. S. Livengood, born in 1861, helped his parents pull flax. Inventories from the 1860s list spinning wheels, both small and large; that they were actively used and not just relics is suggested by the presence in the same inventories of flax thread, heckels, and so on. Local artisan Joel B. Miller's daybook shows that he was making new flax and wool wheels into the 1860s. Local manufactories only used a fraction of the total local wool output, so it is likely that the rest was either sold or processed at home. Casselman Valley resident Ollie Peachy used a wool wheel until 1900. On the Wagerline farm, a weaving house dates from 1824—erected just as the "Age of Homespun" was on the wane in other parts of the country (see Fig. 33)—and was in active use for at least another generation. As late as 1900, local merchant J. H. Sifford advertised "HOME SPUNS," and urged customers to hurry in because these sought-after items sold out quickly. It isn't clear if these items were woolen, linen, or some combination of the two, but their very appearance would have been anachronistic in most places. More indirect acknowledgment that people still spun and

FIG. 34
There is little in this late-nineteenth-century view of Kantner's Woollen Mill to suggest mass production; indeed, this enterprise resembled the old artisan workshop more than the modern factory. Somerset Historical Center.

wove their own fiber came in a 1900 advertisement run by S. Kantner, wool miller (see Fig. 34): "Do you intend having your wool worked up this season. . . . We will card, spin, twist and work it up for you much cheaper than you can at home." Kantner must have had reason to believe that many "farmers and wool growers" indeed did still "work up" their wool at home.[26]

Even the local "factories" that turned out satinett, flannel, and blankets were barely more than large-scale hand producers. An interior view of Kantner's mill from the late nineteenth century (Fig. 35) offers a fascinating glimpse of "factory" life. In the close quarters of this room, two men work, warmed by a stove. A dog curls up comfortably on the floor. One man spins at a wool wheel, while the other operates a hand loom. A second hand loom appears on the left of the photo. Clearly this is much more like the artisan shops of an earlier day than it is a factory—nothing but human handpower is in evidence. Even considering that the typical U.S. manufacturing concern of 1870 had an average of only eight employees, this one falls far short of the conventional definition of "factory" for its day. That local people thought about it and spoke of it as a "factory" is a measure of their perspective. In the context of their lives, the Kantner mill looked big, because so much local enterprise was conducted on an even smaller scale. Woolen mills shared in the old ways by doing custom carding and fulling, often bartering rather than exchanging cash, and offering their patrons meals and even lodging while they waited for processing to be completed.[27]

FIG. 35
Inside Kantner's Woollen Mill, male workers produced yarn and cloth by hand. Somerset Historical Center.

Home clothmaking, perhaps more than any other activity, evoked and symbolized the old values of self-sufficiency, frugality, and personal self-effacement: the county historian wrote that "The wearing of store clothes was thought by many to be an evidence of vanity." Of course, as before, clothmaking did not always work toward self-sufficiency; instead, cloth was traded for commodities. Nonetheless, the symbolism of homespun was deeply rooted.

Other examples of holding to old values of self-sufficiency appear in the county's folk customs. Women made *satz* (the rising agent for their bread) with hops or tansy, growing their own rather than purchasing manufactured rising agents. A writer in the *Casselman Chronicle* remembered that her grandmother always made laundry starch from potatoes: "with little effort and no outlay you could use the starch which 'the Good Lord put in the potatoes.'"[28]

The self-conscious celebration of home cloth production, the reluctance to mechanize, and the attachment to old work customs all suggest a critique of the new order. Such resistance was not unusual in nineteenth-century America. Many people were uneasy with the changes that were in the air. They objected to the loss of self-sufficiency, the impersonal nature of the cash system, the erosion of communal prerogatives. Occasionally they expressed their frustrations in outbursts of violence, but more often, resistance took other forms. The appeal of Mormonism, America's first truly indigenous religion, has been partially explained by its rejection of competitive individualism and its embrace of community. In New England, defenders of traditional water rights fought with factory owners who wanted a riparian law that would favor the interests of capital over those of subsistence communities. In Somerset County, resistance to the new order was expressed in a milder but no less insistent way. The tiny scale of woolen "factories," the persistence of weaving sheds on farmsteads, and even the small, uneven, hand-cultivated fields offered subtle visual defenses of the old order.

Resistance, however, wasn't the only stance taken by local people. The traditionalists stood in conflict with their many neighbors who rushed to purchase imported calico, muslin, silk, gingham, and tweed fabrics from local merchants such as Cover & Hays of Somerset. Consider for a moment the implications of buying cotton textiles—by midcentury, they were available cheaply in huge quantities and myriad varieties. Although the farm wife would still have to sew garments, the significance of buying factory-made cloth from England or New England could not have been lost on her friends and neighbors. Some may have thought her "vain," but enough agreed with her to keep a brisk trade going at the stores. Clearly, many local residents were rejecting the older notions of personal self-effacement and homespun self-sufficiency. The purchaser of mass manufactured goods pursued personal expression (though ironically also participated in a standardizing and homogenizing process, buying the identical item that others were purchasing in Kentucky or New York City). The clash between traditionalists and consumers evident in Somerset County echoed a rhetorical battle that was played out all over the east coast. Critics bemoaned the disappearance of the spinning wheel and equated the consumption of factory-produced textiles with moral decline. In most places their lamentations were ignored, but in Somerset County, the old view was strongly held.[29]

The price system also engendered tension. Global industrial capitalism not only reshaped relationships between employers and workers but also created mounting pressures for cash exchange. Rural people still traded labor, goods, and services in a wide and dense network of non-cash exchange relationships. But though in-kind trade persisted quite a bit longer here than in New England and New York State, cash transactions were definitely on the rise in Somerset County. Cash offered people a chance to relate to each other in different ways. Cash exchanges didn't carry the same continuity of obligation as the old long-term credit system; payment was once—and done. This was an advantage for someone who wanted to escape the dense web of accumulated obligation that the old system brought. But it also meant greater risk. Local retailers such as Cook & Beerits, for example, who themselves increasingly had to pay cash for supplies, began in turn to pressure their debtors: "[W]ho says it does *not* take money to buy Flour, Grain, and Feed by car loads for cash on delivery? Who ever said we agreed to sell these goods on credit for a longer term than thirty days? We are giving our debtors due notice." The spreading cash system, then, contributed to the erosion of old ties and values. We can also note a current of tension between "debtors" operating under the old system of long-term credit and barter exchange and storekeepers forced to adhere to newer short-term and cash standards. Moreover, to some extent, these tensions took on a "countryside versus town" dimension, as town merchants got incorporated into the cash economy sooner.[30]

As these complaints suggest, the price system—though clearly in evidence—had certainly not conquered the countryside completely. Gristmill processing offers an example. The 1870 manuscript manufacturing census listed numerous gristmills, nearly all water-powered, run by just two or three "hands." These mills catered to the new style of farming in that they served the intensifying livestock industry by grinding large amounts of farmers' grains into feed—"chop," "chop bran and shorts," and so on. At the same time, these records evoke an unmistakably precapitalist outlook: when the millers were asked to state the quantities of grain processed, their response was "all custom work, no idea of Quantity produced." Quantity, profit, and productivity were low priorities in this context, in which milling was a neighborly service, conducted according to the old terms of barter and labor exchange. These mills also ground flour for farmers' families, which helped perpetuate self-sufficiency.[31]

Maple sugaring, too, illustrates the incomplete impact of the price system. On the one hand, maple sugar served to insulate farm families from the market economy, because it kept rural residents supplied with sweetener for home use—for direct consumption and for curing meat. The equipment (even when purchased) was relatively inexpensive and simple and continued to be locally made if not farm-made. By the nineteenth century, a distinctive, Pennsylvania German culture of sugar and sugar making had evolved. "Spotza" parties at the sugar camp provided a setting for the old-time mingling of sociability and work. At these festive events, fresh maple syrup was mixed with new-fallen snow to make a deliciously sweet party treat. Yet maple sugar also provided a substantial part of rural folks' livelihood in Somerset; throughout the period—and well into the next century—local stores routinely accepted maple sugar for cash or goods, and families could realize considerable purchasing power from their sugar.[32]

Communal work customs seemed less disrupted by new economic imperatives. Rural neighbors still butchered together, moving from farm to farm, with men cutting and gutting, and women cleaning, scraping, and cooking. From their efforts, they obtained many products: smoked bacon and ham; lard; tallow for candles and soap; sausage (a few midcentury inventories mention "sausage machines"); and liverwurst, for example. When fall arrived, the local paper noted the "rage" for snitzings, huskings, and butcherings. Raisings for barns and other farm buildings attracted dozens and sometimes hundreds of people. German immigrant Wilhelm Krumme marveled, in an 1840 letter home, that his "double barn" cost him only $250 "as well as my neighbors' help for which they will take only food and drink." On 4 July 1883, the Somerset *Democrat* reported that "Mr. Peter Hay has erected a large frame for a new barn. The boys turned out lively at the raising and after the work was over Mr. Hay gave them a large party." Of course it was the neighborhood women (not Mr. Hay) who prepared the party repast, and the paper also was filled with raillery about courtship flirtations following the party.[33]

Frequently, machinery modified but did not destroy group work; threshing, for example, carried over communal customs. Even with mechanical threshers and "threshermen" who worked by contract, neighbors still gathered to thresh each farm's crop in turn; there is also evidence that people owned threshing machines jointly. In Lavansville, a company of half a dozen people formed to purchase and share a steam thresher (Fig. 36); in November 1883, the local paper reported that a Mr. Dencer had seen a wild cat while bringing a threshing machine home from a neighbor's—suggesting that he and the neighbor shared the machine.[34]

Corn husking was a communal task that probably increased in frequency as corn assumed a more important place in the farm economy. Interestingly, even at the turn of the century, Somerset County farmers were still holding huskings: in 1900, the local paper reported that "There was a very enjoyable evening spent last night in Peter Heffley's barn, . . . where a large party of friends gathered to assist him in husking corn." Naturally, the expected dance and feast followed.[35]

Everyone associates quilting with cooperative work. Quilting, in various forms, was a skill commonly learned by girls in the colonial period, but it was transformed by the industrialization of textile production in the nineteenth century. Quilting "bees" seem to have become more popular

FIG. 36
Several men pause as they use a steam thresher to fill a granary. Mechanization replaced hand labor, but old-fashioned cooperation continued when people shared machinery. Somerset Historical Center.

in the latter half of the century. These occasions easily became part of communal work customs. Nineteenth-century quilting is thus a good example of "blending" old and new, since it adapted communal work to industrially produced goods. Quilters generally used new materials (either special purchases or scraps leftover from sewing new garments). Nineteenth-century women everywhere in America made familiar patterns, such as "Log Cabin," "Drunkard's Path," and the like. Researchers have tentatively identified several locally distinctive characteristics, including the "Feathered Star" pattern, multiple borders, and dark blue backgrounds.[36]

Within the individual household, work organization combined pioneer-era subsistence practices with the emerging market orientation. Women baked bread; besides the hens, they raised ducks, geese, and turkeys, which furnished families with meat, eggs, and feathers. Many farm wives made "crock" or soft cheese in the German tradition. As in preindustrial days, many people worked at more than one occupation. Francis Cable, for example, often spent time in the winter months at his trade of shoemaking. Others combined farming with milling and other small-scale industries.[37]

The new world of work affected the gender division of labor. The need for cooperation between men and women intensified, if anything, with commercial production. Both men and women were involved in commercial and subsistence production, and they shared many tasks such as gardening, butchering, livestock care, and dairying. Haymaking time still called for all available hands (see Fig. 37). Yet in some realms, the gender division of labor seemed to be shifting. For example, the adoption of cranes in sugarmaking made it easier for women and children to perform the work. On the other hand, as horse rakes and corn cultivators came into use and as fewer farms raised flax, women were seen in the field less frequently. With their other work escalating, women probably had less time to devote to these tasks anyway. By 1880, Heinrich Möller, a German immigrant to the county, wrote in a letter home that "Here in America the women are better off than the men, a woman has only to do her housework, no woman has to work in the fields." Of course he underestimated and mislabeled "housework," but his observation that women were leaving the fields is telling. To a recent immigrant from Germany, this would be striking, because in nineteenth-century Germany many women *did* work extensively in the fields.[38]

The intensified food processing work in which women were so deeply involved was affected by a major technological change: the availability of the mass-produced cookstove. The stove gradually replaced the open-hearth cooking fireplace with its trammels, kettles, pots, stillyards, and so on; by the 1840s, cooking stoves appeared in estate inventories fairly often, and local foundries advertised them in the newspapers (Fig. 38). The 1860 manuscript manufacturing census shows that in Berlin, Charles Stoner operated a steam power foundry that produced 100 cooking stoves and 150 coal and wood [heating] stoves. In Stoystown, Samuel Custer produced 70 threshing machines, 30 cookstoves, 75 plows, and 80 sugar kettles. The Hathaway stove, well respected throughout the region, was manufactured in Berlin.[39]

Cookstoves demanded far less heavy lifting and stooping than the old open hearth had. They were also less dangerous and more fuel-efficient. At the same time, cookstoves required frequent cleaning and blacking, and they made it possible to replace one-pot meals with more elaborate

FIG. 37
This late-nineteenth-century photograph of haying on the Lehman farm captures a family's pride in their work. It also reminds us that at haying time, men, women, and children all worked to get in the valuable crop. Somerset Historical Center.

fare—which also helped elevate standards of diet. Somerset County farm wives lucky enough to have cookstoves no longer needed to lift, carry, and manipulate cumbersome cast-iron equipment over a dangerous fire. But the abundant variety of goods on exhibit at the 1876 fair was made possible in large part by the cookstove.[40] Chances are that Mrs. F. C. Sampsell's grandmother hadn't had the equipment to create "cranberry tarts, apple pie, and apple butter tarts," nor had Mrs. H. P. Kimmel's forebears put up "canned corn, canned apples, elderberry jelly, blackberry jam, [and] canned quinces."

Other implements that were probably less widespread and therefore less influential included the sewing machine and washing machine. The 1864 *Herald and Whig* compared the washing machines to threshing and mowing machines, arguing that "no head of a family who regards the health and strength of his wife and daughters as objects of his care, will longer be without one." This is notable not only for its appeal on the basis of labor-saving, but also for the assumption that men made purchasing decisions. An accompanying advertisement promoted clothes wringers that fit into wash tubs: "Any washerwoman can use it. A child ten years old can work it." It also stressed the device's simple construction, low breakdown rate, and warranty.[41]

The cookstove transformed the housewife's work. No longer did she have to cope with an open hearth; she redirected her energies toward making more elaborate meals and maintaining the new equipment. Somerset foundries energetically produced stoves for local sale. Advertisement from Somerset *Herald and Whig,* 6 January 1869. Somerset Historical Center.

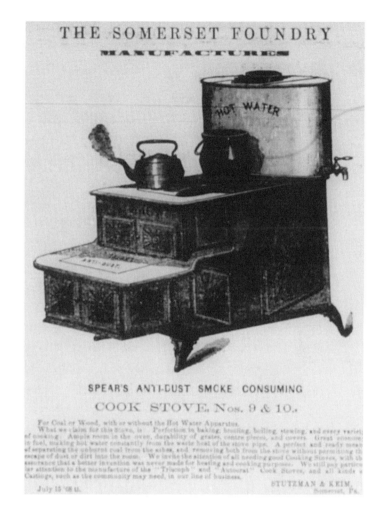

As the advertisements suggest, patriarchal control of women's and children's work was still very common. In the 1820s and 1830s, Harrison and Caroline Tedrow hoed corn; Caroline received no separate credit of her own but instead was credited under Harrison's name. This prac-tice continued into the late 1860s and early 1870s, when merchant Daniel Wright listed work done by Aaron Hay's wife and daughters. The women dug potatoes, planted corn, sheared sheep, and picked apples, and in turn, Aaron was credited with payment. Mary Elizabeth Kay worked for Samuel Flick in the 1870s; she earned from $1.00 to $1.50 per week. For one week in February, her employer allowed her to "work . . . for herself."[42]

In general, independent wage work for women was very scarce. A few "worked out," hauling sugar water and chasing cows. Widows sewed, knitted, sheared sheep, traded honey, and so on for credit at Wright's store, and though farm wives traded butter and eggs for goods or cash, they did not always have control over this income. Even schoolteaching—a highly feminized activity in many other areas of the North—was essentially closed to women in Somerset County. In the 1880s, only 33 of 203 grade school teachers in the county were female.[43]

The persistence of such a dominating patriarchal gender structure is a reminder of the limits of mutuality. Men and women might cooperate, but cooperation did not automatically translate into ideas of gender equality. In this respect, Somerset County's path was different from those taken in rural New England and elsewhere in the mid-Atlantic, where rural women were able to "loosen the bonds" of patriarchy. In New England, cottage industries such as palm-leaf hatmaking afforded young women opportunities to establish store accounts and earn an independent wage, however miniscule. Farm girls in dairy country were often able to parlay their essential expertise into expanded educational opportunities, and academies sprang up to meet the demand. Eventually many of these women withdrew from agriculture, either pursuing non-farming occupations in a rural setting (teaching, for example) or migrating to cities. This process of pursuing even a limited independence often created considerable gender conflict within farm households, as daughters' priorities clashed with household needs. In turn, farm households ventured still further into capitalist organization (substituting wage labor for family labor, for example) as a solution to these conflicts.[44]

In Somerset County, matters took on a different complexion. Rural society here was not so open to independent opportunities for young women—or to autonomy for wives. The fact that this situation of male dominance prevailed in a place where adherence to the old order was highly valued is worth pondering; it was certainly not a coincidence. The old subsistence order rested on the existing gender division of labor, so to defend one was to preserve the other. In this respect, Somerset County calls to mind the yeoman country of antebellum lowcountry South Carolina, in which male household heads were "masters of small worlds." Of course, the comparison can't be taken too far, since one was a slave society and the other was not. In both cases, though, yeomen's resistance to capitalism was strengthened by their dominance within the household.[45]

No matter the task or the worker, farmwork was still shaped by the rhythms of the seasons. Diaries, daybooks, and even the local newspaper columns chronicled the annual rounds, ever watchful for the early frost, the unusual rains, the late harvest. For weather and crop prognostications, the farm family could still consult the almanac. They could check on the "Probable State of the Weather," or on the moon's phases, if they were inclined to believe that this mattered when they planted their potatoes. For the more visually inclined, the almanac woodcuts offered artistic reminders of seasonal activities. Winter pictures showed how families gathered by the fire to wait out the dark and cold, spinning, reading, cracking nuts, telling stories. The late-winter months depicted fence repairing, and then by summer and fall the images show workers making hay, harvesting grain, and sowing winter wheat. Almanac publishers everywhere (Fig. 39) followed a fairly standard formula. To some extent, the images were idealized and generalized—and somewhat anachronistic too. But over time, they did accommodate and reflect cultural changes. By the 1840s, for instance, depictions of oxen were replaced by those of horses; the flower garden appeared. Later in the century, fanciful cherubs replaced scenes of workaday life, and the implicitly didactic and ascetic messages gave way to more secular, lighthearted themes.

As the nineteenth century wore on, seasonality continued to be a major force in rural people's lives, but it was experienced differently. This occurred most noticeably on a workaday level: far more work was packed into the seasonal round than was the case during the preindustrial period. A look at Landreth's almanac for 1878, for instance (Fig. 40), will show minute instructions for

FIG. 39
Seasonality remained an important feature of rural Somerset life, though these almanac woodcuts show some cultural changes. Horses appear in the plowing scene, and the flower garden makes its debut. From *Baer's Agricultural Almanac* for 1843, these scenes show (A) plowing in September, (B) gardening in June, (C) fencing in March, and (D) indoor activities for January. Somerset County farmers read Hagerstown almanacs with illustrations identical to the ones in *Baer's*. Rare Books and Manuscripts, The Pennsylvania State University Libraries.

FIG. 39A

FIG. 39B

FIG. 39C

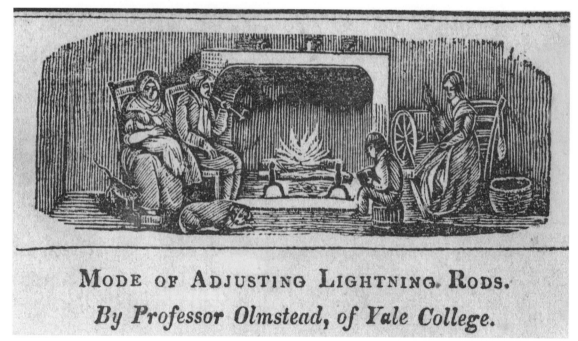

MODE OF ADJUSTING LIGHTNING RODS.
By Professor Olmstead, of Yale College.

FIG. 39D

tending a plethora of garden crops. More subtly, though, people experienced seasonality differently in the realm of consciousness. The old "animate" cosmos was joined by a more mechanistic, scientific, and capitalist worldview, in which Nature was conceptualized as a collection of physical elements and abstract forces that humans could manipulate. Now it was just as important to keep track of meteorological data as to know the astrological phases. In the almanacs, advice on scientific farming appeared next to the zodiacal map of the human body.[46]

FIG. 40
This page from a prominent Philadelphia nursery firm's almanac suggests that the work of the vegetable garden was getting more time-consuming and intensive. From *Landreth's Rural Register and Almanac* (Philadelphia: McCalla and Stavely, Printers, 1878), 15. Rare Books and Manuscripts, The Pennsylvania State University Libraries.

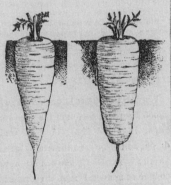

15

MARCH.

KITCHEN-GARDEN CALENDAR.

IN THE MIDDLE STATES, Spring has arrived according to the Calendar, but the experienced gardener is not to be caught by arbitrary terms; and though March and the Almanac may indicate Spring, frost and storm, and biting winds caution him to care and patience. He will wait the progress of the month and bide his time. If the temperature prove mild, let him proceed as indicated below; otherwise, delay until more favorable weather.

Artichokes dress; plant. **Asparagus** sow; plant the **Colossal** roots. **Beets**—Extra Early Philadelphia Turnip and Early Blood Turnip—sow. **Cabbage** sow in a sheltered place, if not already in hot-bed. Test our new varieties—the Wakefield, Early Market, and Bloomsdale Brunswick. **Carrots,** Early Horn, sow. **Cauliflowers**—attend to those under glass. **Celery** sow. **Cress** sow. **Composts** prepare. **Dung** prepare for later hot-beds. **Horse Radish** plant. **Hot-beds** make; also force. **Lettuce** sow; prick out. **Mush-room-beds** attend to. **Mustard** sow. **Onions** put out as sets—those known as "Philadelphia Buttons" much the best. **Parsnips** sow—the Sugar is the best. **Peas—Landreths' Extra Early** and Early Frame—sow. Also, McLean's Advancer and McLean's Little Gem, which we commend with confidence. **Potatoes,** Early, plant. The Early Goodrich continues to secure admirers, but the Early Rose will distance it; it is admirable in every respect. **Radish** —the Long Scarlet and Red and White Turnip—sow. The "Strap-Leaved Long Scarlet," an improvement on the old Long Scarlet, we recommend. **Rhubarb** sow; plant roots. **Sage** sow; plant. **Tomato** sow in hot-bed. **Turnips,** Strap-Leaved Early Dutch, sow; but generally be it observed, so far north as Philadelphia, these directions will apply better to April than March.

THE POINTED-ROOTED HORN, AND BLUNT-ROOTED HORN CARROT differ only in shape, and are raised exclusively for table use, we refer to them simply as desirable for an early Summer supply.

THE LONG ORANGE CARROT is the stand-by for late Summer and Winter use—raise more than is needed for table use and share with the cow—she will make ample return for the kindness, filling the pail with rich milk, and giving the butter the color and flavor of that from grass.

This newer worldview, embodied in agricultural reform or in architectural symmetry, has often been associated with time-consciousness and time-discipline in work. Indeed, in Somerset County (as elsewhere), time-consciousness penetrated even in households where older modes of sociability and work held sway. Inventories commonly mentioned expensive clocks, such as "eight day clocks," by the late 1840s. Some of these clocks would have been imported from elsewhere, but fine ones were available locally through clockmakers in Berlin, especially the Heffley and Hofford families (Fig. 41).[47] The intertwining of old and new was captured in Franz von Löher's account of a night he spent in a cabin with a Pennsylvania German family:

Dinner, mainly fried bacon and hot cornbread, was eaten almost without a word. Then the man and his half-grown son sat by the fire and chewed tobacco. Grandmother sat there, too,

FIG. 41
Samuel Hofford of Berlin made this clock around 1825. The elegant tall case clock bears testimony to a heightened awareness of time in nineteenth-century rural America. Somerset Historical Center.

and smoked a short, black pipe. The farmer's wife sang to her youngest, while the others stood in the middle of the room and stared at me, hair hanging around their faces, glances flashing shyly but brightly and attentively. Although overfilled with people, the room was so still the clock could be heard: ticktock.[48]

Paradoxically, the decision to retain old customs may even have contributed to intensified time-consciousness, since new products and tasks were added on top of the old subsistence base, not substituted for elements of that base. Perhaps not so much as the pursuit of modernity per se, the decision to enrich a "competency" could, ironically, push rural folk to husband their time, to approach time itself in a more modern way even as they clung to so many of the old practices.

The push for time-consciousness and productivity reached into deeply ingrained habits—among them the habit of drinking. In Somerset County, as in other places, the presence of a new ethos was encapsulated in the rise of the temperance movement. Some farmers attacked the prevalence of whiskey as an accompaniment to work, and they demanded sobriety from their laborers. In 1835, the *Old Franklin Almanac* reported on the founding of the Stoyestown [sic] Temperance Society. Its president, Henry Little, triumphantly celebrated a harvest of sobriety:

The grain was cut in less time and with less waste than formerly, and of course in peace and quietness. Some of them [the farmers] heretofore used from 5 to 20 gallons a harvest—now they are well satisfied that any kind of spirituous liquors, is neither needful, nor useful. . . . [T]hey are determined henceforth that their harvest fields shall not be disgraced with the presence of the Rum-jug—that the waving, yellow grain, the gift of a bountiful Providence, shall be secured amidst sobriety and innocent hilarity.

There followed a list of farmers in Quemahoning, Jenner, Somerset, and Shade Townships who had completed their harvest without the aid of liquor; one, Jacob Mowry, had even "completed from the foundation, a new bank barn 84 by 64 feet, without one drop of liquor used." Local historian William Welfley thought that temperance was especially strong among the wealthiest farmers. Farmworkers resisted—in one instance, they refused to participate in a barn raising without spirits—but eventually liquor was "banished . . . from the harvest field."[49]

The temperance agitation revealed new types of fissures in the social structure. If indeed temperance advocates owned large farms and probably hired wage workers (this was the tendency elsewhere, and available evidence indicates it held true here too), this shows a widening class gap between workers and employers. It also implies a new relationship that was governed more by the cash nexus than by traditional neighborly reciprocity. There had always been a social hierarchy, but now, as profit became a concern of the more capitalist farmers, that hierarchy was expressed differently. Employers sought order, rationality, control, discipline, productivity. Imbibing on the job didn't fit well with their ideal of systematic work-discipline.

Nineteenth-century rural society in Somerset County was a society in flux, a remarkable hybrid in which preindustrial values, customs, and tasks became intertwined with the growing emphasis upon profit, money, individual self-expression, order, productivity, and discipline. Sometimes the old and new blended smoothly; at other times, they conflicted, and the confrontation engendered social tensions. These cultural characteristics were expressed in equally complex spatial patterns.

EXPRESSIONS IN BUILDING AND SPACE: A BLENDED LANDSCAPE

Let us begin, as before, with landscapes. In 1829, when Englishwoman Anne Royall traversed the Allegheny ridges, development in the vales impressed her. The central valley was "enclosed, for the most part; overgrown with timothy, and thickly studded with lofty sugar-maples . . . [the] beautiful umbrella-topped sugar-tree, standing, as it were, by magic, on the smooth shorne green."[50] These highly visible pockets of cultivation revealed an ordered, human-dominated landscape. Fences enclosed fields. Timothy, not soft wild grass, now dominated the meadows; it is no coincidence that the hay from it was called "tame." Even the sugar maples gave the inescapable impression of having been selectively allowed to stand, of being isolated through clearing the underbrush (Fig. 42). The impress of human activity was everywhere apparent.

The organizing impact of people on the landscape appeared quite clearly in maps. Nineteenth-century maps celebrated Victorian ideals of improvement and progress. These maps not only indicated useful (and increasingly detailed) information about the locations of villages, river

FIG. 42
This sugar bush was photographed in 1994. It can give us an idea of how the highly cultivated sugar bushes of the nineteenth century must have appeared. Photograph by the author.

systems, and the like, but they also revealed what their makers thought was important in the landscape. The free interpretations of the eighteenth century had given way to a much more structured presentation, in keeping with new values of improvement, regularity, and order (Fig. 43). To be sure, topographic features still loomed, but roads, farms, mills, shops, and churches appeared much more prominently. Connections between and among farmsteads had become much more dense, numerous, and elaborate than before, allowing greater ease of mobility; real estate ads of the period often mention proximity to church, mill site, school, and village among the advantages of a property.[51] Toll gates marked better roads (Fig. 44) and symbolized farmers' connections to distant markets. An 1854 road map of the route from Lobingers Mills to Stoystown located a steam tannery, sawmill, barn, and old furnace; it also showed sites that suggest new concerns about recreation and health (a "mineral spring and salt well") and popular curiosity about natural history ("fossil limestone").

The rise of public schools was reflected in the cartographer's decision to show the school district as a basic unit of each township. This was a major change from earlier days. As long as education had been supported solely by subscription, no school system as such had existed, and educational opportunities were uneven. Schooling took place haphazardly in improvised structures or in private homes or church buildings. In 1834, Pennsylvania enacted a law allocating some

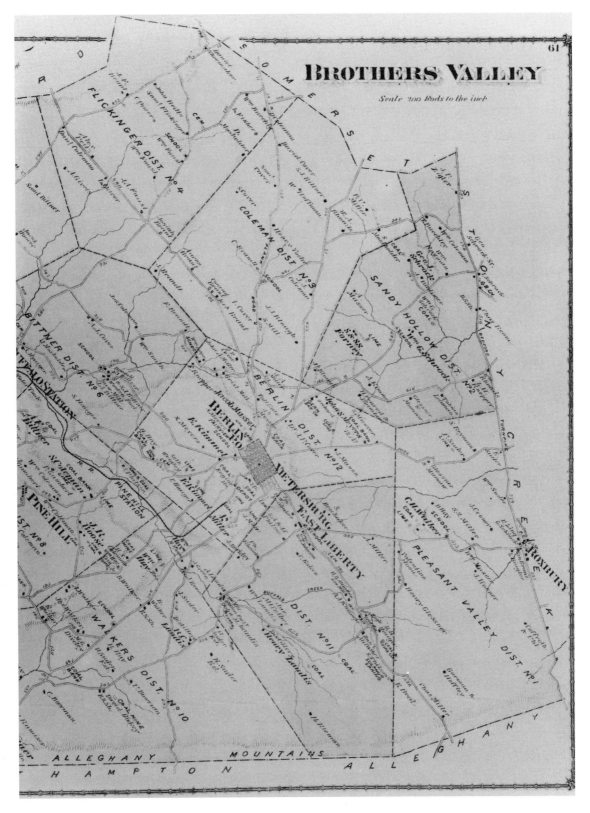

FIG. 43

This view from the 1876 county atlas shows how abstract political boundaries, rigorously platted towns, roads, and industries now appear as prominent landscape features. This visualization shows not only actual physical changes from the settlement era but also a new mentality in organizing and depicting the landscape. From F. W. Beers, *County Atlas of Somerset, Pennsylvania* (New York: F. W. Beers, 1876), 61. Author's collection.

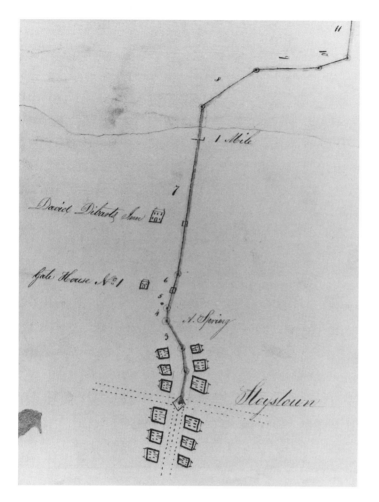

FIG. 44
This 1836 map of a section of the Stoystown and Greensburgh Pike shows "Gate House Nº 1," as well as an inn and springs—all important parts of the turnpike's support system. Map W115, section 1, from State Road and Turnpike Maps, 1706–1873, Records of the Department of Highways (Record Group 12). Pennsylvania State Archives, Harrisburg, Pennsylvania.

financial support for localities that chose to set up public schools. This public-school law was vigorously resisted in many parts of the state, including Somerset, where "guns were loaded to shoot the tax collector" over the schools issue. Several townships held out until the 1850s, but after that, there was a steady rise in the number of public schools countywide. By 1876, 226 schools in the county served 8,800 pupils. This massive organizing effort resulted in a new pattern on the landscape, one in which institutional public space became ubiquitous and accepted. Schoolhouses (Fig. 45), often erected from standardized plans, soon dotted the land, each located conveniently for its rural neighborhood. The school was controlled locally, as public schools still are, but it also reminded citizens of their ties to the larger polities of state and nation.[52]

Like schools, religious buildings and cemeteries were much more numerous and elaborate than during the settler period. Most church organizations in the county were founded after 1840. A wave of church building occurred in the 1840s, and another took place from the mid-1870s into the 1880s. In 1860, there were 91 church organizations in the county; by 1890, that number had more than doubled, reaching 193. The pace of church growth had outstripped that of the population; indeed, optimistically, the seating capacity of churches in 1890 significantly exceeded the county's entire population![53]

FIG. 45
The one-room schoolhouse became a familiar sight at rural crossroads after local opposition to public schools waned. Somerset Historical Center.

This boom in religion was part of a wider trend. Historian Jon Butler has suggested that nationwide, the "phenomenal increases in the number of Christian congregations" meant "more landscape sacralization. . . . In numbers alone, the church building became a ubiquitous feature of the early national and antebellum landscape."[54] We can extend Butler's imaginative observation to Somerset County. As rural neighborhoods took shape, they often coalesced around crossroads centers that consisted of church, school, or cemetery, and often all three.

One 1860 landownership map of the county had a border lined with crude engravings of Somerset County churches. These were executed by an untrained hand; the perspective was slightly skewed and the shading had a shaky quality to it. Yet the artist captured each building's essential features. Most of the churches were a single story tall, and the main entrance was located in the gable end. They were two or three bays wide and from three to five bays deep, with rectangular, regularly spaced window openings. It is difficult to tell from the worn images, but it seems that most of these windows had six-over-six lights. Some were shuttered. A few churches had hexagonal steeples, always placed over the entrance and always topped with a lightning rod or a weather vane. Quite a few of these churches had two symmetrically placed entrances, presumably separating men from women. This was a reminder that patriarchalism still flourished; the German Reformed and Lutheran denominations, of which there were many local congregations, never feminized as heavily as other Protestant organizations in the nineteenth century. Nearly all of the churches were depicted as surrounded by fences, lending the church space a pronounced quality of separation. These midcentury depictions emphasized simplicity. The first generation of rural church edifices was probably erected on a tight budget—and in any case reflected the religious conservatism of the dominant German Reformed and Lutheran faiths.

In the second wave of building, the basic form remained the same, but greater attention to architectural detail marked these buildings as meaningful to the community. The Jersey Baptist Church (c. 1877) in Lower Turkeyfoot Township, for example (Fig. 46), had a pedimented gable with classical cornice, and tall, thin pointed windows with wooden drip moldings. Zion Lutheran Church, in Wellersburg (Fig. 47), had gable returns and a projecting bell tower; the tower was decorated with Doric columns and topped with a steeple. In scale, materials, and design, these rural churches expressed well the local, overwhelmingly Protestant culture. Catholic congregations were so rare that in the 1876 Beers atlas a Catholic church was labeled "Romish church," doubtless the work of a mapmaker who had inherited anti-Catholic attitudes and terminology.

Cemeteries also appeared at this time. Jon Butler points to the rise of what he calls "sanctified graveyards," which replaced individual burial sites; in Somerset County, too, this trend was apparent. Most of the new cemeteries were connected with churches, but there were also several

FIG. 46
Jersey Baptist Church, Lower Turkeyfoot Township, built c. 1877, photographed 1999. By the late nineteenth century, new church buildings boasted more architectural detail. Photograph by Lu Donnelly for the Heinz Architectural Center.

FIG. 47
Zion Lutheran Church, Wellersburg, late nineteenth century. Another example of relative sophistication in rural church architecture. Photograph by David Brumble for the Heinz Architectural Center.

prominent independent cemeteries, including one that was sponsored by the Odd Fellows. Most contained rows of stones laid out in regular geometric patterns, usually on a grid; tree plantings helped soften their linear qualities (Fig. 48). Sometimes they were enclosed with elaborate, beautifully worked stone walls. These cemeteries enhanced the sacralization of the landscape. They created highly visible, public memorial spaces that could become sites for rituals of commemoration, connecting the living with the dead. Cemeteries were carefully tended, and their grooming also marked them out as socially significant spaces. The linear and gridlike arrangement of the country cemetery should perhaps be interpreted as a repudiation of the contemporary romantically inspired trend in cemetery design, which incorporated curvilinear pathways, varied topography, and dense plantings. Certainly the country cemetery, with its highly visible hilltop location, relatively open aspect, and regularity, bespoke a very different sensibility at work.[55]

Along with educational and religious institutions, commercial buildings such as artisans' shops, mills, distilleries, and factories were distributed widely across the countryside. The 1876 atlas showed that the county was thoroughly laced with coal banks and iron deposits; though they were small in scale, they still testified to the growing importance of industry in the local economy (Fig. 49). In Stilesville, for example, a small-scale company town appeared (Fig. 50), with all of the elements that would appear on a much larger scale in the twentieth century.

FIG. 48
Church cemetery, near Jennerstown, 1998. A finely worked stone wall encloses the nineteenth- and twentieth-century gravestones in this country cemetery. Photograph by the author.

Viewing these tidy geographic idealizations, a modern observer can easily forget that at mid-century the forest still covered much of the county's land area. German traveler Franz von Löher captured a more three-dimensional—and more accurate—perspective during his 1846 journey to the area: "In valleys, which communicate with a much-traveled thoroughfare, farmers already have elegant homes and gardens. Yet these beginnings of culture are like a few specks scattered about the forest that runs for hundreds of miles unbroken over stretches of hills and mountains in which there are, even now, wooded acres and craggy slopes where no human sets foot the year round, where only deer and bear roam." The thick forest cover deeply affected von Löher's experience of the landscape. "A deep sylvan desolation surrounded me," he wrote. "Even in these early-settled places, towns will have virgin forests at their doors for a long while. . . . What a relief to leave the dark-green night of a forest and reach open places higher up!"[56]

These descriptions are credible: as late as 1877, nearly half of the county's entire land area was forested. Less than half of the farm acreage of 1850 had been put under the plow, turned into pasture, or used as meadow. By 1880, that figure was only up to 56 percent. In that year, Somerset farms had 228,000 acres in woodland and forest—one of the largest areas in the state, both in absolute and percentage terms.[57]

One can get a feel for the experience of moving in this landscape by examining road maps. In 1842, for example, a road was laid out from the Maryland state line to Centreville (Fig. 51). The road inspectors noted the forested areas along the route as well as where the roadside had been cleared or fenced. Traversing these county roads on foot or on horseback, the nineteenth-century traveler would still encounter long stretches in which the woods closed in from either side; the cleared areas must have felt all the more pronouncedly open.

Some local residents thought that the land was woefully underused. In 1845, a group of local citizens urged the formation of an agricultural society. The marshy areas, they complained, "yield

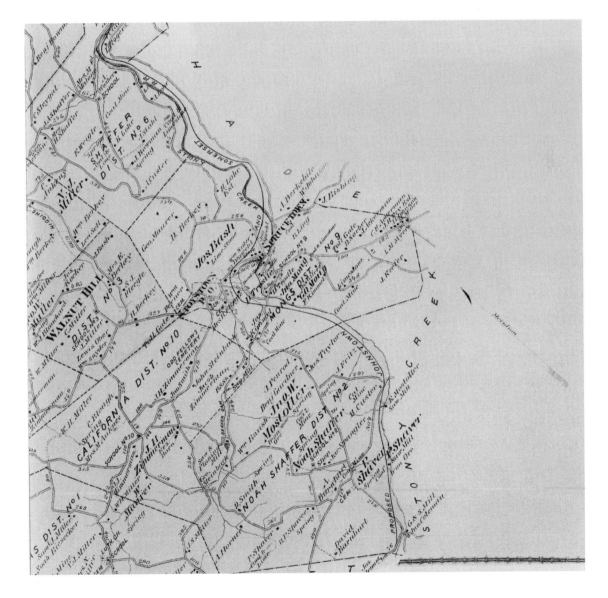

FIG. 49
This map of Stoystown and vicinity from the 1876 Beers atlas shows the area laced with iron ore, coal mines, and limestone banks, indicating not only increased industrial activity but also a transformation of the landscape. From Beers, *County Atlas*, 31. Author's collection.

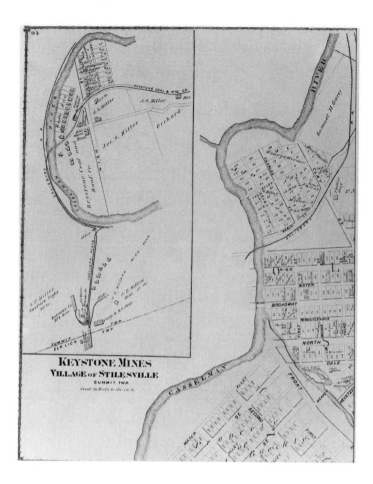

FIG. 50
This map of Keystone Mines in the village of Stilesville shows a small company town, complete with housing, shops, and railheads—and of course the mine itself. From Beers, *County Atlas, 94.* Author's collection.

nought but sour-grass and alders," and ought to be drained, while the mountains, "till now untouched by the husbandman's implements," should be cultivated or at least turned into pasture. Though rural reformers decried what they saw as a deplorable lack of "improving" spirit, most farmers rejected their exhortations. Their strategy of limited clearing made eminent sense, given the importance of woodland to the local economy, and it underscored the subtle refusal to embrace capitalist farming wholeheartedly. Not only did maple sugar production actually increase even as farm size decreased, but the woodlands also continued to serve as a pantry for free-ranging animals; as late as 1883, the Somerset *Democrat* reported that a long, fine autumn had meant that the local farmers were in no hurry to pen up their hogs. All of this suggests that an undercurrent of resistance to new ways still flourished in Somerset County. Local farmers weren't blindly following the dictates of rationalized farm management: they were making choices that were consistent with their commitment to a self-sufficient farming that was only partly capitalist.[58]

When we turn to the individual farmstead, the same tension between the ideal of improvement—the impulse to master nature—and the old ways plays itself out in the daily imperatives of ordinary farm activity. By the end of the period, the celebratory engravings in the published county history speak to the high value placed upon order, regularity, cultivation. Animals graze peacefully, confined by long stretches of fencing constructed of boards, wire, or old-style snake

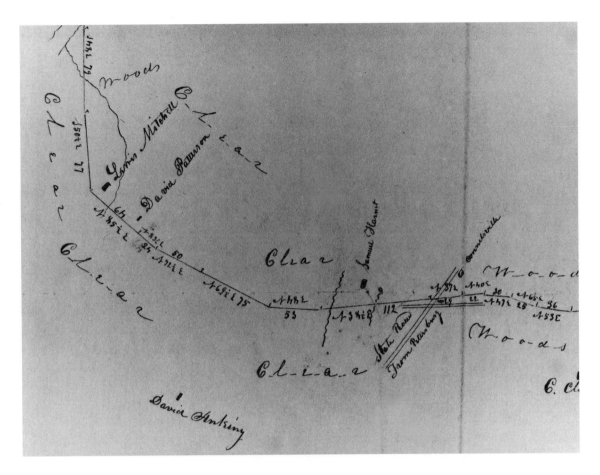

FIG. 51
An 1842 surveyor's map proposed a road from the state line to Centreville. The person who drafted the map thought it important to indicate where the roadside was "clear" and where it was "woods." Half of the county's land area was forested in 1880. Map W150, section 3, from Road and Turnpike Maps, Records of the Department of Highways (Record Group 12). Pennsylvania State Archives, Harrisburg, Pennsylvania.

rails (Fig. 52). Indeed, there is evidence that the local farm landscape did become more tidy over time. In real estate ads, many farms were touted as "well fenced." Mechanization likely brought with it the necessity for new types of fencing in cropland areas and in meadows. Human harvesters or haymakers could cut in between the zigzags of a stake-and-rider fence, but horse-drawn machinery couldn't. Gradually, straight fencing such as post-and-rail or wire fencing replaced older types in tillage areas. The Somerset *Democrat* indulgently reported in 1883 that a local farmer, Mr. John Gumbert, had recently installed wire fencing. The paper chided him for being "a little timid in making any new departure."[59]

The gradual appearance of straighter fencing did not necessarily mean that the fields themselves became more regular, however. The scale of horse-drawn machinery did not require the huge turnaround spaces that later motorized machinery would need. A late-nineteenth-century photograph of Somerset from the country shows this vividly. Within easy view of town, haying

RESIDENCE OF ALEX. WALKER,
STONEY CREEK TP.,   SOMERSET CO., PA.

FIG. 52A

RESIDENCE OF S.S. FLICKINGER, ELK LICK TP, SOMERSET CO., PA.

FIG. 52B

FIG. 52

These views of Somerset County farmsteads celebrate order and prosperity. Different types of fencing establish some areas (e.g., the house) as having higher social prestige than fields or pastures; the farther from the core, the cruder the fencing. The typical Pennsylvania barn and double-decker porches are much in evidence here. The residences of (A) Alex. Walker, (B) S. S. Flickinger, (C) W. H. Miller, (D) S. F. Rieman, (E) Jacob Musser, and (F) William G. Schrock all show a combination of banked houses with double-decker porches, plus Pennsylvania barn. Those of (G) George Dumbauld, (H) J. J. Walker, and (I) John H. Zimmerman show different house forms, but keep the Pennsylvania barn. All of these farmsteads show refined picket fences nearest the house, palings for garden or orchard, and post-and-rail or worm fencing for livestock. From *History of Bedford, Somerset, and Fulton Counties, Pennsylvania* (Chicago: Waterman, Watkins, and Co., 1884). Rare Books and Manuscripts, The Pennsylvania State University Libraries.

JOSEPH MILLER HOMESTEAD.

RESIDENCE OF Wᵐ H. MILLER ESQ. QUEMAHONING TP., SOMERSET CO., PA.

FMG

FIG. 52C

RESIDENCE OF S. F. RIEMAN,
BROTHERS VALLEY TP.,   SOMERSET CO., PA.

FIG. 52D

RESIDENCE OF JACOB MUSSER,
BROTHERS VALLEY,   SOMERSET CO., PA.

FIG. 52E

RESIDENCE OF WILLIAM G. SCHROCK, BROTHERS VALLEY, P.A.

FIG. 52F

RESIDENCE OF GEORGE DUMBAULD.

FIG. 52G

RESIDENCE OF J. J. WALKER, STONEY CREEK TP., SOMERSET CO., PA

FIG. 52H

RESIDENCE OF JOHN H. ZIMMERMAN, QUEMAHONING TP., SOMERSET CO., PA.

FIG. 52I

takes place along a sinuous waterway (Fig. 53). Wire fencing—which took up so much less land area than the old-style space-eating worm fence—may actually have made it worthwhile to cultivate this highly irregularly shaped patch of land.

Cropland accounted for a relatively small proportion of the overall farmstead landscape. Hay meadow would usually consume as much as thirty improved acres on a typical farm. Pasture for cattle and sheep would be at least equally visible. Where tillable cropland was concerned, the only crop that took up much more than fifteen or twenty acres was oats; most crops would occupy considerably less space. Wheat and buckwheat, for example, would normally be sown on patches of fewer than five acres.[60]

Normally, the spatial layout of the farmstead followed a roughly hierarchical arrangement. The woodlot and sugar camp occupied the outer periphery. Pasture and hay meadow were next, and still closer in were orchard, cropland, and garden spaces. The farm building complex, of course, stood at the functional center—if not the geographic center—of the farmstead. Not surprisingly, buildings related to food processing (smokehouse, butcher house, kitchen, springhouse,

FIG. 53
Within easy view of town, haying takes place along a sinuous waterway. Mechanization didn't always mean a more linear landscape; wire fences could make it worthwhile to mow an irregular area. Somerset Historical Center.

ice house) and laundering (wash house) were sited near the main house, as was the privy. A Casselman Valley resident recalled a wash house located near the ice house; the wash house served for boiling apple butter, butchering, storing liverwurst, sugaring off, and, of course, washing. Water came from the overflow from the house cellar. At the east end of this wash house, a hutch held wood ashes stored for soap making. Orchards usually appeared near the house, as depicted in engravings of farms belonging to S. S. Flickinger and Calvin Hay. Gardens were also handy to the house (Fig. 54). Buildings for housing crops, machinery, and livestock clustered near and around the barn, which more often than not was oriented southward to exploit the warm winter sun. The farm landscape changed subtly as crop mixes changed. For example, cornfields—which would have been less familiar to earlier generations—were more common (Fig. 55). The haystack in this photo reminds us that not all farm crops were stored in barns.[61]

Closer to the farmhouse, spaces became more carefully elaborated and they received finer finishes. Picket fences served to demarcate the yard and establish a sense of hierarchy: the best (usually painted) fence surrounded the domestic space. Newspaper ads for lawnmowers suggest that at least some local people had absorbed new standards of refinement. Log construction was still very common

FIG. 54
Somerset County farmhouse and garden, 1892. In this farm's extensive garden, a fenced-in portion close to the house appears to hold peas and beans, while just outside the fenced area are cabbages and corn. The farm garden grew ever more varied and extensive as time went on. Somerset Historical Center.

FIG. 55
Farm with cornfields near Confluence, Lower Turkeyfoot Township, late in the nineteenth century. Cornfields were relatively novel in the area; they appeared only after local farmers had developed short-season strains that would mature before the area's extra-early frosts. Somerset Historical Center.

(ads in 1869 and again in 1883 mentioned "new" log houses), but real estate ads show an unmistakable shift to frame and plank construction, with a sprinkling of brick and stone buildings.[62]

This shift occurred as a more sophisticated milling industry made machine-produced components (such as shingles, doors, sashes and blinds, moldings, and so on) for local consumption. For example, the 1876 Beers atlas listed many a hamlet with sawmills, planing mills, and sash-and-blind works; most were water-powered, but a few were run by steam. In Meyersdale, the Freedline brothers advertised that their planing mill could produce "all kinds of work done to order," and that their business also included "contracting and building." Carpenters' and masons' shops appeared, suggesting that the building trades were acquiring greater specialization. Carpenters, builders, and contractors advertised their skills in the atlas; H. Musselman advertised himself as a "Carpenter and Builder" in the town of Paint. In Somerset, W. Megahan was a "contractor for all kinds of stone, brick or Plaster Work."[63]

Clearly, then, the local pattern resembled trends elsewhere, as rougher, simpler houses gave way to more substantial, larger, more elaborate structures. If families couldn't afford to build anew, often they would improve the old; advertisements commonly mentioned that log houses had been

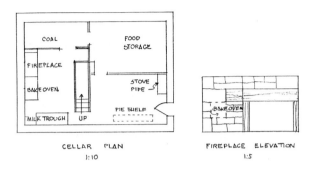

FIG. 56A

FIG. 56
Plan of the John and Anne Beachley house,
Brothersvalley Township, about 1838. This
house reflects the increasingly sophisticated
output of the nineteenth-century farm, with its
facilities for dairying, winemaking, and food
storage. The cellar plan (A) shows facilities for
farm production, and the first and second
floors (B) give evidence of increasing
refinement. Somerset Historical Center.

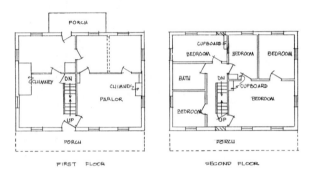

FIG. 56B

weatherboarded, and the newspapers ran ads for paint products such as "Buck's Cottage Colors"
in a range of thirty shades. This improving impulse was part of a broad trend affecting much of
nineteenth-century rural society and agriculture from Maine to Delaware. Ideals of "refinement,"
attainable only by the elite in the eighteenth century, were spreading to the middle social orders
by the nineteenth century. Rural and urban people alike sought gentility through manners,
deportment, and conversation, and they constructed new social spaces such as the parlor and the
dining room.[64]

Surviving vernacular farmhouses amply document the addition of layers of "improvement"
onto preindustrial forms. The John and Anne Beachley house (Fig. 56) adapted to frame construction the principles earlier expressed in log. This two-story house was not banked, but it had
a four-room cellar with cooking fireplace, bake oven, milk trough, and storage space. In 1850, the
residents of this farm tended nine horses, ten cows, thirty-three sheep, and twenty-one pigs, in
addition to raising the usual grains, churning eight hundred pounds of butter, making wine, and
boiling maple sugar. The basement was almost certainly the site for buttermaking; we may specu-
late that winemaking or at least storage also took place there. In this way, traditional arrangements
were adapted to commercial production. On the first floor, we find the familiar proxemic traits of
the earlier society: direct entrance to the living spaces, direct access among living spaces, asym-
metry. Yet a layer of improvement has been added, too. On the main doorway, two of the panels
featured a carved wreath motif. Once inside, a visitor would immediately see a visual relationship
between the doorway and the carved stair banister (Fig. 57). Second-floor rooms had simpler

FIG. 57
John and Anne Beachley house, Brothersvalley
Township, front door (A) and stair banister (B).
Farm families built practical houses, but they
also showed their yearning for refinement in the
decorative details they chose, such as the egg-
and-dart motif of the door and the leaf motif on
the newel post. Somerset Historical Center.

FIG. 58
All over America, rural families—no less than their urban counterparts—experimented with new aesthetic choices. The front door of the Ananias and Ann Landis house, c. 1867, is executed in handsome Italianate paneling. Somerset Historical Center.

bull's-eye door frame molding. These embellishments announced that the family shared values of gentility and suggested that their lives within were properly conducted.

The Ananias and Ann Landis house, c. 1867, shows another up-to-date farm family's interpretation of its architectural needs. Banked, but built as an "L," the house showed the popular "bent" form that appeared frequently on the landscape in this period. Elegant Italianate ornament (Fig. 58) expressed sophistication for the time and place; Palladian windows ornamented the exterior gables, and Doric pilasters extended beneath the cornice returns. The front door, transomed, had four panels, the top two of which were rendered in full Italianate arches. Inside, a visitor entered a central hallway with a staircase, flanked on one side by a kitchen and on the other by a parlor.

The most striking architectural development of this period was the banked two-story house with porch, which became a signature of the region's vernacular. These farmhouses emphatically called attention to themselves. They were sizable, and their construction and ornamentation were conspicuous. The Friedline house, for example, built in 1858 (Fig. 59), was made of brick fired on the site. It measured 23' × 38' without the porches, and this imposing structure had a five-bay front. Its central exterior entrance had a transom and sidelights, set off with simple yet elegant molding and Doric pilasters. The unusually large-proportioned window openings had wide, substantial molded wooden lintels. The front facade featured Flemish-bond brickwork, while the sides were worked in the more common English bond. Paired brackets ornamented the cornice.

The house's most arresting feature was its double-decker porch. It consisted of highly idiosyncratic and very decorative wooden openwork posts, topped by simple molding with an appliqué pattern beneath. The posts (four sets of them) were linked across the base by turned balusters and at the top by three pairs of gracefully curving, thin wooden scrolls. The porch was integral; this created irregular gable-end fenestration, since the first- and second-story gable-end windows had to be "pushed back" to an off-center position in order to create space for the porch. The attic-level windows remained centered. Inside, the plan consisted of a central hallway flanked by pairs of rooms on either side. The front rooms had recessed-panel wainscoting, and there were folding doors between the two west-side rooms.

The Biesecker family farmhouse in Jenner Township (Fig. 60) shows the same type of design and ornamentation, even though it was executed in plank: irregular gable fenestration, integral multistory porch, and main entrance with transom and sidelight. Here, the porch trim is less elaborate, consisting of six simple posts connected at the bottom by balusters and at the top by a scalloped frieze. The Baker farm in Lincoln Township (Fig. 61) fits into this pattern as well. It has four rather than five bays, and thus, its center hall is asymmetrically placed; its integral multistory porch has decorative elements similar to those on the Biesecker house. The Wagerline family's 1867 house (Fig. 62) was built of brick fired on-site, with a cut-stone foundation (the stone was hauled from another nearby farm). The house had a three-bay appearance in the front but five openings in the rear side. It still had a central hall plan. Its builder solved the problem of symmetry in gable fenestration by making double-decker porches on both sides of the house. These porches were enclosed with latticework rather than spindlework.

These architectural changes of the nineteenth century assimilated elements of more widely known architectural styles. The porches' decorative elements are immediately recognizable as "Victorian" in style; they possess the same qualities of machine-tooled, ornate balusters, spandrels, and openwork that can be found on Victorian houses almost anywhere in the nation. Yet while Somerset County porches surely share the language of style, they do so with a localistic tone. Here architectural historian Dell Upton's distinction between "style" and "mode" is helpful. "Style," Upton says, "is pervasive. It provides a context, or system of common understanding, within which the active participants of a society can operate in a coordinated manner." Thus, style provides a common architectural vocabulary. "Mode," on the other hand, "refers to the divisions in society. . . . [M]odes can be created by groups of any social status wishing to set themselves apart." So, we can say that the banked house with double-decker porch represents the mindset of Somerset County's prosperous rural elite, both in style—in the choice of widely popular Victorian detailing—and mode—in the disposition of this detailing within the context of elaborate, multi-tiered porches.[65]

These houses became popular enough to set a trend in the county and to help create a characteristic local landscape. Of course, banked houses had emerged during the preindustrial period

FIG. 59A

FIG. 59B

FIG. 59
The mid-nineteenth century saw the rise of
Somerset County's distinctive double-decker
porch. This example in Jefferson Township,
about 1858, epitomizes the exuberance and
flair of this locally distinctive type. The
elevations (A, above, and C, opposite) show
the full effect and the realignment of gable
windows to accommodate the porches, while
the detail (B) shows gracefully curving
woodwork. Somerset Historical Center.

and were common elsewhere, so in this respect, nineteenth-century builders drew on longstanding traditions that went back at least to eastern Pennsylvania if not to Europe. In other words,
these features were a part of the localistic architectural vocabulary that was employed in accommodating new national trends. Double-decker porches are also found in other locales, such as eastern Pennsylvania and across the Maryland border. But in Somerset County, the banked house
with full-width front facade double-decker porches was a form more elaborately developed and
more commonly built than in other places.

FIG. 59C

FIG. 60
Biesecker (Steinkirchner) house, about 1860, Jenner Township. Somerset Historical Center.

FIG. 61
This midcentury farmhouse in Lincoln
Township shows a four-bay variation on the
theme. Somerset Historical Center.

In the cellars of these banked structures we find equipment for the same work that had gone on before, though in more spacious surroundings. They contain familiar features such as cooking fireplaces, root cellars, cupboards for storage, and water troughs, reflecting the intensified women's work. Many had two doors, one into the kitchen and the other at the other end of the basement. These doors could be approached on the basement level; this public presentation of major work-spaces on the front, public side of the house also recalls earlier times. Local tradition, as well as architectural evidence, suggests that families ate their meals in these basements, again preserving old modes of sociability.

It is when we rise to the first floor that we sense a marked departure from the sociable past. At their most formal and extreme, these arrangements were designed not to encourage mingling but to keep people apart. Take for example the house on the Schrock family farm (Fig. 63). A nineteenth-century visitor would have to ascend the porch stairs to get access to the main entrance: from the outset, the design forced visitors to move *up*, symbolically distancing residents from outsiders—and basement work from upper-level activities. An imposing, symmetrical facade gave no clue to the internal arrangement. Once arriving at the central entrance, a visitor would enter a hallway, a socially neutral space. The four rooms on either side of this hallway could be entered only from the hallway, not from each other. One would hesitate to wander from room to room without an invitation. The same was true on the second floor.

The interiors of these newer farmhouses communicated a range of uses and social messages. On the main floor of the Schrock family house, for example, the rooms had hand-grained wood-work and tongue-and-groove flooring. Two-panel doors separated the rooms. Fluted Greek Revival door framing, with a recessed diamond motif at the corners, announced the social impor-tance of these rooms for entertainment and display (Fig. 64). The basement had four spacious rooms with built-in cupboards. These were surmounted by molded mantelpieces. The window frames had matching molding, and the entire southwest room was wainscoted as well. Layers of paint (gray, blue, red) indicate that the Pennsylvania German penchant for color was indulged

FIG. 62
The Wagerline house in Brothersvalley Township, 1867, sported two sets of porches, front and back. Somerset Historical Center.

here. The built-in cupboards, too, suggest Pennsylvania German custom. Clearly this was not simply a space for rough, dirty work; perhaps the family dined here. The Schrock family house blended "improvement," ornament, and formality with cherished Pennsylvania German spatial conventions. The pattern is common and clear. Similar arrangements appear in the Jacob Smith house, the Weigley/Hauger farm (Fig. 65), and others.

The parlor was only one of the new specialized spaces in the nineteenth-century farmhouse. Dining rooms and sitting rooms sometimes appeared as well. The emergence of these new proxemic patterns was part of a nationwide trend. Increasingly, middling families—in keeping with the culture of refinement—aspired to separate grimy, low-status work from social and family amusements.[66] Somerset County building of the nineteenth century shows a particularly local twist on these themes.

The 1870 estate inventory of Abraham Overholt of West Overton (in bordering Westmoreland County) suggests how people circulated within these spaces. Luckily for our purposes, the

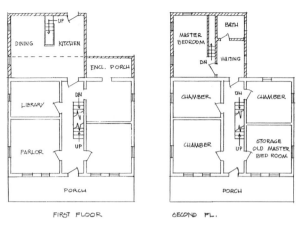

FIG. 63A

FIG. 63
New farmhouses in nineteenth-century
Somerset County had plans that separated
people—representing a departure from the
past. This is especially well illustrated in the
plan of the Schrock family farmhouse in
Brothersvalley; the upper floors (A) contain
hallways and clearly separated rooms,
suggesting greater formality, while the
basement (B) is organized for production.
Somerset Historical Center.

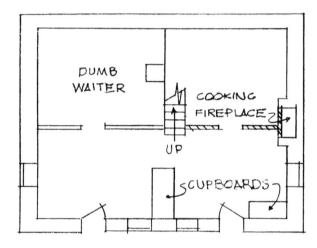

FIG. 63B   BASEMENT

assessors listed Overholt's goods room by room, and from their description, it seems fairly certain
that the house had a center hall with four rooms on each level. This house was built in 1838,
banked, with full porches extending over both the first floor and basement; the main entrance,
located in the center of the facade, opened onto the upper porch. Significantly, the Overholts had
both a first-floor kitchen and a basement kitchen (whether this was part of the original plan is
unknown). The basement was filled with the equipment associated with the nineteenth-century
farm wife's duties: a dough tray (this was found in the basement hall, along with a cupboard and
table), cookstove (less valuable than the one upstairs), cupboard, canned fruits, barrels of vinegar
(all of these in the front cellar), crocks of jam and pickles, and two hundred pounds of lard in the
back cellar.

    In the first-floor kitchen stood a cooking stove and fixtures, cupboards, and tablecloths. A
separate, carpeted dining room was furnished with dining room cupboard, dining table, clock, and
heating stove. The parlor furnishings conjure up our stereotypical images of the Victorian horror

FIG. 64
This simple but elegant interior trim signified a room with social importance. Schrock family farmhouse, Somerset Historical Center.

of voids: the parlor was stuffed with piano, sofa, center table, rocking chairs, rug, upholstery, and so on. The fourth ground-floor room was called the "front chamber," and it contained beds, washstands, and the like. The second story had three chambers and a room simply called the "room 2nd floor," which contained a Franklin stove, secretary, cupboard, wardrobe, stand, sheets, tablecloths, quilts, coverlets, carpet, cane seat chairs, and knives, forks, and spoons. (Could this have been the transmuted *stube*?) Four more bedchambers occupied a third story.

Surely Abraham Overholt was not typical; his property was worth tens of thousands of dollars. So we can't know if his use of space was typical, either. All we can say is that the profile of goods found in the basement fits well with what we know of women's work, and that the two kitchens also find parallels in the emerging differentiation of "heavy" and "light" work. It seems likely that most people had one room they called a "parlor," the "best" room, reserved for special company or for ceremonial occasions such as weddings and funerals. Church weddings did not become popular until the twentieth century, and death had not yet become commercialized in funeral "parlors" (the name is in fact a holdover). The Overholts' specialized dining room is interesting, because it suggests a mentality of refinement, a desire to separate the work of cooking from the social activity of eating. The presence of a "front chamber" carries over longstanding traditions: it recalls the *kammer* of old, and surely represents yet another example of "blending."[67]

Thus just as agriculture, rural life, and farmwork in this period blended elements of old and new, so did houses. House builders of the period retained important traditional social spaces such as the *stube* ("the room"). They enlarged and elaborated to reflect the new drive for order and system in work, but they clung to massive basement kitchen workspaces. At the same time, they placed a higher value on appearances and created new spaces that communicated order, system, and regularity. The center-hall plans also tended toward a more overtly spatial and visual expression of

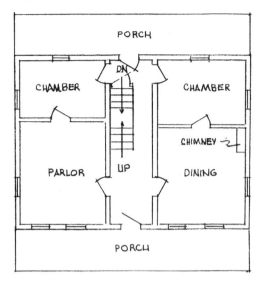

FIG. 65A   FIRST FLOOR

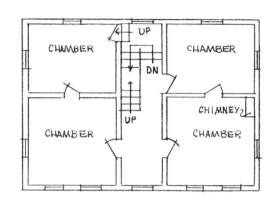

SECOND FLOOR

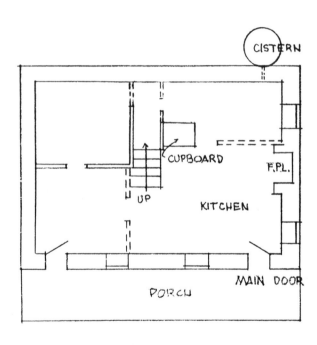

FIG. 65B

FIG. 65
The Weigley/Hauger farm, about 1858, also shows more formal rooms on the first and second floors (A) combined with a production-oriented basement (B). Somerset Historical Center.

social hierarchy and formality, "filtering" people through formal, neutral spaces as one's social status came to be expressed through housing. These spaces offered a striking contrast to the roughness and extreme disorder of the frontier era, introducing a new refinement. They accommodated a richer texture of material and social life and permitted people to express individual tastes. The enforced sociability of the preindustrial period had had its merits, but now that a new prosperity permitted it, nineteenth-century houses afforded expanded options for sociability *and* privacy, for public *and* personal space.

The vast front porches encapsulated all of these tendencies and blended them together. These elaborate structures often spanned the entire front (and sometimes the back, too) over one, two, or even three levels. While some houses had porches relatively early in the century, most appeared later. Sometimes they were added onto existing houses;[68] sometimes they were built as integral parts of new buildings.

This, too, was part of a broader trend. The porch was a vastly popular new architectural form in nineteenth-century America. By midcentury, families all over the country were building new houses with integral porches, or adding porches onto existing houses. The mechanization of wood-working in the post–Civil War period meant that a huge range of elements could be obtained inexpensively: balusters, spandrels, brackets, scrollwork. Romantic aesthetics and a more favorable attitude toward "Nature" helped fuel the enthusiasm for porches. Architectural historians have amply documented the technological and stylistic basis for American porches, even claiming that they represent a uniquely American contribution to vernacular architecture. But few scholars have devoted sustained attention to the porch's social meaning. Yet surely this is significant; after all, a porch often added hundreds of square feet to a house's area. It seems clear that in some cases, porches functioned as "outdoor parlors," extending the parlor space outward to allow refinement to touch the grounds and landscape. On some farms, the porch helped differentiate the house from the rougher barnyard. In the antebellum South, the porch served as a "filtering" space, reinforcing the social hierarchy in a slave society.[69]

In Somerset County, the double-decker porch had complex cultural meanings and social functions. One function of these structures was probably to provide an alternative entrance to the banked basement doors. The new values of refinement were not compatible with having the main entrance open onto a kitchen (as it had earlier). And in any event, the ever-busy farm wife may not have wanted too many interruptions. In practical terms, the porch had to span the facade, or the basement dooryard would be obstructed. This alternative entrance directed traffic away from work areas to living spaces. The upper porch layers offered outdoor social and work space. One Somerset County oral-history informant, born in 1909, remembered that her grandparents hosted social gatherings on the porches. Porches accommodated the ongoing social gatherings of the day and shared work activities as well. People used porches to sit and peel apples (Fig. 66) or cut beans; they shook rugs and hung out wash. Another informant recalled very specific uses for porches on all three levels; while he was growing up, the top porch was used for shaking rugs; the middle porch had a settee and chairs for informal socializing; the basement had a swing. On the basement level, women also used the hand-powered separator, shelled peas, and snapped beans. Sometimes, during visits, men might go to one porch and women to another.[70] In this way the porches preserved the old architecture of sociability: outdoor space is informal (and, of course, open to view) and hence continues the old values in a new context, while still accommodating the pursuit of symmetry, regularity, refinement, and control.

The use of ornamentally formal, sophisticated-looking porches for everyday, mundane purposes points up how ideals of refinement bumped up against competing realities. This was true across the farm landscape. Fencing in many places was only "tolerably good," if the numerous advertisements for stray cattle are any indication. Road surveyors looked to "stone piles" in fields for landmarks. What is more, local farm families were deliberate and selective in deciding where

FIG. 66
Women peeling apples on the porch. Though the photograph is obviously posed, the choice of the porch setting was a natural one. Somerset Historical Center.

to make their aesthetic investments. Surviving images from the period are richly suggestive for what they tell about people's pride and preconceptions. Late in the century, itinerant photographers roamed the region, capitalizing on the rage for improvement by promising to capture the accomplishments of their customers forever. Families eagerly embraced the chance. They posed proudly next to their houses and barns. One surviving image (location and date unknown) shows a house with banked construction and front porch, a configuration that suggests Somerset County. This family chose to embellish their house with a bracketed porch, lined with Victorian paneling; they fenced part of the yard, as well. But they didn't mind having their portrait taken showing a yard strewn with rubble, brush, loose boards, and a rain barrel sitting out (Fig. 67). Another local resident, F. W. Mason of Glade, owned one of the more architecturally sophisticated rural dwellings in Somerset County. This Italianate house boasted a hipped roof, brick construction, columned porch, transom, door frame, and bracketed cornice. It too had a picket fence. Yet in the view for posterity, the proud family stood hip deep in grass (Fig. 68).[71]

FIG. 67
Unidentified bank house with family.
This family showed pride of possession
without apparent concern over the front
yard's appearance. Photograph no. 6
from United States View Company
Photographs (Manuscript Group 419).
Pennsylvania State Archives,
Harrisburg, Pennsylvania.

FIG. 68
Even the sophisticated owners of the Mason house in Glade invested more thought in building design than in the
immediately surrounding landscape. Photograph no. 8 from United States View Company Photographs (Manuscript
Group 419). Pennsylvania State Archives, Harrisburg, Pennsylvania.

The landscape choices that these families made testify to their selectivity. While they embraced some types of refinement, they implicitly rejected others. Their house interiors contained parlors, emblematic of gentility, yet they also incorporated basement work and dining spaces. They built elaborate decorative porches but used them for hanging out wash. In short, the domestic landscape in many ways represented a successful blending of old and new, local and national—but it also evoked the inherent tensions in the attempt to reconcile the traditional with the modern.

As we move from the house to the other farmstead spaces and buildings, we find an array of outbuildings that sustained and accommodated changes in agriculture. Not many nineteenth-century outbuildings survive intact, but we know, from such evidence as real estate advertisements, that they were varied and numerous. Springhouses were crucial spaces on the nineteenth-century farm, since through them ran the water necessary for dairying and other food processing as well as cleaning up. Springhouses were women's spaces. They proliferated with the rise of commercial-scale dairying.[72]

Mentioned as frequently as springhouses are stables.[73] These are usually mentioned along with barns, so it seems as though stables and barns were conceptually and spatially separate. Their appearance reflects the increased reliance on horses for pulling farm machinery and for transportation. Some of the buildings pictured in the 1884 county history may possibly have served as stables; see, for example, the engraving of the John H. Zimmerman residence, which shows a structure with stalls outside.

Other outbuildings mentioned in the real estate ads included granaries,[74] stillhouses, tanyards, hog pens, woodhouses, and smokehouses. Sometimes smokehouses were combined with other facilities, resulting in such multipurpose structures as the "smoke & wash house." All farms had smokehouses at one time, since home butchering and meat preservation were an enduring part of rural life in Somerset County, but few extant examples can be securely dated to the nineteenth century. Inside, meat was suspended in the smokehouse by chains, hooks, or poles (Fig. 69). A fire was built

FIG. 69
This twentieth-century smokehouse interior from the Jacob Walker farm shows meat hooks projecting from the rafters. At the end of the butchering season, there would be hams and sausages hanging here for curing. Somerset Historical Center.

FIG. 70
The outdoor privy was a part of rural Somerset life long after townfolk had indoor plumbing. Somerset Historical Center.

on the dirt floor inside a brick or stone ring or a discarded container. A metal plate laid on top kept the fire low. Smoke exited through cracks in the building. Smokehouses were sited at some distance from the house, but still clearly within the orbit of house (rather than barn) functions.

Sugar camps were mentioned in real estate ads throughout the period. One ad even mentioned a "sugar orchard," suggesting that people regarded the sugar bush as a cultivated space. Nineteenth-century sugar camps (especially after the Civil War, as the trade boomed) were usually located near water, within range of the wood's edge, and frequently at the base of a hill, with ramps to make it easier to unload sugar water. Since they were only used once a year, sugar camps were crude sheds of rough scantling with minimal foundations. Inside, an arch (of stone or brick) and large boiling pan dominated the space, but some camps also had settling stands, finishing kettles, and sugar troughs as sugar-making techniques were refined. Later in the period, metal grates allowed the use of coal as fuel.[75]

Of course, every yard would have a privy, located at a discreet distance from the house (Fig. 70).

By the end of this period, as agriculture changed, other outbuildings became more common in the landscape (though certainly not all farms would have had all of these buildings). Wagon sheds and carriage or buggy houses reflected farm mechanization and improved transportation. Ice houses permitted some families to store ice for summer use. Tool houses sheltered the farm's growing

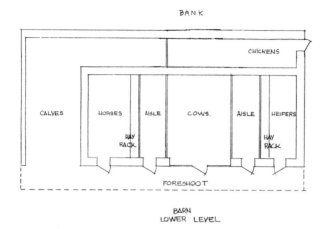

FIG . 71A

FIG. 71
This log double-crib barn in Brothersvalley Township, dating from the early nineteenth century, was designed for a multiplicity of functions: it provided a central focus for livestock shelter, grain and hay storage, and threshing. The lower level (A) accommodated animals, while the upper-level cribs and threshing floor (B) provided space for hay and grain storage and threshing. Somerset Historical Center.

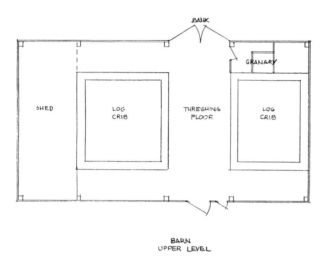

FIG . 71B

collection of implements. Corncribs appeared alongside short-season corn. Sheep stables separated sheep from other livestock. Finally, chicken houses sheltered the larger flocks of the late nineteenth century.[76]

Another interesting development dating from the post–Civil War era is the appearance of a "tenant house."[77] Advertisements from the period 1865–80 were much more likely to mention these structures than before. Tenancy did not rise substantially in this period. Rather, the appearance of "tenant houses" should probably be interpreted as yet another indication of the changing agricultural and social scene. Tenants could no longer be sure of climbing the "agricultural ladder" to full landownership, and so their social status had a more permanent character. Separate tenant houses would codify this change. An increased value attached to privacy probably reinforced this trend; tenant houses would permit privacy for both landlord and tenant families.

Few detached kitchens date from this period, and real estate ads do not often mention a separate kitchen. But we should not read this evidence to mean that home builders lost interest in this *type* of facility, because some earlier structures continued to function; moreover, a number of houses dating from the period had extensive basement facilities and would not necessarily require a detached kitchen.[78] Some farmhouses combined first-floor kitchens with older detached kitchens, so that the emerging differentiation between "light" and "heavy" kitchen work appeared in the first-floor and detached kitchens (paralleling the division, in banked houses, between first-floor and basement kitchens).

Barns were easily the most prominent buildings in the nineteenth-century agrarian landscape. As might be expected, several types appear. One is the double-crib log barn. Two massive log double-crib barns survive in Somerset County. Both are variations on the "Sweitzer" barn, which was a forebay barn with asymmetrical gable silhouettes, conventional livestock pens below, and double cribs plus threshing floor on the upper level (see Figs. 71, 72, and 73). Each has V-notching (the most common type of corner joining in the log construction of this region). The logs were covered with vertical board.

The classic Pennsylvania barn form was the most common. This famous building type originated in Switzerland, whence it migrated to America in the eighteenth century; it became established first in eastern Pennsylvania. Its diagnostic characteristics are the prominent forebay, or overshoot, extending out over the length of the barn; the banked construction, with ramp or bridge entrance to the upper-level threshing floor; and granaries in the forebay.

As people migrated westward from the "core" in southeastern Pennsylvania, they took the Pennsylvania barn with them. In Somerset County, most surviving examples date from the middle

FIG. 72
The interior of this magnificent double-crib log barn shows typical V-notching and massive square cribs. Somerset Historical Center.

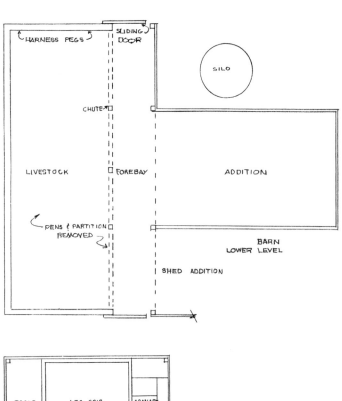

FIG. 73
This banked double-crib log barn in Lower Turkeyfoot Township probably was built around the mid-nineteenth century. It has a granary in the forebay, as was customary in the eastern part of the state. The shed addition is later.

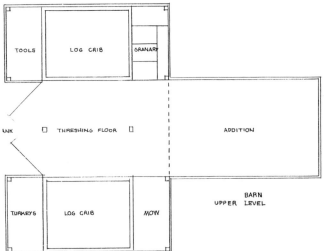

and late nineteenth century. The banked barn had gained favor in the east as an accompaniment to a mixed, commercial-scale, grain-and-livestock economy. (As commercial agriculture emerged in the nineteenth century, a similar process occurred in Somerset County.) Like the banked two-story house, the banked barn appears at a particular point in the county's economic development.

These banked barns (Figs. 74 and 75) generally were constructed of timber framing—that is, of huge, square hewn posts and beams held together not with nails but with pegs, which pinned together mortise-and-tenon joints. A variety of bent forms (a "bent" is one complete cross section of framing posts and beams) can be found in Somerset County, but most seem to echo Germanic traditions, such as double reinforcements on top plates and diagonal reinforcing timbers reaching from one horizontal to another. The upper level contained the threshing floor; this was the area immediately beyond the "bank." A variety of activities took place here, including, of course, threshing. On either side, mows held hay. The location of granaries differed from the customary Pennsylvania-barn placement over the forebay; in southwest Pennsylvania, granaries were just as often on the bank side. The reason for this local variation is still unknown. Yet several examples, including the Baer barn in Brothersvalley Township (c. 1840) and the Moses barn in Shade Township (1877), had forebay granaries.

Below, animals were housed. Few lower-level arrangements have survived intact, so we need to rely on descriptions to understand function. An article in the 1851 *Pennsylvania Farm Journal* (Fig. 76) shows, on the bottom level, stables for farm horses and "strange" horses (H and A), cattle (C), and oxen (O); harness room (G), turnip storage (T), potato storage (P), feed mixing room (F), and aisles (a). The upper level shows the customary threshing floors (F), mows (M), granaries (G), and doors (D).[79]

For the latter part of the period, a valuable document survives in the form of Francis F. Cable's diary. Cable was a young farmer just starting out in the early 1880s, and he left a detailed account of how his barn was constructed. After the structure's skeleton was in place, he began to work on

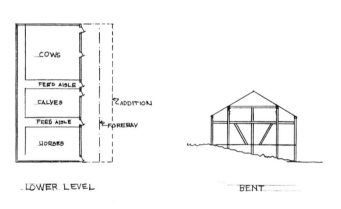

FIG. 74
This Pennsylvania barn in Jefferson Township, probably built in the 1830s, had characteristic local features, including Germanic timber framing and a forebay granary. The lower level is organized with aisles horizontal to the roof ridge; the bent configuration is typical for its day. Somerset Historical Center.

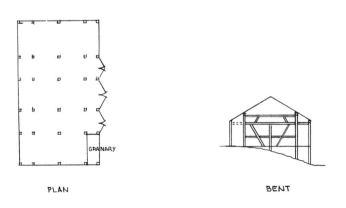

FIG. 75
A Pennsylvania barn in Shade Township, dating from 1877, shows the essential continuity in local barn building. Built nearly fifty years after the one depicted in Fig. 74, it still has the same lower-level plan and a bent configuration that differs in the details—but not in the essentials—of timber framing. Somerset Historical Center.

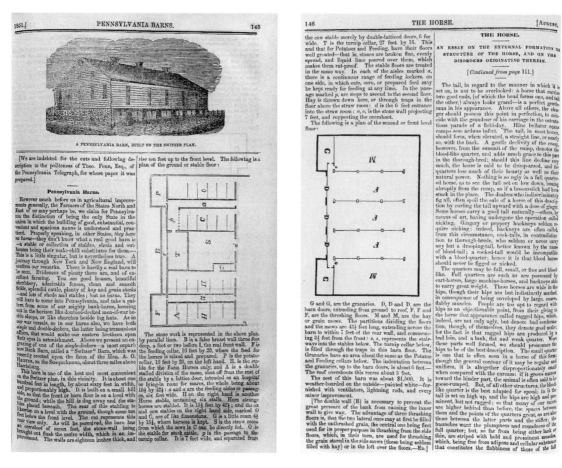

FIG. 76
This diagram of a Pennsylvania barn offers important insights into the actual functioning of the barns in the period
in which they were built. This is particularly valuable since few contemporary barns have survived unaltered.
Interesting features of this plan (depicting a barn built around 1850 near Harrisburg, Pennsylvania) include a "lying-
in" stable for mares, stables for "strange horses," and storage for turnips and potatoes. The lower level *(left)* is devoted
to crop storage and animal shelter, and the upper level *(right)* to hay and grain storage and to space for threshing.
"Pennsylvania Barns," *Pennsylvania Farm Journal* (August 1851), 145–46. Rare Books and Manuscripts, The
Pennsylvania State University Libraries.

the internal partitions. They included a feeding room, cow "staples" (one can just hear Cable's
thick Pennsylvania German accent), horse stables (these had stalls), sheep stable, an oxen stable
(a real anachronism), and a calf stable.[80] These were likely arranged crosswise perpendicular to the
roof ridge, with feed aisles between and perhaps a side access aisle. Hogs and hens may have shared
barn space with the other animals. Doors led out into the barnyard. This is probably where milking took place, since stanchions did not appear in barn interiors until later.[81]

Within the basic barn form, there was wide variation. Samuel Boger's midcentury barn (Fig.
77) possessed the defining features of this period. At 88' × 46', it was amply proportioned. Its
heavy beams were pinned together. The granaries were on the bank side. In keeping with the new
fondness for architectural ornament, the ashlar stone foundation consisted of regular stones, laid

in contrasting shades to form a patterned effect. A decorative diamond was cut into the gable end of the barn. Daniel Baer built a barn around the same time; it, too, was a banked Pennsylvania barn with open forebay. At 65' × 30', it was smaller than the Boger barn, but had some of the same characteristics nevertheless. Its framing system consisted of hewn timbers with mortise-and-tenon joints. It also had a dressed stone foundation and a decorative cut-diamond pattern in the gable. The barn on the Koontz farm conformed to the same overall characteristics. Its decorative feature in the gable consisted of two cut-out hearts and a cut-out circle.

Whether of double-crib or classic Pennsylvania design, all of these barns suited well the diversified commercial agriculture of the period. For example, John and Mary Wagner built a 54' × 84' Pennsylvania barn in 1877. In 1880, they reported for the census a total of eighteen cattle, twenty-seven sheep, seventeen pigs, and thirty hens. They churned 1,000 pounds of butter. The barn doubtless housed most of the stock and also served as storage for the 20 tons of hay, 100 bushels of buckwheat, 300 bushels of oats, 25 bushels of rye, 30 bushels of wheat, and perhaps also the 140 bushels of potatoes. The family also boiled 1,200 pounds of maple sugar and gathered 300 bushels of apples. Other local manuscript census records that are tied to known Pennsylvania barns show a similar mix of crops and processed products. These barns and associated farms appear to be typical in terms of the crop mix, but they operated on a significantly larger scale, producing more commercial quantities than the average; thus, they represent the wealthier, more prosperous farms.

FIG. 77
Samuel Boger barn. Note the decorative cross design in the foundation; a small diamond-shaped cutout in the gable end is barely visible. Somerset Historical Center.

FIG. 78
Family photograph showing farm family, barn, animals, and road. Somerset Historical Center.

On many nineteenth-century Somerset County farmsteads, the visual correspondence between house and barn was noticeable. The farmstead's two main poles of activity echoed each other visually and architecturally to communicate messages about their intimate relationship. It is no coincidence that house and barn both were constructed in the same idiom. Banked, cut-stone foundations defined a major characteristic of each; so did projecting elements, whether fore-bay or porch. Exterior cladding materials were often similar—weatherboarding, for example. At least some barns were painted, further lending visual continuity between house and barn. Architectural ornament made its way into the decorative repertoire of both house and barn at this time; though the barn's ornament was more subdued, it still tied the barn visually to the house. In terms of scale and siting, the barn was larger than the house, but not dramatically so. Nineteenth-century photographs capture a pronounced level of comfort with barnyard and home grounds (Fig. 78); people pose in either or both (Fig. 79), mingling with livestock in many cases. Their pride in their farms and their products is evident. Contemporary photos suggest that for ordinary farm people, rigorously separating people and animals was not a high priority, and "improvement" was fully consistent with a producerist ethic.

The photos also suggest that a gendered "domestic sphere" was not part of Somerset County farm people's spatial vocabulary or experience. The farm husband and wife, children, and hired hands continually circulated throughout the farm. Although women may have worked less in the haymeadow or grain fields than before (and men spent a considerable amount of time there), they still shared the field at critical harvest times. In the barn, too, men and women worked, often in

FIG. 79
Family photograph on the Wagerline farmstead, late nineteenth century. Here is the complete package, a harmonious blending of architectural elements relating house to barn and vice versa. Somerset Historical Center.

large, mixed-sex groups. Indeed, from time to time men and women came together and actively used just about every space on the farmstead. Women milked in the barn or barnyard, while men and women together shared butchering and apple butter making (Fig. 80). Orchard, wash house, smokehouse, and flax patch were all communal workspaces. Thus, even though there was a fairly clear (though not by any means completely rigid) gender division of *labor* on the farm, in almost no case was there a rigid gender division of *space*.

A few examples from two local diaries will illustrate. Francis F. Cable's diary is a rich source that shows him often working with his wife, Maria:[82]

21 April 1883: "I helped Maria in the Garden."

15 July 1883: "I & Maria went to Shanksville, for some coloring Dye and got Lottie shod, then

home & I help to color some yarn. Mother-in-law was here. She came yesterday."

10 September 1883: "I, Maria & Katie [the horse] finished up tying up oats for this year."

5 October 1883: "I & Maria pick apples for cider all day."

14 November 1883: "I & Maria helped Schrock's to butcher 3 hogs."

19 November 1883: "I helped Maria to scrub the kitchen."

20 February 1884: "I & Maria cleaned 25 bushels of seed oats."

20 May 1884: "I helped Maria to clean house."

28 September 1884: "I & Maria cleaned some wheat over at Schrock's & then home & in the

Eve. we went over & we made some sourkrout together."

And from Sarah Garee Armstrong's diary, we find that on 24 September 1879, "Newton and me cut peaches to dry"; on 11 October 1879, "we dug potatoes"; and—on 19 October 1879—"I went to see Lonie Hill. Newton kept the baby."[83]

When we consider the visual parity between house and barn, we should take care not to assume that it was a marker of gender equality. Remember that men still controlled women's lives very closely. In fact, we might consider the relatively high architectural status of the house as an indication that *men* still frequented the *house* as much as the barn. They were willing, then, to invest barn and house with equal visual and architectural status. Perhaps we even ought to consider the equation of house and barn as part of a masculine critique of bourgeois "domesticity" that emphatically separated the (women's) domestic domain from the (men's) workplace.

FIG. 80
This wonderfully evocative photograph taken at apple-butter-making time shows three generations enjoying the seasonal task. Somerset Historical Center.

The nineteenth-century rural landscape was shaped by a dynamic mix of neighborhood reciprocity, consumerism, and individualism. Preindustrial customs and spatial patterns mingled with the newer tasks and spaces of the modernizing era. The farmstead of this period vividly captures this blending. Within the house, new ideas of refinement meshed with old values of production, and this combination achieved spatial expression in parlors and basement kitchens, respectively. Vast informal porches offered areas for old-style social gatherings, but they coexisted with formal parlors and dining rooms that expressed social formality and display. The center-hall plan itself, which could be found all over the continent and across the ocean, reflected the nascent trend toward standardization.

Outdoor space was similarly blended. The Pennsylvania barn accommodated mixed agriculture on a commercial scale. Well-defined fields, meadows, pastures, tillage areas, and woodlots organized farming spatially. Outbuildings facilitated the diverse functions of the mixed subsistence-and-commercial farm. In all of these spaces, activities occurred that both recalled older days (collectively accomplished butchering, for instance) and newer developments (including commercial dairying, laboring for cash wages, or raking by machine). Men and women fully shared farm spaces.

Most of the time, this blending achieved a satisfying balance, aesthetically and socially. However, the very need for selectivity also implied tension, because sometimes the old and new ways just weren't compatible. So in the landscape, we see statements that embrace the new order and others that just as insistently critique it. Overall, we could say that nineteenth-century Somerset County rural people succeeded in creating a distinctive place. It surely borrowed from the vocabulary of the national, the capitalist, the individualistic; note the machine-carved decoration, the formal plans, the picket fences, the centralized barn, the roads and schools. But the elements of the local, the precapitalist, and the communal were communicated with an unusually high level of relief. Extensive woodland, tiny blotches of cropland, banked buildings, and neighborhood churches and cemeteries offered a competing vision.

This local idiom flourished and reached a peak just as a wave of industrialization was about to break over the county. No sooner had the new landscape emerged than miners and railroad builders would transform it yet again.

3 ★ *An Industrial Order, 1880–1940*

If the nineteenth century was the farmer's age, the twentieth century belonged to the city dweller. As the industrial economy matured, the proportion of the population living in cities grew apace, reaching majority status early in the century. Now the economy was nationally integrated—and unequivocally so. The cities formed the organizational and information centers for huge corporations that were established on an unprecedented scale, using mass production and distribution techniques. A white-collar middle class staffed these corporate bureaucracies in sales, accounting, and (increasingly) advertising departments, while the working-class experience now included assembly-line work in huge plants. The separation of home and work became more pronounced. Not only the national economy but also national politics and culture commanded more and more authority. Shifting definitions of citizenship afforded political rights to white women, but brutal exclusions based on race persisted. Progressive Era reforms and their New Deal successors addressed the dislocations inherent in an economy that forced so many people to live on the edge. In the process they made the federal state a force in daily life as never before.

In this atmosphere, rural people faced special challenges. For a brief period from about 1910 to 1920, farm families enjoyed a "golden age": high prices and new conveniences promised to bring rural America into the modern era. During the twenties, however, the agricultural sector plunged into a deep depression that anticipated what the thirties would be like for the rest of the economy. The number of farms dropped rapidly.[1] Their political and cultural power on the decline, rural people struggled to keep up in a fiercely competitive economy. Larger-scale, efficient, heavily capital-intensive operations crowded out less profitable farms caught in the price-cost squeeze (farmers paid retail prices for goods they bought, but received wholesale prices for the products they sold). Mechanization allowed more land to be cultivated; the tractor accelerated this trend. Regional specializations grew more pronounced—for example, fluid-milk dairying was carried on in the East, corn and hog production in Iowa, and wheat in the bonanza fields of the Dakotas.

The government (especially the U.S. Department of Agriculture) and its associated land-grant research arm came to claim a greater presence in agriculture and rural life. It surely had not yet taken on the proportions it has now assumed, but began to assert more influence and power than ever before. After the Hatch (1887) and Smith-Lever (1914) Acts established agricultural research and extension, respectively, the land-grant complex initiated and disseminated research aimed mostly at farmers with large, capital- and technology-intensive operations. Both of these movements were regarded with skepticism and even hostility in many rural areas.[2]

The rural landscape reflected these realities. Everywhere, the impress of the urbanizing national culture was evident. As national transport and communications networks consolidated, and as architectural professionalism gained power, the range of housing forms diminished. The result was a greater convergence between rural and urban areas; one could find foursquares or bungalows in rural Iowa or in suburban Detroit. The modern house expressed values of individualism, conformity, expertise, and consumption; it was assumed to be occupied by a nuclear family. Of necessity, there was greater regional differentiation in farm outbuildings, depending on the type of farming in a given area. But even these varying structures were built with modern materials, techniques, and social processes.

These years saw the triumph of the new order in rural Somerset County. In the nineteenth century, rural families here had successfully straddled the old and the new, but in the twentieth century, the industrial order was just too powerful—and in some instances, too seductive—to resist. This was true even though Somerset County farming typically continued to be diversified and to have a subsistence dimension. These remnants of precapitalist life receded into relative insignificance in the face of the changes wrought by the coal industry. The salient fact was that on the whole, farm families benefited from the coal companies' presence, and this generation became more willing allies of business interests than their parents and grandparents had been. If the watchword for the nineteenth century had been selectivity, the theme of the twentieth century was accommodation.

The twentieth-century coal-patch towns in the Somerset County landscape bespoke coal's power loudly and unambiguously. But the farmstead landscape was much more enigmatic. Some of its elements extended the nineteenth-century pattern of selective localistic response to new conditions; the summer kitchen is a good example. But other elements of the farmscape strangely obscured some underlying realities. The highly visible star barns are an exemplary case. Their size and finish belied the modest scale of most Somerset County farming. In fact, the rise of the star barn owed much to coal money, and its prominence arguably functioned as much to separate farming folk from miners and coal patches as to reflect a high level of agricultural activity. Again, we can look at the processes of landscape formation in the county to understand these forces at work.

AGRICULTURAL MODERNIZATION

The boom in coal mining set the agenda for twentieth-century rural life in the county. A burst of railroad building in the 1890s and early 1900s occurred in conjunction with the rise of large coal mining operations such as those in Windber and Garrett. Eight major companies established extensive mining operations in the county, using outside capital. For example, the Consolidation

Coal Company (which was controlled by John D. Rockefeller and his associates) opened forty-seven mines in the county between 1904 and 1917. Over one hundred other locally financed companies operated on a smaller scale. These enterprises produced high-quality, low-ash coal destined for steam locomotives, light and power companies, and steamships.[3]

The county's total population reflects these developments and the jobs they created: from thirty-seven thousand in 1890, the population rose, by 1920, to over eighty thousand (see Fig. 24). The 1919–20 report of the state Department of Mines counted over twelve thousand miners working in Somerset County mines. By 1930, only 21 percent of the county's population fell into the "rural farm" category, while 58 percent was classified as "rural nonfarm" and 21 percent as "urban." Much of this "urban" population lived in company-controlled coal-patch towns. The contrast with the recent past was staggering; at the turn of the century, only 6 percent of the county's population had lived in "urban" areas.[4] Aside from sheer numbers, another major population change occurred with the influx of immigrants of eastern and southern European birth—from a negligible number to about 12 percent of the county's population—and these newcomers were concentrated in the coal towns.

Industrial capitalism had arrived with a vengeance; the labor struggles that marked the era came to Somerset too. The coal companies exerted an increasing and ruthless power in the county. Especially in non-union areas (the central part of the county was not unionized), they subjected workers to wage cuts, refused to pay for "dead work," and tried to control consumption through company stores. The coal companies' neglect of fundamental health and safety standards was deeply resented. Somerset County mines had twenty-nine fatalities in 1920 alone. Mine police enforced company rule with the threat or reality of violence. Unionized workers responded with major actions in 1903 and again in 1906. These met with determined resistance from the coal companies, and they failed. In 1922, thousands of non-union miners in Somerset County struck in response to an invitation by the national United Mine Workers to join the union's national strike. The Somerset County strike attracted wide attention as a struggle for basic union recognition. Even though local miners were eventually isolated by the national union, they persisted for over a year. They won a vague sort of recognition, but at great cost: union organizers estimated that a third of the labor force quit the county's mine pits, and another third left the county altogether. In general, the embattled coal miners could not sustain their efforts in the face of employer collusion, government hostility, and a divided union leadership. Hardship, poverty, and class differences, already apparent in the nineteenth century, became enduring features of Somerset County rural life.[5]

Despite the rise of coal towns, the county remained essentially rural; the number of farms in the county dropped only slightly, and the land area in farming remained high (Fig. 81). But during these years, Somerset County farm families also experienced the full impact of industrialization, for better and for worse. The percentage of the county's population living on farms declined significantly. Those who remained shifted decisively toward capital-intensive farming. Money expenditures on fertilizer, feed, labor, and equipment rose to unprecedented levels.[6] Capital

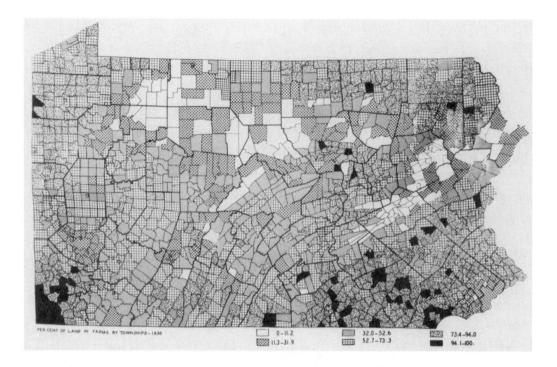

FIG. 81
"Percent of Land in Pennsylvania Devoted to Agriculture by Townships, 1930." Somerset County in 1930
still had a very rural character despite the extent of mining operations; sixteen of its twenty-six townships
had more than half of their land in agriculture. Austin Vardell Edwards, "Agricultural Land Use Changes in
Pennsylvania by Minor Civil Divisions, 1930–1940" (master's thesis, The Pennsylvania State University,
1953), 21. The Pennsylvania State University Libraries.

outlay on buildings and machinery escalated. The cash economy almost completely absorbed most
farm operations, in the sense that farms now produced most items for sale and received cash
income, which in turn was used to finance purchases. In other words, profit-and-loss assumed a
critical place. Thus, not only did crop and livestock patterns shift, but the way farming was organized and conducted also changed profoundly during this period. Agrarian life everywhere felt the
impact of capitalism, mechanization, urbanization, and science.

Somerset County farming still could be characterized as general or mixed, but within this
scheme, the relative importance of dairying, poultry, and (for a few) beef cattle increased, while
other enterprises (such as sheep raising and rye production) essentially disappeared. Subsistence
activity and old social customs still persisted, but market and cash transactions accounted for most
of the farm's income. Farm families benefited from the mining boom, not only because they could
sell mineral rights but because migrants to the area created local markets for farm produce.
Improved transportation also helped some farmers get fluid milk to more distant urban centers.[7]

Transportation in the region—and indeed, in the nation—was completely transformed in this
era with the advent of the automobile. The chronicle of Henry Ford and his inexpensive Model
T is familiar; in 1924, an astounding 94 percent of Somerset County farms had automobiles. This

era also marked the beginning of the tractor revolution in agriculture. Fourteen percent of county farmers used tractors; 27 percent possessed stationary gasoline engines; 13 percent owned trucks. These vehicles mostly bumped over unimproved dirt roads. (Rural Pennsylvanians resisted road bond issues, citing fear of indebtedness and unfair benefits to urban areas.) But even so, geographic mobility took on a new meaning for rural people.[8] More than any other development, the auto transformed rural space. Historian Joseph Interrante points out that in rural America the auto rapidly went from a "farm *convenience* to a farm *necessity*." The auto helped spur the growth of rural villages and towns and the decline of smaller crossroads communities: "These larger villages became the centers of rural space." People did not necessarily travel farther, but they made far more frequent, shorter trips. Women's lives, in particular, were changed; they made more trips to town, and their opportunities for socializing increased.[9]

The shift to farm horsepower mechanization, which had begun in the late nineteenth century, was thoroughgoing by the 1920s.[10] By 1924 the average farm used nearly eight hundred dollars' worth of implements, including patent plows, manure spreaders, grain drills, horse-powered mowers, hay rakes, tedders, and hay forks (horse-powered devices for lifting hay into the barn). Other implements that local farmers used included the corn planter, steam hay baler, spring tooth harrow, and horsepower or steam threshers. An auction announcement for 1907 gives some sense of the range; it included "a McCormick hay tedder, Empire grain drill, 1 disc harrow, 1 cast iron roller, 1 hay rake, fanning mill, feed cutter, ploughs, harrows, corn planter, horse hay forks, hay ladders, 1 two-horse wagon, 1 sled, two sets of double harness." This was on a farm with four milk cows, just the average.[11]

However, farm specialization was not as pervasive as in many other parts of the country. In 1934, a Pennsylvania State College survey of "Types of Farming in Pennsylvania" mapped the state, using census data from 1929. The maps produced are revealing (Fig. 82). The only sign of specialization in Somerset County was a small patch of "crop specialty" area that represented the remnants of maple sugaring. The "predominant types of farms" were "general" farms, dairy farms, "self-sufficing farms," and "abnormal" farms. "General" farms were defined as those in which no single source of income accounted for 40 percent or more of farm income; conversely, on dairy farms, dairy products made up at least 40 percent of farm income. On "self-sufficing farms," at least 50 percent of farm produce was consumed by the family. "Abnormal" farms (the terminology is interesting) were mostly part-time farms, in which the owner worked more than 150 days off the farm. This undoubtedly reflects the opportunity for work in the mining industry.

Yet while Somerset County agriculture certainly qualified as "mixed" farming, the number of elements in the "mix" was on the decline. Between 1880 and 1925, Somerset County farm families stuck to the old standbys of potatoes, hay, apples, poultry, dairy cows, swine, corn, and oats. However, they severely curtailed their production of wheat, rye, peaches, maple sugar, beef cattle, and sheep. Thus, the overall farm enterprise was markedly less diversified than it was at its nineteenth-century peak (see Fig. 28).[12] The reasons for these shifts in production patterns offer insights into the modernizing landscape of farming.

FIG. 33.—THE PREDOMINANT TYPES OF FARMS, 1929

Dairy farms occur in greatest numbers in the counties near Philadelphia, in the northern tier of counties, in the Appalachian Valley, and around Pittsburgh. In the remainder of the State the most common type is the farm where dairying is supplemented by two or three other important enterprises, which places it in the class of general farms.

FIG. 34.—THE SECOND MOST PREDOMINANT TYPES OF FARMS, 1929

FIG. 82

"The Predominant Types of Farms, 1929." A few Somerset County farms were described as "dairy farms," but most were either "general," "self-sufficing," or "abnormal." "General" farms produced a wide variety of products for market, while "self-sufficing" farms relied less on market sales. "Abnormal" farms were essentially part-time farms: their owners worked off the farm at least 150 days a year. From "Types of Farming in Pennsylvania," *Pennsylvania State College Agricultural Experiment Station Bulletin*, no. 305 (April 1934), 46–47. The Pennsylvania State University Libraries.

Oats were now about the only major grain crop of any consequence. The average farm raised 355 bushels in 1924. Wheat production in the area had little chance, since it was competing against the western bonanza fields, and Prohibition reduced the market for rye. The buckwheat crop remained about constant at a 52-bushel-per-farm average. Data that would indicate how these items were used are surprisingly scarce, but it seems likely that both grains were fed on the farm to livestock in this era of horsepower. Much of the rise in Indian corn production would go to feed milch cows. Corn production continued to rise; by 1924, the average farm produced 236 bushels on about 6 acres (up from 167 bushels on 4 acres only a decade before). By the end of the period, a larger percentage of the Indian corn ended up as ensilage. Ensilage represented an innovation with tremendous significance for the county, because converting (green) corn to ensilage eliminated the risk of losing the crop to frost. As a result, Somerset County surged ahead of the rest of the state in adopting the silo. In 1924, 20 percent—at most—of farms statewide had silos, but in Somerset County, the figure was 33 percent. The county was seventh in the state in acreage of corn grown for silage, with 8,800 acres. The pattern of the past was reversed in this case; for the first time, Somerset County was ahead in agricultural innovation rather than lagging behind. Climatic factors played a large part in this particular instance.

Potatoes continued to be a popular crop. By 1924–25, the average farm raised two hundred bushels of potatoes, and the county ranked highly in per-acre yield. Again, as before, local and regional markets figured prominently in this trend. Railcar loads of potatoes regularly ran from local terminals to the cities. The Cooperative Extension system, established by the federal government to disseminate the results of agricultural research, played a role in improving yields; local farmers embraced extension service work on potatoes, even as they resisted other initiatives.[13] The locally developed "Mason" was the favorite variety, but others were popular, too, and extension workers promoted spraying and certified seed stock programs.

Though fewer farms produced beef cattle overall, there was a significant pocket of specialization in this enterprise. Rural sociologist Ralph L. Watts ranked Somerset fourth in the state in this category and characterized the county as a leader in livestock raising. The 1924 manuscript agricultural census shows that in the vicinity of the village of Berlin and in Somerset Township, a large number of farms—perhaps as many as five hundred—raised and fattened steers and other cattle; many of these farms had no dairy cows at all. Though this concentration was significant in the local economy, it must be placed within a general context of a declining beef industry for the eastern states.[14]

Gardening flourished in this period—perhaps even more than before. The county home economics extension agent reported in 1934 that the average farm gardener raised twenty-one varieties of vegetables alone. A small patch near the house held such items as onions, lettuce, radishes, beets, tomatoes, and carrots, while farther off, a "truck" patch accommodated sprawling vines of squash, pumpkins, and other space-consuming crops, such as sweet corn. People also grew small fruits such as gooseberries, raspberries, and blackberries. Rhubarb occupied a separate spot. Canning increased significantly, as techniques became easier and safer and as war and depression stimulated home preservation.[15]

The farm's apple orchard remained a source of sustenance for the farm family; over 90 percent of farms reported having apple trees in 1924. In fact, the county was a leader statewide in the number of bearing-age trees. The fruits, as before, furnished the material for a wide variety of local delicacies such as applesauce, apple butter, schnitz, and cider—and, of course, they were eaten fresh. As such, the farm orchard represents the traditions of self-reliance and ethnic identity as expressed through food. But at the same time, the percentage of farms reporting peaches declined. Peach tree plantings fluctuated more than apple tree plantings, but it is nevertheless likely that commercial orchards were replacing homegrown peaches. In any case, the climate wasn't really favorable for peaches.

The drastic dropoff in maple sugar production demands more extended comment, since this article had occupied such an important place in pioneer and nineteenth-century farm economies. Though the county was still a leader in 1924, overall production was only about a third of its 1880 level.[16] What accounts for the demise of the maple sugar industry? The availability of cheap, mass quantities of industrially refined cane sugar (from the newly acquired U.S. territories in Cuba and the Philippines) played a pivotal role, as did the rise of beet sugar. In these tropical places, "factories in the fields" practiced capitalist, industrialized farming with its most exploitative force. Historian Stevenson Fletcher, examining the decline of maple sugaring, also cites the "scarcity and high cost of labor, pasturing of sugar bushes, [and] high prices paid for maple logs."[17] These factors, in turn, were related to industrialization, as coal mining drew labor away, new markets encouraged greater investment in livestock, and mines and other buyers raised prices for lumber and mine props. By 1940, sugarmaking showed only a vestige of its former stature. Only four hundred farms reported maple sugar that year.[18] The implications should be apparent: while the tradition undeniably persists even down to the present, it now has more of a ritual significance than a real presence in the local economy. With it went folk customs, social structures, and one more remnant of the preindustrial way of life.

Another traditional pursuit, dairying, actually increased its presence in the local economy, but it too was transformed by the commercial revolution. By 1929, the Pennsylvania Department of Agriculture termed Somerset one of the "newer dairy counties."[19] Somerset was still not among the leading dairy counties, but it had gained in relative position. Several major changes occurred in dairying generally during this period, and they affected Somerset County to one degree or another. Buttermaking shifted from home to centralized plants, and fluid milk production rose. Per-cow productivity increased markedly, achieved mostly by intensified feeding and better shelter. These transformations in turn had social consequences.

Until the late nineteenth century, the pace of dairy centralization in Somerset County followed the rest of the state very closely. Creameries (centralized processing points for making butter and sometimes cheese) appeared in Somerset County late in the century, as they did elsewhere in the state. By the 1880s, local newspapers announced spring openings and fall closings for a half-dozen creameries scattered throughout the county. The decade of greatest change was from 1880 to 1890. In 1880, Somerset County processed 85 percent of farm milk into butter on the farm; by 1890, only about 56 percent of the milk was made into butter on the farm.[20]

The centralizing tendency in buttermaking had profound implications for the dairy industry generally and for the way farmwork was organized. At the creamery, a number of scientific and technological innovations transformed buttermaking. Large-scale equipment, tended by men, made mass production possible. The Babcock test for butterfat content—a product of the emerging land-grant agricultural research system—first became available in the 1890s. This test allowed creamery personnel to screen milk, excluding milk with low butterfat content. Whether the offending farmers had deliberately watered their milk or whether their cows just didn't give rich milk, the result was that creameries exerted an unprecedented measure of control over farmers' day-to-day practices. Besides using the Babcock test, creamery owners tried to impose rules about how the milk should be treated in order to avoid contamination; after the initial dissemination of the germ theory of disease in the 1880s, the industry groped toward solutions to the problems of sanitation. Later, the state passed sanitation laws that applied to dairying.[21]

More profound than the scientific or technical achievements of centralized creameries were their social implications. Wherever they were adopted in the United States, centralized creameries transferred buttermaking from women to men. In the process, the rhetoric of factory buttermaking also devalued home buttermaking (and, by extension, the buttermakers) as unscientific, unsystematic, and dirty. A tradition of women's work was under attack. On farms where milk or cream was sent to the creamery, women no longer made butter except during the off-season, when the creamery was closed. In the Nanticoke Valley of New York, women adapted "strategies of mutuality" to accommodate changes in dairy work, sharing the work of milking, caring for livestock, off-season processing, and so on. And in central New York State (where cheese factories replaced home cheesemaking), women responded by increasing poultry work and by expanding their activity in community organizations.[22]

We can get a few glimpses of the impact of creameries in southwest Pennsylvania from the diary of Francis Cable. A few months after his marriage to Maria Lambert, Cable recorded this entry in his diary: "April 16, 1883, I & father walked over the farm &c. He left after dinner. John Feig was here to see what I intended to do with our Butter. I told him I would try the creamery. He wanded [sic] me to go in as a partner and ship our Butter to Johnstown all Summer, once a week. I told him I wouldn't, then I fixed fence."

This intriguing passage raises as many questions as it answers. Did Maria refuse to make butter during the months that the creamery was open? Or did Francis decide independently? Their partnership in dairying and in other agricultural pursuits seems to have embraced "mutuality" fully, as they shared work and space all over the farm. Indeed, the next day, Francis noted: "I & Maria went to Peter Keefer's to buy a cow." Maria appears to have exerted considerable influence over stock buying, so it is possible that she had some input in decision making about the creamery. Yet the nature of Francis's conversation with his neighbor also reveals the limitations of mutuality; in the end, two men negotiated about it, with Maria out of the picture. Certainly for those farms that patronized creameries,[23] the organization of work changed significantly. Women were relieved of the heavy, time-consuming, and vexing work of hand churning—and also of a central role in the household economy.

But Somerset County creamery production hit a plateau after about 1890, when the county began to diverge from the rest of Pennsylvania; by 1920, county farms still processed about half of their milk into butter on the farm, while statewide, only about 25 percent of milk was processed into butter on farms. (The rest was either sent to creameries or sold as fluid milk.) It was not until the late 1930s that Somerset County began to close the gap with the rest of the state.[24]

This pattern relates to specific local circumstances. The period during which home butter-making stayed on this plateau coincided very closely with the period of the most rapid population growth in the county. Local markets appeared in the coal-patch towns, and farm families responded by treating butter as one element in a mix of products that was marketed locally and personally by the members of farm families. In a system like this, it would be illogical to devote special effort to delivering milk to creameries. Instead, as the 1924 census statistics show, most farms possessed mechanical cream separators (Fig. 83), which eased the labor of home butter-making. The presence of home separators suggests that families were perfectly willing to embrace

FIG. 83
Home separator, early twentieth century. This device efficiently separated cream from milk. It aided dairying women in home butter production for local markets in the booming coal-patch towns. The centralization of butter production in Somerset County was retarded; families chose to use home separators and retain control of producing and marketing their own butter. Somerset Historical Center.

FIG. 84
This photograph of Emanuel and Christine Varner has no date, but evidently was taken when they were still fairly young. Their choice of props is very evocative; the old-style worm fence, an increasingly rare sight, now evoked nostalgia and pastoral rusticity. Emanuel Varner's diary reveals that he and "Tenie" worked very closely together on the farm, realizing an ideal of mutuality in their everyday lives. Somerset Historical Center.

a new home technology for what they regarded as an important commercial enterprise. Here again, the nineteenth-century theme of selectivity lingered: families used technology to perpetuate an older system of informal marketing, permitting Somerset County dairying to remain part of a farmstead-based economy and to avoid fuller incorporation into an industrial system.[25]

Though most sources note that home buttermaking was women's work, there is also some interesting evidence that men were beginning to do some churning. Emanuel Varner, a local diarist, often noted that "This day I churned butter," leaving no doubt that he, and not a female member of the family, did the work. Yet his wife, "Tenie," also churned (Fig. 84). Probably the most accurate interpretation of this evidence would be to say that men definitely did some churning, but that the specific division of labor was worked out on each farm. Even so, the fact that men churned at all marked a significant change in the gendering of the work.[26]

The milk that was not processed on the farm was sold in fluid form. Between 1910 and 1924, this amount zoomed from a mere 160 gallons to 811 gallons per farm in the county. This too can be attributed to the boom in the nonfarm population created by the mining industry. Not only did local towns spring up, but Johnstown, easily accessible by rail and road, was also growing quickly.

The increased importance of fluid milk also would tend to shift the overall work responsibility from women to men. Certainly women still milked, but the associated crop raising, feeding, and marketing were men's jobs.

The rising importance of milk production (whether for fluid milk sale, cream sale, or home buttermaking) was accompanied by a host of changes in dairy farming practice. The major accomplishment here was a substantial increase in per-cow productivity. In Somerset County, for example, the average cow in 1880 produced about 2,000 pounds of milk per year; by 1924, that figure stood at about 4,400. Everywhere it occurred, this increase was achieved *without* much impact from the infant science of animal breeding. (Blooded dairy cattle made their appearance here late in the nineteenth century, as elsewhere, but their numbers were tiny and had little effect on overall productivity.) Rather, increased productivity was achieved through better feeding and shelter; this not only increased cows' output because of better nutrition, but also resulted in a lengthened milking season.[27] We will consider shelter in the section on building, so let us look here at the case of feeding. Besides continuing to grow feed on the farm, farmers invested more and more money in purchased feed. In 1910, over two thousand county farms reported having spent $160,000 on feed; in 1924, the total had risen to $544,000. These feed concentrates, probably made of cheap grain originating farther westward, helped boost milking totals.

The tonnage of hay harvested in the county also jumped from about 70,000 to 90,000 tons between 1880 and 1924, and from an average of 16 to 25 tons per farm. Yields rose from 1.15 tons per acre in the 1880s to 1.26 tons per acre in 1924. The quality of the hay also probably improved; most farms now produced hay grown from improved strains of clover and timothy. They probably also harvested it earlier and tended and stored it better, thereby capturing more of its nutritive value.

Along with dairying, poultry raising showed a dramatic increase; that farms all over Pennsylvania shifted to the poultry enterprise during this period reflects the impact of industrialization (through national competition in grain farming and the opening of nearby urban markets). Somerset County was no exception: the poultry industry grew tremendously during this period. By 1924 the average farm was home to over seventy-five increasingly productive hens, which altogether laid nearly five hundred dozen eggs per year. Together with receipts from dairying, poultry and egg production accounted for more than half of the farm income on many a farm.

Interest in breeds and productivity accompanied the boom in numbers. The Somerset County Agricultural Society awarded prizes for twelve breeds of chickens at its 1881 fair, but by 1929, the Westmoreland County Poultry and Pet Stock Association listed ten classes with fifty-one standard breeds. The local paper claimed that attendance for the poultry show in 1907 reached three thousand. Oral histories show that farm families marketed their eggs to stores, either through "huckstering" (doing the selling themselves or selling to hucksters) or through the Farm Bureau's marketing agency. Dressed fowl were sold to various outlets.[28]

Most of the oral history interviewees associated the hen and egg business with women's work, though some remembered the work being shared by men and women. When women sold eggs,

FIG. 85
Mrs. Seith of Sand Patch, Somerset County.
Photograph no. 14 from United States View
Company Photographs (Manuscript Group
419). Pennsylvania State Archives, Harrisburg,
Pennsylvania.

they kept at least part of the proceeds. But here too, as with dairying, a few signs of change appeared as the business grew in scale. For instance, a notice in the Somerset *Standard* for 21 January 1897 described a chicken-raising business. The subject of the article was a man whom the paper approvingly portrayed as a progressive farmer using new techniques. By 1907, Ed. M. Shaffer of Somerset advertised "Barred Plymouth Rocks and S. C. White Leghorns . . . Eggs for Hatching. Stock for Sale. I breed the kind that win and lay." Men were predominant among the prize-winners in the 1907 poultry show. Norman Maust, a resident of the Casselman Valley who was born in 1879, operated a small incubator system early in the twentieth century, hatching eggs for himself and for others, so that they could in turn raise the chicks. By the 1930s, (male) Penn State extension agents—*not* (female) home economists—handled poultry work, and boys joined the extension poultry clubs oftener than girls did. Here we can see the very beginnings of a pattern similar to the powerful shift taking place in dairying: as the business became more capitalized and claimed a greater proportion of the farm's profits, men moved in.[29]

Though men made significant inroads into work formerly done exclusively by women, women continued to perform a wide variety of tasks.[30] A photo of a woman identified only as "Mrs. Seith" of Sand Patch, Somerset County (Fig. 85), captures a quintessential image of the rural woman of her generation; surely she led a life full of challenges, yet also she faces the camera with a resolute and steady gaze. Frances Shoemaker Werner, whose parents married in 1911, remembered that she milked cows at age eight. Later, she harrowed, cultivated potatoes, and used the tedder and hay rake. Frances's mother helped load the hay into the wagon, and the family had a hay fork to get it into the barn. The daughters hauled and husked corn. The grandmother milked, fed the calves, washed the separator and milk buckets, churned, and fed the skimmed milk to hogs and calves. Sarah Garee Armstrong's diary (1879–1915) shows that she canned, washed, scrubbed, churned, gardened, berried, raked, cooked for threshers, made jellies, dug potatoes, sewed, and baked.[31] One household enterprise that became more common in the industrializing era was taking in boarders; at one point, in 1900, John and Jane Lehman had no less than eleven "telephone men" boarding. Families also boarded miners (Fig. 86) and construction workers. This, too, was primarily women's work, since women did the cooking and cleaning for these residents.

In general, on the individual farmstead, there was a more marked gender division of labor. Men and women still collaborated on a wide variety of jobs in a wide variety of spaces; overall, though, the tendency was toward greater definition and separation. This was most evident in

FIG. 86
This combination "Miners' house" and potato cellar on the Jacob Walker farmstead encapsulates two new money-making trends in twentieth-century Somerset farming: taking in boarders and raising potatoes. It also suggests the segregation of people according to class. Somerset Historical Center.

dairying and poultry raising—these, after all, were the most important jobs in terms of both work requirements and income. The disappearance of other activities also tended to remove important categories of gender-mixed labor. The decline in subsistence activities and the near-disappearance of maple sugaring are two obvious examples. Indirectly, the mining work was exclusively an opportunity for men; so their wage work, too, contrasted dramatically with women's farmwork. And even when new work for women *was* income-generating, as in the case of taking in boarders, the work was more markedly domestic in character.

Whether through the market (by acquiring goods and machinery from afar) or by accepting scientific knowledge, Somerset County farm people found themselves oriented more and more toward nonlocal, nontraditional information sources. The land-grant colleges widened their sphere of influence through extension. Somerset County farm people approached the land-grant services selectively, as they did other innovations of the day. Early on, they ignored the county agents' advice on corn (and indeed much of their other advice); the local agent's records for the early years shows that very few farmers actually carried through on the agent's recommendations. But once agents familiarized themselves with the territory, their efforts were more successful. Hundreds of women attended the home economists' clinics on canning methods, for instance, and potato growing information was also popular. Extension workers promoted spraying and certified seed stock programs.[32]

Some neighborhood work traditions showed continued vitality, at least into the early twentieth century. The Varners still butchered with their neighbors (who returned the favor). John Lehman and members of his family went to raisings, quiltings, and butcherings. Lehman also shared a threshing machine with neighbors, as did Francis Cable. Interestingly, even some forms of wage labor resembled older customs; in the Depression years, local farmers could work off their fertilizer debts at A. D. Graham and Company's Somerset County Fertilizer Works.[33]

But a noticeable trend in the period, especially during the later years, is that cooperative work and in-kind exchanges of labor and goods slowly diminished; as farming became more thoroughly mechanized, labor (and consumption) more completely integrated into the cash nexus, and diversification diminished, communal work atrophied too. Not coincidentally, German was less frequently spoken as well; English supplanted German as an everyday language. By the 1920s, activities such as haying, reaping, corn husking, apple butter making, and barn raisings were more often performed by individual farm families and hired help, or done in factories, rather than through community effort. H. H. Reitz announced in the 6 September 1895 *Standard* that his cider and apple butter factory had opened in Salisbury. "Instead of making apple butter the old way, the farmers of this locality nearly all bring their apples to the Salisbury factory, where they can have the manufactured goods made while they wait, in a remarkable short time, and at much less expense than is required the old way."[34]

The Somerset *Standard* for 27 August 1908 carried a fascinating advertisement testifying to the commercial challenges to old-style barn raisings. A photo of "The Largest Barn in Somerset County" (65' × 125') was accompanied by a short description, which emphasized that "no barn-raising, with its great trouble and expense, was necessary. The barn was constructed entirely by Mr. [R. G.] Hostetler's force of workmen, not exceeding six, without any outside assistance." The contractor's client, Miss Omie Cable, purchased carpenters' services rather than relying upon neighbors. This process was still not typical, but it foreshadowed the future when barn building would be commercialized like so many other aspects of rural life. Of course the reference to the "trouble and expense" of old-style raisings was self-serving, but also probably carried some force, because in the cash-driven economy, time *was* money. Rural people could less and less afford to take time out to donate an entire day's worth of labor to their neighbors. Another significant dimension to this change is that these forms of group work had been gender-mixed. Their decline reinforced the increasing gender separation of work in the rural community.

This does not mean that people socialized less often, or that socializing was more segregated by gender as well—far from it. Rather, work and socializing were diverging. Informal visiting, community-wide social gatherings (such as Harvest Home picnics), and organizations such as the Grange (Fig. 87) and the Society of Farm Women replaced the older forms of communal work organization. The churches continued to serve as focal points for religious communities. The automobile helped

FIG. 87
Valley Grange Hall, Berlin area, built about 1920. The Grange came to have an important place in rural life, fulfilling social, educational, and political functions. Grange buildings were an important new part of the rural landscape. Somerset Historical Center.

sustain social networks of kin and neighborhood further and further, and it made a wider variety of activities possible. For example, the Penn State Extension Service sponsored auto outings to State College in which literally hundreds of cars joined a caravan to tour the countryside and the agricultural college. Extension also sponsored local gatherings for farm women; thus, new social forms arose in keeping with the new era.[35]

The rise of the Grange and its associated buildings symbolizes important shifts in rural life. To be sure, churches were still vital institutions, but in this era the Grange more fully signified the principal social forces at work. The organization tended to attract the more prosperous elements of rural society, and its emphasis was more secular, stressing educational and cultural programs and citizenship. Women were a strong force in Granges everywhere. On a local level, the Grange signified a subtle shift in orientation away from neighborhoods and toward village centers. Along with this shift came a diminution in the power of kinship ties and an increase in the importance of class ties. Indeed, the Grange buildings symbolized ties to the national culture, too, because they shared the basic attributes of thousands of Grange halls all over the country.[36]

Not only was work separating from social life, but leisure was taking on an independent life of its own. Commercial entertainments replaced preindustrial pastimes. Residents could go to the movies, see plays, or dance. Even before autos were common, train excursions to resorts such as Niagara Falls offered new opportunities for travel and social experience.

A less attractive side to rural life of this period was the provincialism expressed in anti-immigrant, Prohibitionist, and pro–child labor sentiment. Local Granges frequently passed resolutions favoring immigration restriction. Incidents of nativist violence flared up from time to time, and the Ku Klux Klan was also quite active in the region, tapping into deep currents of intolerance, insularity, and racism. The temperance movement, with its nativist and middle-class base, was strong in the county. The Society of Farm Women passed a resolution condemning child-labor laws as inimical to the values of work and character building. The conservatism of the local society is evident here; people responded to the presence of Eastern European people with pressure for immigration restriction, and ignored the exploitation (especially in coal mining) that led to child-labor laws.[37]

Tensions between newcomers and old-timers only increased during times of stress. While some local people worked in the coal industry and sympathized with the union movement, unionism was generally unpopular in this conservative place. Reportedly, strikebreakers in 1922 were recruited from among young farm men—one account characterized scabs as "native Americans from the farms and hill country"[38]—who sought work during the slow winter months. They could always return to their farms, unlike the coal-patch residents. Mine owners also hired many extra members for their police forces during the strike year, and doubtless the local farm population was one promising field for recruitment.

Less overt forms of tension must have manifested themselves in everyday relationships between mining and farming communities. For example, the mining communities furnished markets for farm produce. When "hucksters" sold produce directly to miners' households, they offered an alternative to the company store; however, farmers also supplied the detested company stores with produce. Either way, it must have often seemed that farming households benefited at the expense of miners and their families.

★   ★   ★

Rural life in Somerset County moved decisively away from the past in this period. Diversification on the farm diminished. Farm residents relied more on the outside world for equipment, fertilizer, feed, and labor. Market production ruled. Class conflicts erupted openly, and the gender division of labor began to change. Farming had converted almost entirely over to horsepower; with less need for human energy, cooperative work customs diminished. Many traditions that remained were altered to fit new circumstances. For example, visiting—now carried out with the help of the automobile—flourished. Overall, though, local people were more integrated than ever before into the national economy and culture.

EXPRESSIONS IN BUILDING AND SPACE: AN ARCHITECTURE OF INDUSTRIALIZATION

Forces of modernization wrenched the rural landscape in this industrial era. Mining and lumbering wrought fundamental transformations, reshaping the landscape through deforestation, mine excavations, and the sudden, mushroom-like appearance of coal-patch towns. Farmers began to find profit in selling mineral rights to the resources that lay below the tilled soil; sometimes coal-patch

FIG. 88
Map of Somerset County, 1902, showing rail lines. By the turn of the twentieth century, rail lines had completely penetrated the county; even tiny villages enjoyed direct or nearby rail access. *Map of Somerset County Pennsylvania 1902,* compiled and published by William G. Schrock and Charles Staniford. Historical Collections and Labor Archives, The Pennsylvania State University Libraries.

FIG. 89
Pennsylvania Department of Forestry photograph, dated 15 January 1920, showing "farmland and forest in vicinity of Shaulis Farm and properties of United Lumber Company." Even making allowances for the winter date of the photograph, the devastation of clear-cutting is apparent. Pennsylvania State Archives, Record Group 6, Department of Forests and Waters, Farmland and Forest Section (negative no. 1246).

towns literally intertwined with former farmsteads. Rail lines and highway networks (Fig. 88) also contributed to the transformation of rural space, at once bringing rural people closer together and transforming the ways in which they interacted.

The forests, ever a prominent part of local experience, were profoundly affected by the arrival of industrialization. In the late nineteenth and early twentieth centuries, industrially organized lumbering came to Somerset County. Spurred by the availability of rail transport and the regional demand for mine props, railroad ties, and tanbark, large-scale corporations set up in the county and began systematically to fell trees and saw lumber. In a matter of decades, the supply of marketable timber was much reduced. It is very difficult to tell, however, just how much—or even whether—these activities reduced the county's total forest cover, because even as lumbering was eliminating some forest areas, new growth was taking place in others as the proportion of the county's land area in farms declined. Total forest cover remained more or less steady at about half the county's land area. Indeed, the 1897 Annual Report of the Department of Forests and Waters declared that "From the forester's standpoint," "Somerset must be set down as 'good.'" The report added that although some of the "better timber" had been cut, the interior still had strips and "compact parcels of fine woodland."

Nevertheless, the landscape did show a marked change; the pace and character of deforestation had accelerated. Rather than nibbling away slowly and imperceptibly, as farm clearing did, industrial-scale lumbering clear-cut great swaths from along the ridge slopes, resulting in a new and visually arresting sight. Negro Mountain, for example, was reported in 1895 as "completely robbed" in some areas. A Pennsylvania Department of Forestry photo, dated 1920, showed "farmland and forest . . . in vicinity of Shaulis Farm" (Fig. 89), showing properties belonging to the

United Lumber Company. This winter scene showed a thin line of trees serving as a field boundary line, with a clear-cut area beyond.

Equally important, the species composition and ages of the county's forest shifted. "Originally," contended the state's Forestry Division in 1895, the county "contained much good white pine. This is practically gone now." Hemlock now could be found only in scattered, small stands and as isolated individual trees. Rock oak was being harvested for tanbark, and white oak was in demand for ties. In other areas, a second growth of twenty- to thirty-year-old trees had taken root, together with an undergrowth of brush and shrubs that did not create the layers of humus and leaves typical of the older stands of tall trees.[39]

The mining industry brought even more drastic changes to the county's landscape (Fig. 90). At the turn of the century, when mining activity really began to heat up, Somerset newspapers captured the excitement that rural people felt about their new prospects. Farm life "will be more congenial than heretofore," declared the Somerset *Democrat*; $500,000 had recently been paid to local farmers for the rights to coal beneath their land. Later that season, the paper reported that A. A. Stutzman was in town settling up with farmers; payments ranged from $2,000 to $8,000, and there reportedly were eighty to ninety thousand acres under option. It is hard to know precisely how much of the county's agricultural acreage was converted to mining (either outright or indirectly, through separation of mineral rights from landownership). Local histories suggest that over one hundred thousand acres were affected—almost a sixth of the entire land area in the county.[40] Not all of this acreage was actually mined, but farmers' relationship to it was forever altered. For many farming families, the arrival of coal interests brought a novel source of income, in sums

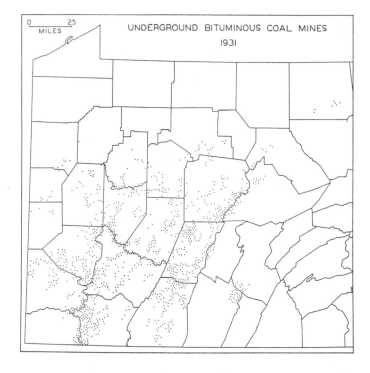

FIG. 90
"Underground Bituminous Coal Mines, 1931." Somerset County was laced with coal mines by the 1930s. The accompaniments of coal mining—tipples, slag heaps, company towns—also appeared. From George Deasy and Phyllis Griess, "Atlas of Pennsylvania Coal and Coal Mining, Part I: Bituminous Coal," *Bulletin of the Pennsylvania State University Mineral Industries Experiment Station*, no. 73 (1959), 34. The Pennsylvania State University Libraries.

which to them must have been fabulous. (After all, many farms were not even worth $8,000 with all their land and buildings.) This new "crop" involved no labor on their part; it simply brought in money. It could, potentially, also reduce farm families' control over their land. It is doubtful, though, that many could foresee consequences that included water pollution, subsidence, and "boney piles." They focused, understandably, on their miraculous windfall. For them it was a landscape of serendipity.

This incursion of coal operations onto former farmland reshaped the rural landscape in dramatic ways. Photographic images from the period sum up these changes graphically. A postcard from around 1910 (Fig. 91) captured in its brand-new condition the coal-patch town of Jerome, established 1904. Perhaps nowhere is the juxtaposition of farm and coal patch more dramatically illustrated. In coal-patch towns like Jerome, the company built housing for workers or contracted with real estate companies to erect houses.[41] Uniform, rigidly straight lines of company housing march along the rolling topography of a former farm site, seemingly oblivious to the contours of the land. These particular houses appear to be standardized two-story duplexes (built into the hillside in many instances, interestingly enough). At the right of the picture, institutional buildings proclaim the presence and power of the United Coal Corporation. Right in the middle of it all—

UNITED COAL CORPORATION
PART OF TOWN, JEROME MINES

FIG. 91
Postcard of Jerome, Somerset County, about 1910. Amid the homogeneous company-town housing, a nineteenth-century Pennsylvania barn incongruously sits. Pennsylvania State Archives, Manuscript Group 213, Postcard Collection, Somerset County, Box 31.

Merchants Coal Co.   Tipple, Finest in United States.   Built of Steel   BOSWELL

FIG. 92
Boswell coal tipple, postcard view, about 1910.
Structures like this brought a new and massive
industrial element to the rural landscape.
Pennsylvania State Archives, Manuscript
Group 213, Postcard Collection, Somerset
County, Box 31.

and noticeable because its orientation does not conform to that of the town streets—is a classic
Pennsylvania barn, almost lost and surely overwhelmed in the new crop of company houses.
Beyond, in the distance, two thin, ragged lines of trees straggle skyward from the open hillside,
testifying to the newly open character of the industrial-era rural landscape.

For a time, nearby Boswell claimed the world's largest coal tipple (Fig. 92). The enormous
dimensions of this structure guaranteed that it made an emphatic statement on the landscape all
by itself. Huge stone pylons in a ravine supported a towering steel superstructure. This tipple and
other, smaller ones proliferated rapidly, beginning around 1900. They served immediate notice
that new forces would shape the local landscape and economy.

The coal-patch towns inscribed in the landscape the brute force of industrial-era economic
power. The unvarying, hastily built company housing proclaimed the company's control over its
workers. Since the company owned the buildings, tenants were not permitted to make alterations
that would lend some variety to the monotonous streetscapes (or even merely tailor a house more
closely to meet a specific family's needs). The visual monotony was more than a matter of cost-
efficiency; it announced the company's domination. Typically crowded, poorly insulated, often
lacking plumbing and electricity, these houses were occupied only at the company's pleasure. The
threat of eviction was an ever-present deterrent to union activism. The miners' tenuous hold on
their built environment contrasted sharply with even the moderately prosperous farm people's relatively secure tenure on the land; even if they lost control of what went on underneath their feet,
they still could build and farm on the surface as they pleased.

Despite their general lack of power over labor conditions and housing, Eastern European
immigrants succeeded in keeping some important facets of their lives beyond the reach of the coal
companies. Wherever they could, they avoided company-owned lands as sites for their social halls
and churches. The buildings they erected contributed to reshaping the built landscape. Immigrants' churches for Catholic or Orthodox congregations often stood in subtle contrast to the

FIG. 93
Church of St. Michael the Archangel, north of Salisbury, west facade. Courtesy of Heinz Architectural Center, Carnegie Mellon University, Pittsburgh, Pennsylvania.

plainer mode of the long-established dominant Protestant congregations. The Catholic church of St. Michael the Archangel, for example (Fig. 93), prominently displayed a cross both on the steeple and in the main church entrance. Other churches had onion domes, echoing Eastern European motifs. Such architectural elements must have seemed exotic in this context; to some locals, at least, they represented unwelcome reminders of a new and—to the insular local people—alien presence in the community.

In places like Boswell and Jerome, mining overran and even obliterated agrarian spaces. But what evolved more typically over the next few decades was a landscape in which the boundaries between farms and industrial landscapes were continually defined and redefined, creating a vital ambiguity. Sometimes there was overlap at the boundaries between farms and mines. For example, the Dombrowski farm in Jenner Township had the coal mined out from under it during the 1920s, but this only temporarily disrupted farming activity. In the end, a subtly changed landscape resulted. A careful eye can detect smooth, linear slopes of former mining areas where fields of hay now grow. On the Blough farm, a coal mining company financed the erection of a steam-powered water pump with a small outhouse to protect it. The pump house, which looks like any agricultural outbuilding, served to link farm and mine vertically, through the layers of coal and rock that bound them together.

Powers Hapgood, a labor organizer with the United Mine Workers of America, spent some time in the county in 1921. His *In Non-Union Mines: Diary of a Coal Digger* aptly captured the contrast between farm and mine (and, implicitly, the resentments of miners toward the farmers they perceived as more privileged):

> I walked slowly along the road toward the boarding house, gazing off over the valley and the sparkling stream near the high hill on the other side. It is somewhere under that green hill with the farmer driving his team and plow over it in the sunlight that the miners in the third right dip spend their days, in the blackness and in the dust. . . . All during the hours when the sun is shining brightest on the meadows and fields of that green hill, the miners, hundreds of feet below, are working with their backs bent at right angles.[42]

The new regime had created a landscape in which most remaining farms kept their integrity, but the countryside was no longer an expanse of forest punctuated by cleared agrarian landscapes. Instead, it was a startling patchwork, juxtaposing farms, remnant patches of woodland, and mining complexes. Because of the county's hilly topography, travelers on the main roads might see bucolic rural scenery one minute and turn a corner to encounter a ragged patch town, tipple, and

FIG. 94
Boswell from Jennerstown. This early-twentieth-century postcard view captures the patchwork admixture of mine and farm in the new rural landscape. Pennsylvania State Archives, Postcard Collection, Manuscript Group 213, Somerset County, Box 31.

headhouse. A postcard view of "Boswell from Jennerstown" (Fig. 94) captures this disjuncture well. In the foreground is a field with patches of woodlot; from this hilltop vantage point, a smoke plume of Boswell is visible, as are the outlines of the village.

Within this context, the overall disposition of farmland was relatively stable. Fencing laws in the late nineteenth century had finally codified the livestock owner's responsibility for fencing animals in. By the Depression era, permanent pastures were well fenced. County farms showed the same basic organization as in the earlier period—woodlands and pasturelands at the periphery, cropland next in toward the farmstead, and gardens or truck patches closest to the functional center of the farm. At harvesttime, one would see shocks of wheat standing in the fields—just as they had in the previous century—on farms lacking adequate barn space. Nor is there much evidence that the size or shape of the fields had changed drastically from the nineteenth century.

When we look at the patterns of building on the farmstead in this period, however, the scene was significantly altered: this was an era of grand barns and modest houses. Few new farmhouses were erected in rural Somerset County for the period 1880–1940. In these rare cases of new construction, balloon-frame techniques dominated. Right away we see the ties between building and industrialization, since balloon frames were made of standardized pieces fabricated in factories

FIG. 95
Lehman/Walker house, built 1909, porch added later. A hipped roof, large dormer, and two-bay facade signify the arrival of modern house forms. Somerset Historical Center.

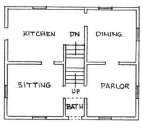

FIRST FLOOR   SECOND FLOOR

FIG. 96
Harvey and Margaret Friedline farmhouse, built about 1901, plan. Informal planning was making a comeback in the county; here, the kitchen is connected to two other rooms and also has exterior access. Somerset Historical Center.

with the capacity to mill wood in fantastic amounts and at high speeds. Auxiliary enterprises, such as sash-and-blind works, created the trim. The contrast to heavy, labor-intensive timber framing could hardly be greater. Balloon framing demanded less skill; standardized members were simply nailed together. Far less on-site work (fashioning mortise-and-tenon joints, for example) was required. It is even possible that the wood itself came from outside the state.

Not only were construction techniques standardized, but so (to a great extent) was exterior appearance. New or remodeled farmhouses of the period lacked the double-decker porches and the banked construction of the nineteenth century. Instead, they were plain and sparsely ornamented. Some borrowed from nationally popular styles. The Lehman/Walker house, for example (Fig. 95), had a hipped roof, with dormer and side gable. Later, a porch was enclosed—signifying a notable departure from the open, public porches of the nineteenth century.

In their internal arrangement, most of these houses didn't show radically new floor plans; the builders stuck to tried-and-true arrangements that were modifications of such old standbys as the "I" house or the Georgian plan. But the assignment of room functions solidified trends begun earlier. Most important was that most of these houses included an integral ground floor kitchen in the original plan. This kitchen usually occupied a back room, and cases opened onto a dining room. On the Harvey and Margaret Friedline farm in Jefferson Township, built 1901, for instance (Fig. 96), the kitchen occupies the back room in this modified Georgian plan; it opens onto both a dining and a sitting room and to the outside. The Knepper family farmhouse, c. 1911, Brothersvalley Township, had a back kitchen opening onto a small dining area. Though these houses were banked, only vestigial traces of the old workspaces remained in the basement.

These ground-floor kitchens functioned as multipurpose rooms, not exclusively as workspaces. Family meals, family socializing, and informal visits with others took place there. The cookstove and kitchen table provided the room's focal points. Chairs, sinks, cupboards, and rugs filled up the remainder of the space. Of course, women cooked, baked, and performed innumerable processing tasks there—shelling beans, peeling apples, and so on. All the while they cared for children as well.

The Germanic tradition of "the room" continued into this era; John Lehman carefully noted when he lit the stove in "the room" and Francis Cable expressed delight when he bought a "No.

3, for $11.00, then home & set up the stove, done splendid. It seems like home." William Woys Weaver has emphasized the depth of Pennsylvania Germans' psychological and cultural attachment to "the room," and we find echoes of it here.[43]

Although these spaces were informal, others were strictly reserved. Even when families had dining rooms, they didn't normally eat daily meals there; these rooms were for special meals or for company. The same was true for rooms called "living rooms" or "parlors." As in the nineteenth century, these spaces held ritual and ceremonial significance and were off-limits for everyday activity, especially where children were concerned. Indeed, the Somerset County home economics extension agent in 1931 explicitly tried to reform these persistent customs by holding a session on "Making the Living Room More Livable."[44]

Oral histories reveal another interesting aspect of these twentieth-century houses: as with the ground floor, family members fully utilized only part of the upper floor bedroom space. Few girls joined the home economics extension's "own room clubs" in the 1930s, probably because the whole idea was irrelevant to most. Bedrooms functioned as spare rooms, or were used by hired men, long-term visitors, relatives, schoolteachers, boarders, and so on. This pattern indicates that the farmhouse never lost its character as a place open to the community. At no point in our entire survey period did it function exclusively as "domestic" space for a nuclear family. This strong continuity (modified, to be sure, by hallways and formal spaces) characterized rural life in Somerset County.

Why did so many families essentially live in only half the available space? On the face of it, this seems irrational and wasteful, but people had compelling reasons to live this way. Some conducted funerals in the parlor; in this case it would be important to maintain a sacred space, even if these occasions were few. Special dining rooms suggest a deeply felt desire to separate the social, refined process of eating—and the dinner guests themselves—from the work of preparing the meal. From a twenty-first-century perspective, there is an element of fastidiousness here, but also one of politeness and deference to guests' sensibilities. The contrast to the earlier, inconsistent pursuit of refinement in the nineteenth century is notable.

FIG. 97
Lehman/Walker farmhouse, 1909, plan. The hired man was segregated from the family, even though this plan is otherwise quite informal. Somerset Historical Center.

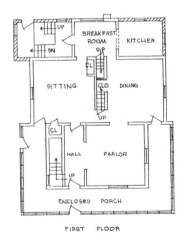

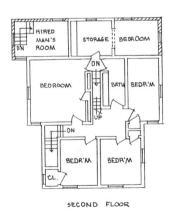

Like the formal visiting and eating spaces, separate areas for hired hands continued into the twentieth century and perhaps became more pronounced in their degree of segregation. Oral histories indicate that about half of the families with live-in hired men provided sleeping quarters in the same space with the family's. The rest overtly separated their hired hands from the family. Some workers reached their quarters through a separate stairway, as on the Lehman/Walker farm (Figs. 95 and 97). The Flick house was remodeled in about 1900 to provide a hired man's room in the attic. Other farm workers lived in small houses that were completely distinct from the main house. It seems that in this very mixed pattern, we have the persistence of old customs, in which hired laborers were treated as part of the family, and newer ones in which the hierarchy of class is very apparent and spatially enforced.

Remodeling was more common than new house building in this period. Frequently, it was financed by women's poultry and egg money. Progressive Era critics argued that the contrast between grand barns and modest houses paralleled the relative power of men and women on the farm. This was surely the visual message imparted. Despite farm women's continuing commitment to the farm enterprise, the devaluation of women's work and the more emphatic gender division of labor had literally visible consequences in the farmstead's buildings. Yet the visual demotion of the house did not necessarily imply that women's status had *worsened* from the nineteenth century into the twentieth; men's work had always had more prestige and status than women's. The difference was in the newly emerging gender division of labor. Men were now less likely to be found at work in and around the house. Instead, their work took place on farm grounds and in outbuildings—and even off the farm altogether, for those employed in mining. Thus, they were less inclined to invest in the house itself.

The main thrust of remodeling usually involved rearranging kitchen space. For example, on the Schrock family farm, the owners added a kitchen and dining room wing in 1910, significantly modifying this classic nineteenth-century Georgian basement house. An 1890 extension on the Walker farm similarly modified a house built around 1830. On the Benning farm, in Lower Turkeyfoot Township, a kitchen wing was added around 1920. This pattern is consistent with the appearance of integral kitchens in the newly built houses of the period, and holds the same social significance.

Along with kitchen wings came a resurgence of interest in detached kitchens. In 1894, Emanuel Varner made entries in his diary that chronicled the construction of a new building he variously called a "spring house" or "summer house." After it was clad with reused siding and painted, he and his wife "moved in Summer house" on 12 June. Varner's experience was repeated all over the county, as a rebuilding process resulted in the appearance of summer kitchens. It is not clear just when (or where, or more important, why) the term "summer kitchen" was coined, but in Somerset County, advertisements first began to use it late in the nineteenth century. Among the "improvements" noticed in the 1889 Somerset *Standard* were separate buildings for baking, washing, and storing fuel.[45]

Varner's summer kitchen was only one of many that appeared around the same time. In addition, it is likely that older detached kitchens began to function as "summer kitchens." First, let us

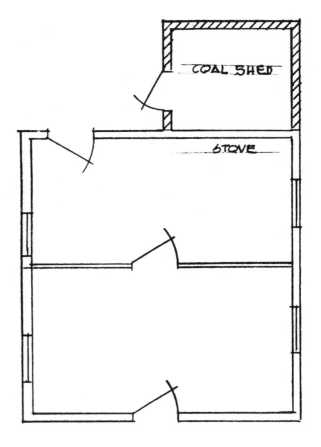

FIG. 98
Walker farm, plan of summer kitchen, c. 1890. The summer kitchen had its heyday in the late nineteenth and early twentieth centuries. A hundred years earlier, detatched kitchens had mainly supported artisan activity, but these later summer kitchens represented the full flowering of farm-based production. Somerset Historical Center.

SUMMER KITCHEN

examine some of these buildings and their uses, and then we can consider what this flurry of building means. Most of these new summer kitchens were of balloon-frame construction, and most were located near the house to the back or side (see Fig. 99). Built for cookstoves, they lacked the huge fireplaces of their early-nineteenth-century predecessors. For example, the Walkers erected a balloon-frame summer kitchen (Fig. 98) around the same time that they added a kitchen wing onto their house—in the last decade of the nineteenth century. This sixteen-foot-square building never had a fireplace but instead had a coal-fueled cookstove. At this point, the Walker farm was operated on a substantial scale with multigenerational cooperation, producing a mix of crops and livestock products typical for the time.

Another late-nineteenth-century balloon-frame summer kitchen, 24' × 16', had two stories each with two rooms. In Shade Township, on the Statler Tavern property, a 15' × 30' summer kitchen was divided into two rooms, in which stood cookstoves, laundry tubs, tables, iron kettles, and milk cans. Later summer kitchens do not seem to have differed in their essentials from the turn-of-the-century examples. A 1922 building on the Schrock family farm, for instance (Fig. 100),

FIG. 99
Summer kitchen, unidentified location, Somerset County, 1994. Farm men and women spent many hours cooking, butchering, and doing other heavy work in these spaces. Photograph by the author.

combined springhouse with summer kitchen functions. Inside, the building was divided into two levels by a single step; residents used the upper level (supplied with springwater) for laundering, butchering, apple butter and soap making, and for finishing off maple sugar. On the lower level, a furnace supplied heat for maple sugar boiling.

Information on these buildings' uses is fairly plentiful, although there are some problems in accurately pinning down dates. Oral histories suggest that initially, these buildings were used for the same "heavy" food preservation and processing work that had been conducted in earlier basement or detached kitchens. Canning, pickling (including sauerkraut making), baking, apple butter making, washing, butchering (and probably associated tasks such as rendering lard, sausage stuffing, scrapple making, and the like), maple sugar finishing, and sometimes dairying took place there. Amos Long's interviewees in the Lancaster County area also mentioned using the cream separator there as well as plucking chickens and cutting up meat. Long's subjects also recalled that during the warm months, the family ate either right in the summer kitchen or on the lawn nearby,

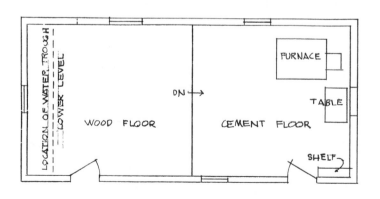

SPRING HOUSE/SUMMER KITCHEN

FIG. 100
Schrock family farm, plan of combination summer kitchen and springhouse, c. 1922. This arrangement centralized laundering, apple buttering, soapmaking, and maple sugaring. Somerset Historical Center.

and he went so far as to state that "only occasionally was the big house used during the summer months." Lofts often served to house family members or hired help. Many summer kitchens also offered storage space for roots, crocks of pickles, and so on.[46]

Conventional folklore holds that the summer kitchen served to remove confusion, mess, disorder, heat, etc., from the main kitchen. To this apparently accurate characterization we may add some context. It is no coincidence that a spate of summer kitchen building occurred precisely as people were rearranging their "big houses" to either abandon or curtail the use of basement space. The correlation is not perfect, but on the farmsteads where we can document the form of the "big house" for the same period, we find that in several cases people erected summer kitchens on farmsteads where the houses were not banked but instead had integral ground-floor kitchens (frequently newly added or newly built). In other words, summer kitchens replaced basement kitchens. Summer kitchens therefore continued and amplified the differentiation between "heavy," "messy" work and day-to-day cooking. They separated "dirty" tasks more emphatically from the house, thereby symbolically helping to associate the house more strongly with ceremonial and social uses—and perhaps with women's work. At the same time they also helped perpetuate the informal, all-comers-welcome ways of earlier years with their eating facilities. So the strong division between formal and informal, refined and dirty, carried through every aspect of domestic space. The summer kitchen continued the nineteenth-century custom of selectivity, adapting an old form to new social values.

Within this newly configured household space, the role of consumption expanded from the nineteenth century, as people increasingly bought consumer goods not only for themselves but also for their homes. The mail-order revolution helped bring an ever-widening variety of goods to the nearest railhead. But the modern era came to Somerset County farmhouses most dramatically with the new household conveniences available by the 1920s. According to the 1924 census, 60 percent of the county's farms had telephones; 40 percent had some type of heating system; a third had running water; a quarter had electricity; 17 percent had a bathroom; and 10 percent had radios. Here is another reason why so little new house building took place: families concentrated on investing in internal improvements.

These families' priorities present interpretive challenges. When considering their choices from the ever-expanding range of technological wonders, we must take into account the entire range, since as always, budgets were not infinite. Clearly autos claimed the highest priority. As elsewhere in rural America, Somerset County families chose mobility over the domestic comfort and convenience offered by plumbing and electricity. Everybody could justify telephones, from a business and social point of view. Heating in the chilly Somerset County hills was a compelling priority, no doubt. Families eased women's work by purchasing cream separators.

During this period, government agencies and organizations such as the Country Life Commission decried what they saw as an oppressive system in which men unfairly received the benefits of modern conveniences, while women were left out. More recent scholarship has pointed to the complexity of the issues confronted by farm families, and also to the error of the government's assumption that farm women were like city women, keenly focused on consumption and domesticity rather than on farm production. In fact, in the rural Midwest, farm women consciously chose paths that preserved their productive work and their mobility, even if it meant that they had to forego some domestic conveniences. When queried about her preference for a car over indoor plumbing, one woman exclaimed that "you can't go to town in a bathtub!" This attitude was particularly prevalent in mixed-farming areas, where women's production accounted for a significant portion of farm income.

The Somerset County record suggests a more ambiguous pattern. On the one hand, rural women showed that they conceptualized their activity as an integral part of the farm economy, resisting the home economist's entreaty that they keep separate household accounts. They protested that "we don't know what our income will be . . . something unexpected is always turning up." On the other hand, they openly resented the devaluation of their work and the denial of resources that followed from it. The Somerset County extension agent, imbued with ideas of efficiency, tried to encourage women to remodel their kitchen furnishings to the correct height for working, but she received a skeptical response; as one woman put it, "That's all very nice but now to get my husband to fix things for me." The woman did get her equipment, but had to install it herself. A 1940 series of pictures showed a kitchen remodeling for which "this woman has been saving for thirteen years to get the kitchen improved." The total cost was $160. Especially in the deep Depression of the 1920s and 1930s, many farm women felt that they had no choice but to put the farm's economic survival over their own convenience—a different motive from actively supporting productive activity out of a principled attachment to production over consumption. They substituted labor and time for purchased items wherever they could. In 1935, for example, ninety girls joined the home economics extension's "School Outfit Club," which taught sewing skills.[47]

Thus the twentieth-century house's arrangement (balloon framing, formal spaces, class segregation, and separate summer kitchens) and its contents (telephones, for instance) betokened an architecture of industrialization that expressed the values of standardization, class differentiation, consumerism, and orientation toward the national rather than the local. This was even true of external appearances, as twentieth-century houses shed some of their distinctively local qualities—especially the double-decker porch. But like their grandparents, rural people of the early twentieth century showed a great deal of ambivalence in their actual use of these spaces. They socialized in informal spaces, even if it meant leaving large portions of the house essentially uninhabited. Thus, despite the transformations of these years, people successfully carried many old social values into the modern era.

As we move to the farmstead's outbuildings, the basic nineteenth-century complex remained mostly intact. But newer types joined the others, so that the farmstead became more elaborate. Families continued to need and use many structures. Butcher houses continued to be built. Springhouses continued to be useful (even after the hand-powered cream separator appeared), since they still offered space for cold storage, meat processing, and the like. Smokehouses were still built—

sometimes by immigrants using Eastern European methods. Pigpens housed the hogs before butchering. Most of the surviving sugar camps date from the early twentieth century onward, but since sugar had diminished so in quantity and importance, far fewer farms would have had them. On farmsteads without other facilities, kettle places provided temporary structures for such tasks as apple butter making. And of course, the inevitable privy persisted.

Newer additions to the complex reflected shifts in the agricultural economy. Among these were potato caves (Fig. 101) to accommodate the increasing production of this staple. Corncribs did the same for corn; the cribs were much more common in this period than in any of the previous eras. Garages, of course, symbolized the automobile age. Machine sheds accommodated the proliferation of horse-drawn machinery and, for those who acquired them, tractors.

Chicken houses were not new, but they grew more numerous (and perhaps a bit larger and more elaborate) during this period. "Peepy houses" were a new building type in the poultry industry, intended to provide warm, efficiently organized space for raising chicks to sell to people who would then raise them on to maturity (see Fig. 103). One, manufactured in Berlin, dates to about 1930 (Fig. 102). This one especially epitomizes industrialized farming, because it was manufactured and purchased, rather than being built from materials available on the farm.

FIG. 101
Potato cave, Lehman/Walker farm. Somerset County farmers increased their potato production significantly in the twentieth century. Somerset Historical Center.

FIG. 102

Peepy house, Brothersvalley Township, about 1930. This hexagonal building had a stove at the center to keep the house warm for the "peepies," or baby chicks. People raised them to sell. This peepy house was prefabricated in Berlin, yet another sign that industry and farming were inextricably linked. Somerset Historical Center.

FIG. 103

Peepy house, Jenner Township, 1998. A few peepy houses survive down to the present. Photograph by the author.

The location of most of these outbuildings on the farmstead followed nineteenth-century precedent in most cases. For example, the butcher house, wash house, and springhouse would be sited nearer to the house, with pigpens, corncribs, and so on closer to the barn, and newer buildings (such as the garage) in an appropriate spot near the road. The location of henhouses and peepy houses wasn't as predictable. In some cases the henhouse could be considered within the house's orbit, but in others it was closer to the barn.

Many more barns than houses were erected or significantly remodeled in this period. Most noticeable were the huge, gorgeously decorated barns that appeared on the landscape. They are justly famous—providing material for many a postcard and calendar. But why did they appear at this particular point in time? Certainly, changes in agriculture help account for them; more capital-intensive farming demanded larger, more elaborate, more expensive buildings than ever before. But we shouldn't overexaggerate the role of farm economics, because Somerset County farming still wasn't highly capital-intensive, relative to other areas of the state. Rather, to explain the efflorescence of huge barns in this period, we should remember that the flush of money from coal rights had a significant impact on the farm landscape. Ironically, the same coal money that brought "boney piles" and patch towns helped finance the erection of the beautiful cathedral and star barns that still adorn the countryside of Somerset County. This money came either in the form of payment for coal rights or as money generated from sales to coal-town markets.

These structures were based on the familiar local Pennsylvania barn form. In this sense they represent yet another use of local idioms to adapt to changing values and conditions. These barns are memorable for their size and their exuberant decorative spirit. On the Blough farm, for example (Figs. 104 and 105), a prominent circular star decorated the gable end, and louvers sported matching decorative trim.[48] A Swiss barn near Meyersdale (Fig. 106) had a large center gable, creating both space and visual variety in the facade; an idiosyncratic cupola finished the building in style. Another barn (Fig. 107) had decorative louvers and not one but three cupolas. Still others (Figs. 108–10) achieved decorative effect through latticework or simply by cutting designs right into the barn walls.

These new barns announced a new relationship between farm and home enterprises. Increasingly, barn and house came to be "divorced"—visually, spatially, and socially. The visual congruity between nineteenth-century house and barn was replaced on twentieth-century farmsteads by greater contrast. The barn overwhelmed the house in scale, and new or remodeled houses in the twentieth century shed the decorative trim and the most prominent and distinctive feature of the nineteenth-century farmhouse, the double-decker porch. When new house and barn building occurred contemporaneously, the result was often a stripped-down, modest vernacular house that did not call attention to itself, sited near a barn that proudly proclaimed its dominance.

The twentieth-century barns represented major modifications to the nineteenth-century Pennsylvania barn form. Overall, the barns were larger, and they had enclosed forebays. New bent forms accommodated horse-powered hay forks and hay tracks. Rainbow roofs and lighter construction afforded more room for storage. In some barns, gable-end doors and lengthwise aisles

FIG. 104
Blough farm barn, built 1900–1920. Money from a sale of land to a mining company helped finance the building of this barn. Somerset Historical Center.

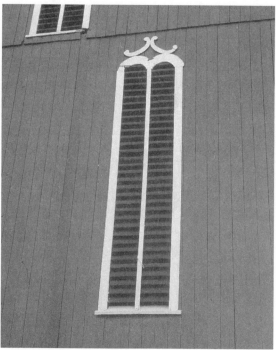

FIG. 105
Blough farm barn, 1998, details. The huge scale of Somerset County "star barns" and their elaborate decoration signaled a new relationship between the barn and the house. Photographs by the author.

FIG. 106
Barn near Meyersdale. Its large center gable and idiosyncratic cupola were in keeping with new trends in barn decoration. Somerset Historical Center.

created more efficient milking and working space. Silos, though technically not part of the barn, were invariably located next to it, essentially providing more storage space for feed.

The enclosure of the forebay marks a definite departure from the familiar signature of the Pennsylvania barn. In many instances, a nineteenth-century open forebay was later enclosed (Fig. 111). Others built new barns with enclosed forebays.

Why did barn builders enclose forebays almost universally between about 1880 and 1930?[49] In the eastern part of the state, farmers had larger dairy herds to care for; they enclosed forebays and rearranged their barn interiors with lengthwise aisles and stanchions to accommodate milking and feeding. But this does not explain enclosed forebays in Somerset County, because the average herd size was still tiny. Between 1880 and 1924, the number of milk cows in the county actually declined (increased quantities of milk came from higher per-cow productivity), and average herd size stayed between three and four cows. Even the largest herd in the county—thirty-nine cows— was modest by dairy industry standards. Thus the traditional Pennsylvania barn layout still suited prevailing agricultural conditions, and enclosure cannot be connected to the need to rearrange the interior. Indeed, most barns in the county retained traditional interior arrangements even if they had enclosed forebays.

The key to the appearance of enclosed forebays in Somerset County is that by the turn of the century it paid to shelter cows better. Forebay enclosures were commonly called "storm sheds," and the enclosed space was used to provide indoor watering facilities for the cattle, to house and

FIG. 107
Late-nineteenth-century image of a large Pennsylvania barn, with louvered openings, star, and three cupolas. Somerset Historical Center, Harris copywork (no identification for the barn).

protect the manure pile from the elements, and also to store some machinery. In the harsh Somerset County winters this indeed would be a rational thing to do. But if this is the explanation, why did farmers wait so long? The timing makes sense, if we recall that this is exactly the period when the financial returns justified farmers' investment in measures that would increase their milking herd's productivity, and that the major means of achieving that increase was through better feed

 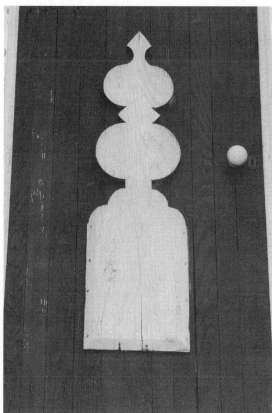

FIG. 108
Decorative details, Faidley barn, 1892–1922. These details were made possible by industrial power jigsaws and sash saws. The louvered window (*left*) is surmounted by delicate incised decoration, while the cut-out motif (*right*) is a simple but effective combination of basic geometrical shapes. Somerset Historical Center.

FIG. 109
Barn star, Jacob Walker farm, date uncertain. Somerset Historical Center.

FIG. 110
Schiller barn, about 1890, Allegheny
Township. Another variation, achieved with
intricate lattice work (A, B). The lattice work
adds a decorative turn to the practical function
of ventilation, while the eight-pointed star acts
as a focal point. Somerset Historical Center.

and shelter. In an age when even small farms typically were operated with a lot of equipment, the storm shelter also provided housing for machinery.[50]

Twentieth-century barns also consistently incorporated new technologies. Nearly all, for example, exhibited modified bents that accommodated hay tracks and hay forks. Some accomplished this with traditional timber framing, but others used newer construction techniques such as lumber trusses bolted together (Fig. 112) to create huge spaces for machinery storage. The builder of Omie Cable's barn boasted that "This barn is built on an entirely new plan, the interior above the floor being without ties or posts, thus permitting the driving of teams over the entire floor space."[51] Rainbow roofs (Fig. 113) also appeared during this period, affording storage facilities for larger hay crops.

FIG. 111
Samuel Flick farm barn, forebay enclosed about 1900. The enclosed forebay—often called a "storm shed"—appeared when it became profitable to provide better shelter for cattle. The plan shows that the traditional arrangement of stalls was left unchanged, while the bent arrangement shows how the forebay was enclosed. Somerset Historical Center.

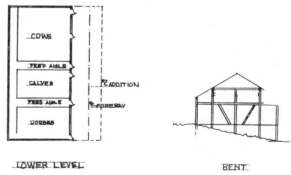

The silo, of course, represented innovation. Early silos were wooden and some were actually incorporated into the barn space. By the late 1920s, tile silos began to appear (Fig. 114). These structures transformed the landscape's appearance substantially, prefiguring the vertical thrust of today's giants.

Looking back over time, we can see that the twentieth-century changes in the rural landscape were especially violent. As the coal industry swept into the county, it imposed large-scale alterations, ranging from rigid lines of company housing to enormous tipples. Its influence washed over into the farm landscape, too, though in an indirect way. Of course those who shaped the farm landscape also responded to the overwhelming forces exerted on twentieth-century agriculture

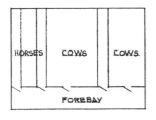

LOWER LEVEL

BENT

FIG. 112
Truss bent, about 1915, Quemahoning Township. Compare the bent to earlier nineteenth-century examples; this one provides much more vertical room and is less cumbersome. Somerset Historical Center.

from far beyond. Enclosed forebays, machine sheds, and peepy houses testified to the forces of capitalist agriculture. Hierarchies of class and gender were much more overtly expressed in the landscape than they had been in the past. The contrast between house and barn emphasized differences in the status of men's and women's work. Separate summer kitchens removed "dirty" work from the house proper—and, in the process, also helped define work spatially according to gender. Separate quarters for hired hands segregated the farm by class. All in all, while the eighteenth- and nineteenth-century Somerset rural community had exercised selectivity with respect to the

FIG. 113
Rainbow-roof barn under construction, undated photograph. This type of roof offered even more room than trusses or conventional framing. Somerset Historical Center.

FIG. 114
Tile silo, Dombrowski farm, 1998. The silo first
appeared in the 1880s, and it was quickly
adopted in Somerset County, because it helped
stretch the feeding season. Tile silos became
popular in the 1930s; the tiles were so
weatherproof that many still stand in excellent
condition. Photograph by the author.

wider culture, by the twentieth century, accommodation was much more in evidence. Agricultural
villages and neighborhoods made landscape statements that could not fail to be understood: their
tidy barns, churches, Granges, and farmsteads were set in self-conscious contrast to the dismal
coal-patch towns. The tensions and contradictions in the Somerset County landscape gave force-
ful expression to the dilemmas of life in twentieth-century rural America.

★ *epilogue*

Over time, forest-dwelling, farming, and industrial societies successively contributed to shaping the landscape in Somerset County. All three left imprints on the land; today's Somerset County is a layered landscape. Contemporary activities continue to reshape the forest, farm, and industrial landscapes in a never-ending process, at once enabling local residents to live in close connection with the past and to create a future suited to new generations.

The earliest human societies in the county, both Native American and Euro-American, created landscapes in which the forest and its products gave shape to everyday life. Remnants of the aboriginal forest-dwelling cultures are least visible in the contemporary landscape. Few, if any, stands of pre-contact-era forest remain, and only a few archaeological sites document the presence of Native Americans in the pre-contact period. Early European settlement is represented by more numerous survivals in the form of scattered small log buildings and perhaps even early clearings marked by fencerows or tree lines. Over the course of the nineteenth century, residents slowly chipped away at the forest cover. Clearing for farms proceeded piecemeal; later, mechanized lumbering operations (for lumber, railroad ties, and mine props) stripped large swaths of hillsides very quickly. Around the turn of the twentieth century, the percentage of the county's land area under forest cover may have hit its lowest point, dipping just under 50 percent. The decline of mining and farming helped restore the county's forest area; a century later, second- and third-growth forest has filled in many of the gaps, returning the total forest area to about two-thirds.[1]

At the beginning of the twenty-first century, Somerset in many respects is once again a forest society, because the woodlands and their resources still play an important role in the contemporary county's economic and cultural life. Of course, today's forest activities differ from those of two hundred years ago; the very modern pursuit of leisure and recreation dominates. Commercial facilities and private retreats make extensive use of the woodlands. The county boasts several ski resorts, and it has become an increasingly popular site for summer homes belonging to city dwellers from Baltimore, Pittsburgh, and Washington, D.C. Serving a much more extensive constituency is the system of state parks and forests. Along the Laurel Highlands ridge, a chain of six state parks straddles the county's western border. These parks are part of a far larger tract of state forest, Forbes Forest. Within the borders of these lands, millions of visitors each year (many from the greater Pittsburgh area) engage in hunting, camping, fishing, water sports, hiking, cross-country skiing, rafting, and picnicking. In northern Somerset County, Gallitzin Forest serves a similar function. Two hundred years ago, settlers trod woodland paths to neighbors' homesteads or to millsites; today, hikers follow trails to seek quiet or to understand natural habitats. Minimal park facilities, often of imitative log construction, are architecturally unobtrusive.[2]

The farming culture has left an equally strong and continuing legacy. In the nineteenth century, Somerset Countians were preeminently a farming people. They pursued a highly varied agriculture, combining a subsistence base (which was nurtured by traditional folkways) with robust market production of items sent long distances to American cities and abroad. Their landscape reflected this combination of the local and the cosmopolitan. It reached its apex with the distinctive two-story farmhouse with double-decker porches, flanked by a substantial Pennsylvania barn, both buildings sharing a common visual vocabulary. A full complement of small outbuildings accommodated the wide variety of agricultural enterprises of the nineteenth-century farm. In the early twentieth century, market-orientation came to dominate, though production was still fairly diversified. But the shift to profit-and-loss farming meant the accentuation of landscape elements that were associated with market products. Thus, barns of this era overshadowed houses—and ancillary structures, such as peepy houses and silos, spoke to values of efficiency and productivity. The rise of mining helped stimulate this trend, both by supplying local markets and by creating an incentive for farmers to distinguish visually their landscapes from those of the coal-patch towns.

Within Pennsylvania, Somerset is still an important agricultural county, ranking in the top ten counties in hay, oats, silage corn, potatoes, dairy production, sheep numbers, and poultry production. Over 200,000 acres of the county remained in farmland as of 1997, and the value of farm products increased markedly between 1992 and 1997. Nevertheless, when we compare the 200,000 acres of the 1990s to the peak of 526,000 acres a century earlier, the diminishing role of agriculture becomes obvious. Fewer than six hundred full-time farms—and less than a thousand farms altogether—remained in Somerset County at the turn of the twenty-first century; again, compare that figure with the peak of over thirty-nine hundred in 1910. Today's Somerset County farms, at about 215 acres per farm, are larger by about 50–75 acres than their nineteenth- and twentieth-century counterparts. They are also far more specialized; livestock products account for 87 percent of the market value of agricultural products sold from Somerset County farms.[3]

These figures of continuity and decline perhaps explain how today's farming families make use of the historically layered landscape they have inherited. Many farms still retain a good bit of the nineteenth-century building stock, especially barns and houses. Tough times for farming since the 1930s have made it prudent to make do with existing buildings rather than to invest heavily in new ones. However, the array of small structures such as smokehouses, peepy houses, summer kitchens, and henhouses is slowly disappearing, along with the subsistence base. In many farm households, at least one adult works off the farm, and the family purchases food rather than growing it, so even large vegetable gardens are scarcer than they once were. At the same time, the new elements that do appear testify to the present-day specialization of Somerset County farms. Most prominent among these are the enormous blue metal silos, often part of a cluster of silos from the fifties, sixties, and seventies. Also common are pit silos (these pits for storing silage are often covered with plastic and old tires) and facilities for handling animal waste. Mechanized milking facilities and computerized feeding systems customize input and output for each cow. Pasture is less important than it was, and so one is less likely to see animals out grazing. Overall, though, in the rapidly changing modern agricultural scene, it is remarkable that the nineteenth- and early-twentieth-century landscape has proven so adaptable.

One new "product" has recently appeared on a Somerset County farm that may be a harbinger of the future. It is wind power. Spurred by the deregulation of the utilities industry, a Pennsylvania power company committed to generating electricity from renewable sources has erected eight state-of-the-art wind turbines. The equipment is imported from Denmark, the world's leading maker of wind-powered generating equipment. The power company's website announced:

> Construction began on December 1, 1999, and the 10.4 megawatt wind facility officially began serving our customers on May 1, 2000. Located on a stretch of vacant farmland and reclaimed strip mine above Garrett, Pennsylvania, this is one of the largest wind facilities ever built in the eastern United States.
>
> There are eight 200-foot high windmills, each with a tubular tower and three blades approximately 95 feet in length. Each turbine has a capacity of 1,300 kilowatts of electricity— the wind farm altogether will generate enough electricity to power 2,500 average Pennsylvania households.[4]

Here is a development that could drastically change the rural Somerset County landscape, at once transforming both the farm and industrial landscapes. The turbines will be visible for quite a distance, and they offer an arresting sight. In the rural environment, they are unprecedented in scale (except perhaps for isolated earlier structures such as coal tipples). Such enterprises could supply a new use for farmland and help counter the environmental degradation of coal mining.

On the ground in Somerset County, the contrasts between farms and mines are more jarring than ever, because open pits and strip mines now have ripped huge gashes in the earth's surface. This is the continuing legacy of the industrial era. It is hard to say just how much of the county's surface area has been excavated, but it is all too evident that strip mining has exerted an enormous impact, visually and environmentally. A century of mining both underground and on the surface has resulted in intractable problems; today's residents struggle with the challenges of groundwater contamination, occupational and environmental health problems, and enormous, bare mounds of mine waste. Mining companies are still powerful, and government regulations have not been fully successful in remedying the environmental damage caused by mining.

Mining is still an important enterprise locally, but not because it is a major employer. Only 41 coal mining establishments operated in Somerset County in 1992 (as opposed to over 150 in the early twentieth century). Mechanization has drastically reduced the need for human laborers. The number of mine employees in the county dropped from 2,624 in 1980 to only 1,093 in 1990. Having replaced workers with machines, the coal companies no longer needed company towns as instruments of labor control, so they have sold company housing to the former employees and their descendants. Mechanization and deindustrialization in the immediate region have added to the area's woes, and in some townships the poverty and unemployment rates are high. Lower-paying service employment now dominates the job market. Many young people feel that they have little choice but to leave; not only has the overall population dropped from early-twentieth-century levels, but it is also aging.[5]

Yet withal, Somerset County remains a rural place, and a lovely one at that, a place of refreshing breezes, pastoral scenery, and breathtaking mountaintop views. Tourism—even ecotourism—and recreational facilities now vie with agriculture and mining as major revenue sources. Urbanites come to Somerset County for rest and rejuvenation, and they delight in the environs that generations of builders worked so hard to create. Local residents take pride in that heritage as well. In Somerset County, past customs and values have retained a strong hold on rural people. Though the economic importance of many old practices has diminished, people remember them. Indeed, historical organizations here are unusually active. By the mid-twentieth century, organized efforts began to preserve the memory and skills of folkways that were integral to cultural identity in this locality, such as handloom weaving and maple sugaring. A new appreciation for the heritage of coal mining helped ease some of the scars occasioned by the social divisions of earlier decades. The Historical and Genealogical Society of Somerset County energetically collects historical materials—not only artifacts but also manuscript collections, printed historical documents, and even folktales. The Society maintains a well-regarded publication, the *Laurel Messenger,* and it organizes many educational and cultural programs. These Somerset County citizens, with others across Pennsylvania and the nation, are striving to find ways of preserving these lands and their buildings for future generations—for the people who will work on the land and for visitors who will enjoy and learn from the landscape.

History has shown that the rural landscape has never been static. Today's Somerset County residents face difficulties, to be sure; but there are also opportunities to reshape the multilayered landscape in response to new needs. Forests can become landscapes of recreation and environmental recovery. At least some agricultural lands will continue to be farmed, even if for "crops" such as electrical power. And former mine lands can be reclaimed for new purposes. Perhaps today's preservation efforts will produce a new generation of vernacular designers who will creatively use the best of their ancestors' handiwork to address contemporary concerns—and, in so doing, will impart new life and vitality to the rural landscape.

★ *notes*

INTRODUCTION

1. The Center for Rural Pennsylvania, "Welcome" <http://www.ruralpa.org> (27 May 1999).
2. See Stuart Brand, *How Buildings Learn* (New York: Penguin Books, 1994), for a wonderfully perceptive articulation of these themes.

CHAPTER 1

1. For prominent revisions of the frontier argument, see, for example, Patricia Limerick, *The Legacy of Conquest: The Unbroken Past of the American West* (New York: Norton, 1987); Alan Taylor, *William Cooper's Town: Power and Persuasion on the Frontier of the Early American Republic* (New York: Vintage, 1995); and Daniel Usner, *Indians, Settlers, and Slaves in a Frontier Exchange Economy: The Lower Mississippi Valley Before 1783* (Chapel Hill: University of North Carolina Press, 1992).
2. Bernard Bailyn, *The Peopling of British North America* (New York: Knopf, 1986); John Mack Faragher, *Daniel Boone: The Life and Legend of an American Pioneer* (New York: Henry Holt, 1992), 121; Taylor, *William Cooper's Town*.
3. Edward Muller et al., *Atlas of Pennsylvania* (Philadelphia: Temple University Press, 1989), 24, 52; Michael Yaworski, *Soil Survey of Somerset County, Pennsylvania* (Washington, D.C.: Soil Conservation Service, 1983), introduction.
4. Paul A. W. Wallace, ed., *Thirty Thousand Miles with John Heckewelder* (Pittsburgh: University of Pittsburgh Press, 1957), 39–40.
5. William H. Welfley, *History of Somerset County*, vol. 2 of *History of Bedford and Somerset Counties, Pennsylvania*, by E. Howard Blackburn and William H. Welfley (New York: Lewis Publishing Co., 1906), 13. Hereafter cited as Welfley, *History*.
6. Mark Hornberger, "Germans in Pennsylvania, 1800, 1850, 1880: A Spatial Perspective," *Yearbook of German-American Studies* 24 (1989): 97–104; Thomas Purvis, "Patterns of Ethnic Settlement in Late Eighteenth-Century Pennsylvania," *Western Pennsylvania Historical Magazine* 70 (1987): 107–22.
7. Israel Shreve, "Journal from Jersey to the Monongahela, August 11, 1788, by Colonel Israel Shreve," reprinted in *Pennsylvania Magazine of History and Biography* 52, no. 3 (1928), 196; John Palmer, *Journal of Travels in the United States of North America . . .* (London: Sherwood, Neely, and Jones, 1818), 41. See also "Journal of Colonel John May, of Boston, Relative to a Journey to the Ohio Country in 1789," reprinted in *Pennsylvania Magazine of History and Biography* 45, no. 2 (1921), 112; Shreve, "Journal from Jersey," 197; and Henry Bradshaw Fearon, *Sketches of America: A narrative of a journey of five thousand miles through the eastern and western states of America*, 2d ed. (London: Longman, Hurst, Rees, Orme, and Brown, 1818), 194.
8. Welfley, *History*, 52; tax assessment records are reproduced on 139–48, 156–58, 176.
9. 1810 tax assessments (notes compiled in Somerset Historical Center files); Welfley, *History*, 177.

10. See Joseph E. Walker, ed., *The Journal of Joshua Gilpin, 1809: Pleasure and Business in Western Pennsylvania* (Harrisburg: Pennsylvania Historical and Museum Commission, 1975), end piece. See also Archer B. Hulbert, *The Old Glade (Forbes's) Road* (Cleveland: A. H. Clark Co., 1903).

11. Aaron Fogleman, *Hopeful Journeys: German Immigration, Settlement, and Political Culture in Colonial America, 1717–1775* (Philadelphia: University of Pennsylvania Press, 1996).

12. "Notes of Travel of William Henry, John Heckewelder, John Rothrock, and Christian Clewell, to Gnadenhuetten on the Muskingum, in the Early Summer of 1797," *Pennsylvania Magazine of History and Biography* 10 (1886), 155–56; Walker, ed., *Journal*, 32.

13. Walker, ed., *Journal*, 33; William Cronon, *Changes in the Land* (New York: Hill and Wang, 1983).

14. For grains and garden produce, see Somerset County estate inventories, especially those of Harmon Husband (1795, no. 1); Peter Clester (1795, no. 2); and Jacob Kooser (1795, no. 4), Somerset Historical Center, microfilm. Gates, quoted in the *Laurel Messenger* 17, no. 44 (1970), 1, 4. See also Walker, ed., *Journal*, 32.

15. Tax assessment records suggest that oxen were never as important here as they were in other regions, such as New England.

16. See inventories mentioned above for samples of the equipment mentioned. These inventories represent comparatively wealthy people; typical farm families would probably have borrowed equipment from neighbors. Samuel Philson, "Old Implements and Methods," Somerset *Standard*, 3 August 1899.

17. Philson, "Old Implements."

18. Welfley, *History*, 106; Lois Ann Mast, ed., *The Peter Leibundgutt Journal* (Elverson, Pa.: Mennonite Family Publishing, 1991), 2–3, vi; Stevenson Fletcher, *Pennsylvania Agriculture and Country Life*, vol. 1 (Harrisburg: Pennsylvania Historical and Museum Commission, 1950), 108; Joan Jensen, *Loosening the Bonds: Mid-Atlantic Farm Women, 1750–1850* (New Haven: Yale University Press, 1986).

19. John Heckewelder, *A narrative of the mission of the United brethren among the Delaware and Mohegan Indians . . . ,* ed. William Elsey Connelley (Cleveland: n.p., 1907), 56; Anna Maust Bender, "The Masts, [Maust] Pioneer Settlers . . . ," *Casselman Chronicle* (Winter 1962), 2–3; Cronon, *Changes in the Land*, 141–42; Welfley, *History*, 85.

20. Mast, ed., *Leibundgutt Journal*; Somerset County estate inventories, John Black (1803, no. 12).

21. Philson, "Old Implements." See also Welfley, *History*, 514.

22. Donald Graves and Michael Colby, "An Overview of Flax and Linen Production in Pennsylvania," *Pennsylvania Folklife* 35 (1986): 108–26.

23. On the origins of maple sugaring, see John Mack Faragher, *Sugar Creek: Life on the Illinois Prairie* (New Haven: Yale University Press, 1986), 15–17. On Somerset County, see "Sugaring in the Casselman Valley," *Casselman Chronicle* (Spring 1961), 1–9; Mark Ware, "Spotza, Keelers, and Stirred Sugar: The Maple Sugar Industry of Southwestern Pennsylvania," *Proceedings of the Association for Living Historical Farms and Museums* 13 (1993), 48–59.

24. In 1798, for example, 213 of Brothersvalley's 261 taxables owned either horses or cattle or both. (See the Somerset County tax assessment records for 1798, Brothersvalley, 158–65.) The actual size of the entire herd may have been larger, since it is unclear whether young animals were counted.

25. See, for example, one German immigrant's criticism of American farm women as too lazy to chase the cows and milk them; he implied that the job was a woman's task. See Walter Kamphoefner et al., eds., *News from the Land of Freedom: German Immigrants Write Home* (Ithaca: Cornell University Press, 1991), 70. Only men were listed on tax assessments as weavers, but since their numbers are much smaller than the number of looms (listed in manufacturing statistics), it is reasonable to assume that women did a great deal of weaving too.

26. François André Michaux, *Travels to the Westward of the Allegheny Mountains . . . in the Year 1802* (London: Richard Phillips, 1805), 24.

27. Somerset County estate inventories, David Ream (1803).

28. Geese turn up in inventories. For example, see the inventories of Harmon Husband (1795, no. 1) and Joseph Berkey (1798, no. 7).

29. Faragher, *Sugar Creek,* especially chapter 12.

30. Carolyn Merchant, *Ecological Revolutions: Nature, Gender, and Science in New England* (Chapel Hill: University of North Carolina Press, 1989), chap. 4.

31. See William A. Hunter, ed., "John Badollet's 'Journal of the Time I Spent in Stony Creek Glades,'" *Pennsylvania Magazine of History and Biography* 104 (1980), 187. See also "Journal of Colonel John May," 113.

32. For Badollet, see Hunter, ed., "John Badollet's 'Journal,'" 171, 166; Michaux, *Travels,* 26.

33. Thomas Vickroy Papers, Somerset Historical Center; Lee Soltow and Kenneth Keller, "Tenancy and Asset-Holding in Late Eighteenth-Century Washington County, Pennsylvania," *Western Pennsylvania Historical Magazine* 65 (January 1982): 1–17.

34. Marylynn Salmon, "Equality or Submersion? Feme Covert Status in Early Pennsylvania," in *Women of America: A History,* ed. Carol Berkin and Mary Beth Norton (Boston: Houghton Mifflin, 1979), 92–111.

35. For example, see the John Deeter account book, Somerset Historical Center; for a good account of the flexibility of prices, see Christopher Clark, *The Roots of Rural Capitalism* (Ithaca: Cornell University Press, 1990).

36. See, for example, the inventories for Harmon Husband (1795, no. 1), John Black (1803, no. 12), and John Cross (1799, no. 8); for Palmer, see his *Journal of Travels,* 43.

In their mobility, women's lives in Somerset differed significantly from those of women in other parts of the country; women in Sugar Creek, Illinois, and women in South Carolina yeoman families, for instance, were confined to the homestead most of the time. See Faragher, *Sugar Creek,* and Stephanie McCurry, *Masters of Small Worlds: Yeoman Households, Gender Relations, and the Political Culture of the Antebellum South Carolina Low Country* (New York: Oxford University Press, 1995). But Martha Ballard, a Maine midwife, traveled all over the countryside; see Laurel Thatcher Ulrich, *A Midwife's Tale* (New York: Vintage, 1991).

37. Bettye Hobbs Pruitt, "Self-Sufficiency and the Agricultural Economy of Eighteenth-Century Massachusetts," *William and Mary Quarterly,* 3d ser., vol. 41, no. 3 (1984): 333–64.

38. Margaret Van Horn (Dwight) Bell, *A Journey to Ohio in 1810* (New Haven: Yale University Press, 1913), 46–47.

39. For the classic formulation of this argument, see James Henretta, "Families and Farms: Mentalité in Pre-Industrial America," *William and Mary Quarterly,* 3d ser., vol. 35, no. 1 (1978): 3–32.

40. Scott T. Swank, ed., *The Arts of the Pennsylvania Germans* (New York: Norton, 1983), 40; Mast, ed., *Leibundgutt Journal,* 4–5. For research on Amish patterns, see Metin M. Coşgel, "Religious Culture and Economic Performance: Agricultural Productivity of the Amish, 1850–1880," *Journal of Economic History* 53 (June 1993): 319–31. On German immigrant patterns, see Walter Kamphoefner, "The German Agricultural Frontier: Crucible or Cocoon," *Ethnic Forum* 4 (Spring 1984): 21–36.

41. Bell, *Journey,* 37; Michaux, *Travels,* 22; Henry Fearon, *Sketches of America,* 190–91; letter of Sally Anderson Hastings (1800), reprinted in John W. Harpster, ed., *Pen Pictures of Early Western Pennsylvania* (Pittsburgh: University of Pittsburgh Press, 1938), 236. See also "A Journey to the West in 1817," *Essex Institute Historical Collections* 8 (1868): 221–50.

42. W. J. Rorabaugh, *The Alcoholic Republic: An American Tradition* (New York: Oxford University Press, 1979).

The Whiskey Rebellion has been interpreted by Thomas Slaughter (*The Whiskey Rebellion* [New York: Oxford University Press, 1986]) as one of the culminating events of the American Revolution, in which backcountry people—underrepresented and increasingly impoverished—protested what they regarded as an unconstitutional internal excise. Especially in the region surrounding Pittsburgh, an increasingly inequitable distribution of wealth, coupled with a lack of markets, underpinned the protest. Much remains unclear about the incident, however. Some of its leaders (such as Harmon Husband) were members of the local elite; Slaughter's distinction between a "mercantile" east and an "agricultural" west is inaccurate; and it is not entirely established that western Pennsylvania was the worst hit by the tax. Moreover, urban large-scale manufacturers in Philadelphia also protested the tax. See Roland Baumann, "Philadelphia's Manufacturers and the Excise Taxes of 1794: The Forging of the Jeffersonian Coalition," *Pennsylvania Magazine of History and Biography* 106 (1982): 3–40.

43. "Travels of Johann David Schoepf," in Harpster, ed., *Pen Pictures*, 134.

44. See Pruitt, "Self-Sufficiency"; Kenneth W. Keller, "From the Rhineland to the Virginia Frontier: Flax Production as a Commercial Enterprise," *Virginia Magazine of History and Biography* 98 (July 1990): 487–511; Elizabeth Perkins, "The Consumer Frontier: Household Consumption in Early Kentucky," *Journal of American History* 78, no. 2 (September 1991): 486–510. On local markets, see Timothy Flint, "Letters to America" (1822), quoted in Ruben Thwaites, ed., *Early Western Travels, 1748–1846*, vol. 9 (Cleveland: A. H. Clark, 1904–7), 78. Nagel Store accounts, Somerset Historical Center, photocopies.

45. Michael S. Knecht, "Early Structure Characteristics," *Laurel Messenger* 24 (February 1983), 65–66.

46. "Notes of Travel," 129–33.

47. Walker, ed., *Journal*, 116.

48. Fearon, *Sketches*, 192–93. See also Shreve, "Journal from Jersey," 202.

49. Walker, ed., *Journal*, 58–59.

50. William Woys Weaver has questioned the label "Continental" for this plan; he argues that this room arrangement may have been a Pennsylvania German adaptation that drew from "Continental" sources only in the sense that it was more related to European urban examples than to rural folk traditions of any specific German region. See William Woys Weaver, "The Pennsylvania German House: European Antecedents and New World Forms," *Winterthur Portfolio* 21, no. 4 (1986): 243–64. For a wonderful study of a particular locality in which German influence was significant, see Philip Pendleton, *Oley Valley Heritage: The Colonial Years, 1700–1770* (Birdsboro, Pa.: Pennsylvania German Society, 1994).

51. Edward Chappell, "Germans and Swiss," in *America's Architectural Roots: Ethnic Groups That Built America*, by Dell Upton (Washington, D.C.: Preservation Press, 1986); Amos Long, "Bank (Multi-Level) Structures in Rural Pennsylvania," *Pennsylvania Folklife* 20 (Winter 1970–71): 31–40; Robert Bucher, "The Swiss Bank House in Pennsylvania," *Pennsylvania Folklife* 13 (Winter 1968–69): 3–11; Henry Glassie, "A Central Chimney Continental Log House," *Pennsylvania Folklife* 13 (Winter 1968–69): 33–39.

52. Other good examples are the Jacob Swank house (Lincoln Township, c. 1820), John Griffith house (Jenner Township, dated 1819), and William Bowman house (Lincoln Township, dated 1813). Though atypical in its stone construction, the Abraham Beachy house (Elk Lick Township, dated 1809) follows the same spatial pattern. (Historical property names are used throughout.)

53. Direct Tax manuscripts for Somerset County; U.S. Bureau of the Census, Heads of Household, 1800 (manuscript census), Somerset Historical Center, microfilm. Nevertheless, the households in these little dwellings show a range of types. Peter Winger, for example, owned a 20' × 25' "House" worth $40, and lived in 1800 with one male between 16 and 25 years of age; two males between 26 and 45; one female between 10 and 15, one female between 16 and 25, and one female over 45 (probably his wife). Nicholas Schultz and his wife, both over 45, lived in an 18' × 25' "Cabin" worth only $15.

54. Ibid. Yoast Lindensmith and his household consisted of the parents, both over 45; one child between 10 and 15; three young people between 16 and 25; and one man between 25 and 45. Their house was described in 1798 as measuring 20' × 25', one and one-half stories, with three windows. It was valued at $100 even.

55. Simon Hay is the anomalous exception; he built a 30' × 35' stone house with 174 lights, valued at $1,000.

56. U.S. Bureau of the Census, Heads of Household, Somerset County, 1800 (manuscript census), Somerset Historical Center, microfilm; Conrad Beamer will, no. 2, from 1801.

57. 1798 Direct Tax manuscripts, Somerset County.

58. Michaux, *Travels,* 26; see that text, too, for another mention of farmers in the region: "every individual is satisfied with cultivating as much land as is necessary for supporting his family" (20). Robert Boyd, *Personal Memoirs . . .* (Cincinnati: Methodist Book Concern, 1868), 64–65.

59. Weaver, "The Pennsylvania German House," 257; Hunter, ed., "John Badollet's 'Journal,'" 174, 172, 185. One wonders if this is the house of "John Huber" in the 1798 tax, described as 30' × 28', with thirteen windows and 165 lights.

60. Lee Soltow, "Egalitarian America and Its Inegalitarian Housing in the Federal Period," *Social Science History* 9 (Spring 1985): 199–213; idem, "Rural Pennsylvania in 1800: A Portrait from the Septennial Census," *Pennsylvania History* 49 (January 1982): 25–48; Walter Lord, "Architectural Characteristics of Houses: Lancaster County, 1798," *Journal of the Lancaster County Historical Society* 85 (Michaelmas 1981): 132–51; Karen Koegler, "Building in Stone in Southwestern Pennsylvania: Pattern and Process," in *Gender, Class, and Shelter: Perspectives in Vernacular Architecture 5,* ed. Elizabeth Collins Cromley and Carter L. Hudgins (Knoxville: University of Tennessee Press, 1995), 193–211.

61. In his *Distribution of Wealth and Income in the United States in 1798* (Pittsburgh: University of Pittsburgh Press, 1989), Lee Soltow argues that frontier areas showed significant inequality at the turn of the nineteenth century. Somerset County did not follow so marked a pattern.

62. Scott T. Swank, "Proxemic Patterns," in *The Arts of the Pennsylvania Germans,* ed. Swank, 45–49. In Somerset County, see, for example, the inventory of Jacob Kooser (1795), in which the single most valuable item was £320 worth of "debts on notes and bonds."

63. For good explications of this, see Henry Glassie, "Vernacular Architecture and Society," *Material Culture* 16 (Spring 1984): 5–25, and Charles Martin, *Hollybush: Folk Building and Social Change in an Appalachian Community* (Knoxville: University of Tennessee Press, 1984). The phrase "architecture of sociability" has been used by Henry Glassie. On "open" houses, see Bernard Herman, *The Stolen House* (Charlottesville: University Press of Virginia, 1992). To read about other instances in which architecture did not reflect social hierarchy, see Clifton Ellis, "Dissenting Faith and Domestic Landscape in Eighteenth-Century Virginia," in *People, Power, Places: Perspectives in Vernacular Architecture 8,* ed. Sally McMurry and Annmarie Adams (Knoxville: University of Tennessee Press, 2000), 23–41; and Fraser Neiman, "Domestic Architecture on the Clifts Plantation: The Social Context of Early Virginia Building," in *Common Places: Readings in American Vernacular Architecture,* ed. Dell Upton and John Michael Vlach (Athens: University of Georgia Press, 1986), 292–314.

64. See Somerset County Historic Resource Survey, Quemahoning Township.

65. Paul Touart, "The Acculturation of German-American Building Practices of Davidson County, North Carolina," in *Perspectives in Vernacular Architecture 2,* ed. Camille Wells (Columbia: University of Missouri Press, 1986), 72–81; Edward Chappell, "Acculturation in the Shenandoah Valley: Rhenish Houses of the Massanutten Settlement," in *Common Places,* ed. Upton and Vlach, 27–58; Bernard Herman, *Architecture and Rural Life in Central Delaware, 1700–1900* (Knoxville: University of Tennessee Press, 1987).

66. Fifteen percent of all taxables in 1800 declared a nonagricultural occupation, but one-third to one-half of kitchen owners were artisans or traders. Of the kitchens that could be definitely matched with owners, twenty-four were owned by artisans or tradespeople and twenty-three were owned by people whose occupations were not recorded (and who were therefore probably farmers or farm laborers).

67. This is, of course, not to say that issues of status do not explain detached kitchens in other regions, especially in the South. But it does suggest that in the North, a growth of artisan activity might be accompanied by a proliferation of "kitchen" outbuildings in specific time periods in rural areas. It would be interesting to conduct a study to find out whether this actually happened and to see how "kitchens" were sited with respect to the main house. For an individual example, see William Woys Weaver, "A Blacksmith's Summer Kitchen," *Pennsylvania Folklife* 22 (Summer 1973): 22–24. The owner actually kept many of his smithing tools in the kitchen.

68. See for example, the inventories of Jacob Kooser (1795, no. 4) and Ebenezer Griffith (probably 1795).

69. Though it seems like a very small figure, the cleared acreage was probably enough in the aggregate to supply the population's basic needs. Most individual families would not be self-sufficient, but as a community, the people could pool and exchange resources to ensure adequate diet, shelter, and clothing. This again points up the critical role of social networks. For example, Bettye Pruitt has found that farms in Massachusetts averaged a *total* of only twenty acres in 1771; individual households exchanged labor, services, and goods to make up what they lacked. James Lemon's estimates for southeastern Pennsylvania are higher, but he underestimates the amount of exchange that went on to meet basic needs. He does, however, point out that many farms probably had a third of their production go to international trade. Analyses by Eugene Harper and Thomas Slaughter of southwestern Pennsylvania ignore the role played by exchange, and so they interpret the figures for average acreage much more pessimistically than I do here. See Pruitt, "Self-Sufficiency"; James Lemon, *The Best Poor Man's Country: A Geographical Study of Early Southeastern Pennsylvania* (Baltimore: Johns Hopkins University Press, 1972); R. Eugene Harper, *The Transformation of Western Pennsylvania, 1770–1800* (Pittsburgh: University of Pittsburgh Press, 1992); and Slaughter, *The Whiskey Rebellion*.

70. Conrad Frank inventory (1802, no.10); Anne Royall, *Mrs. Royall's Pennsylvania* (Washington: printed for the author, 1829), 17; Welfley, *History*, 131; Henry Hartzell inventory (1801, no. 9); Henry Beam inventory (1802, no. 13).

71. John Lorain, "Account of the Modes pursued in clearing Land in Pennsylvania, and on the Fences in new Settlements . . . ," *Memoirs of the Philadelphia Society for Promoting Agriculture* 3 (1814), 117; Bernard Herman, *The Stolen House*, 142–45; Lorain, "Account," 116; Thomas Vickroy Papers, Somerset Historical Center.

72. Tenancy agreements, Thomas Vickroy Papers, Somerset Historical Center.

73. For these interpretations, I am indebted to Herman, *The Stolen House*, chap. 4, and to Paul Bourcier, "In Excellent Order: The Gentleman Farmer Views His Fences, 1790–1860," *Agricultural History* 58 (October 1984): 546–65.

74. Somerset County inventories for Harmon Husband (1795, no. 1), Jacob Kooser (1795, no. 4), and John Markley (1796, no. 8); Knecht, "Early Structure Characteristics," 66.

75. Direct Tax manuscripts, Somerset County; "Diary of [Mennonite] Bishop Christian Newcomer, 1799," *Laurel Messenger* (May 1968), 3.

76. Jon Butler, *Awash in a Sea of Faith: Christianizing the American People* (Cambridge: Harvard University Press, 1990), 283.

CHAPTER 2

1. For a summary, see Charles Sellers, *The Market Revolution: Jacksonian America, 1819–1846* (New York: Oxford University Press, 1991). The conceptualization of a shift from a gendered division of labor to a gendered definition of labor is borrowed from Jeanne Boydston, *Home and Work: Housework, Wages, and the Ideology of Labor in the Early Republic* (New York: Oxford University Press, 1990).

2. Several useful collections give a good overview of current studies of vernacular architecture. See Upton and Vlach, eds., *Common Places*, and the volumes in the series *Perspectives in Vernacular Architecture*. To date, there are eight of the latter; the most recent was published in 2000. The Vernacular Architecture Forum also maintains a searchable bibliography online at <http://www.vernaculararchitecture.org/>.

3. Albert Buffington, "The Pennsylvania German Dialect and Folklore of Somerset County," *Publications of the Pennsylvania German Society* 14 (1980): 6–32. Buffington estimated that as late as 1960, half of the older Somerset County residents could still speak Pennsylvania German. The note about "sharpers" appeared in the Somerset *Democrat*, 9 May 1883.

4. William Welfley reproduces the original 1830 returns in his *History*, 179. The 1830 cleared acreage was still only 11 percent of the county's total acreage.

5. The 1850 agricultural census figures at the county level are reproduced in Welfley, *History*, 181. Some important enterprises, such as poultry raising, are not accounted for in the 1850 census. The maple sugar figures are averaged for *all* farms, not just for maple-producing farms, so the amount for sugar-producing farms would be higher. The figures showing the percentages of farms growing different crops are compiled from the Census of Agriculture, Somerset County, 1850 (manuscript census), which contains data for individual farms. Figures for horses and corn are for Brothersvalley and Quemahoning Townships only.

6. Comparative figures are derived from Kuan-I Chen and Jerome K. Pasto, "Facts on a Century of Agriculture in Pennsylvania," *Pennsylvania Agricultural Experiment Station Bulletin* no. 587 (1954).

7. The aggregate figures for 1880 are reproduced in Welfley, *History*, 186. Statewide comparisons are from Chen and Pasto, "Facts on a Century of Agriculture."

8. The Pennsylvania State College Extension Annual Reports, Somerset County. The Pennsylvania State University Archives, Box 85 (summary narrative for 1917), 4.

9. Fletcher, *Pennsylvania Agriculture and Country Life*, vol. 1, 151–52. Rorabaugh *(The Alcoholic Republic)* points out that consumption declined by midcentury.

10. Liberty Hyde Bailey, *Cyclopedia of Agriculture*, vol. 2 (New York: Macmillan, 1907), 219–20.

11. Somerset *Herald and Whig*, 7 December 1864; Somerset *Democrat*, 24 March 1880. See also the ads in the 4 October 1865 *Herald and Whig* for Goodrich seedling potatoes. The premium lists for the 1876 county fair also show these potato varieties.

12. All or nearly all farms reported hay, milch cows and farm butter, other cattle, poultry and eggs, Indian corn, potatoes, and apples. Two-thirds listed sheep and wool, maple sugar, peaches, wheat, and cordwood. The notice about itinerant workers appeared in the Somerset *Herald*, 12 July 1871. The employment of wage labor could also vary with the family's life cycle and with the seasons.

13. Somerset *Democrat*, 11 November 1876 (droves), 27 June 1883 (Alderney/Short Horn killed by a train), 19 April 1871 (Johnstown livestock fair); F. W. Beers, *County Atlas of Somerset, Pennsylvania* (New York: F. W. Beers, 1876), 107; Somerset *Democrat*, 18 May 1867.

14. Somerset *Herald*, 19 April 1871 (Vick seed endorsed in local column), 1 February 1871 (Brigg's flower and bulb catalogue, Rochester, New York), 23 March 1871 (Buist's garden and flower seed for sale at Blymer's store). For all the fair data, see the Somerset *Democrat*, 18 and 25 October 1876.

15. Somerset *Herald*, 11 January 1871 (nursery advertisement); Somerset *Democrat*, 14 April 1883 (real estate ad mentioning orchard fruits). Thanks to the Landis Valley Farm Museum Heirloom Seed Catalog (Lancaster, Pa.: Landis Valley Farm Museum, 1998), 22, for descriptions of ground-cherries; on the Siberian crab apple, see S. A. Beach, *Apples of New York*, vol. 2 (Albany: Lyon Co., 1905), 264. On ginseng, see the Somerset *Democrat*, 15 November 1876.

16. Somerset *Herald and Farmers and Mechanics Register*, 13 September 1847; John King account book (1861), Somerset Historical Center; *Annual Report of the Secretary of Internal Affairs of the Commonwealth of Pennsylvania*, pt. 3, *Industrial Statistics*, vol. 3 (Harrisburg: B. F. Myers, 1876), 302; Somerset *Democrat*, 12 July 1876.

17. Manufactures Census, Salisbury, Somerset County, 1870 (manuscript census); Somerset *Democrat*, 12 July 1876 and 28 January 1880.

18. See estate inventories for John Kemp (1824), Christian Schrock (1847), and, for "fancy chairs," Margaret Engle (1848); Somerset *Democrat*, 8 March 1876.

19. Somerset *Democrat*, 12 July and 18 October 1876.

20. Thomas Gordon, *A Gazetteer of the State of Pennsylvania* (Philadelphia: T. Belknap, 1832), 423. See also I. Daniel Rupp, *Early History of Western Pennsylvania* (Pittsburgh: P. W. Kauffman, 1846), 331, and Charles B. Trego, *A Geography of Pennsylvania* (Philadelphia: Edward C. Biddle, 1843), 347–49; Somerset *Democrat*, 12 July 1876.

21. Estate inventory for John Rishebarger (1837, no. 26), Jenner Township. This barrel churn was reserved for the widow along with other buttermaking equipment, including several dozen milk pans. An ad for a dog-powered churn appeared in the Somerset *Herald and Whig*, 26 April 1865. In *Loosening the Bonds*, Jensen notes that most patent devices were not major improvements. The Manufactures Census for Somerset County, 1870 (manuscript census), lists makers of butter kegs. The Wilhelm estate documents are reprinted in the *Casselman Chronicle* (Fall 1963). Francis Cable diary, 8 September 1883, Somerset Historical Center.

22. Welfley, *History*, 514, 515; Fletcher, *Pennsylvania Agriculture and Country Life*, vol. 1, 101; Philson, "Early Implements"; Somerset *Herald and Farmers and Mechanics Register*, 9 June 1846; Somerset *Herald and Whig*, 26 April 1865 (local foundry); Somerset *Herald*, 4 January 1871 (ads and endorsements). The Somerset *Herald* of 24 May 1871 noted a barn fire that destroyed new threshing machinery.

23. The Somerset *Herald and Whig*, 13 April 1864, had ads for hay rakes; in the Somerset *Herald and Whig* for 5 July 1865, an ad for Ball's Ohio Mower & Reaper announced that the company had a warehouse in Uniontown.

24. Manufactures Census, Brothersvalley Township, 1870, p. 1, l. 9 (manuscript census); Manufactures Census, Addison Township, 1880 (manuscript census). We do not know what the overall proportion was in the field, since horse rakes purchased by farmers would often come from a national distributor.

25. Somerset *Democrat*, 25 July 1883.

26. Donald Graves and Michael Colby, "An Overview of Flax and Linen Production in Pennsylvania," *Pennsylvania Folklife* (Spring 1986), 108–27; *History of Bedford, Somerset, and Fulton Counties* (Chicago: Waterman, Watkins, and Co., 1884), 401–2; Agriculture Census, Brothersvalley Township, 1880 (manuscript census); *Casselman Chronicle* (December 1961), 4; Somerset County estate inventories for Jacob Sipe (1860) and Frederick Hoofer (1868); Joel B. Miller daybook, Somerset Historical Center. *The People's Guard and Farmer's and Mechanic's Advocate* for 10 July 1844 contained a sale notice for a farm with several acres in flax. The ad for "home spuns" and Kantner's ad were in the Somerset *Democrat*, 16 May 1900.

27. For woolen mill data, see the Somerset County manufacturing censuses for 1850, 1860, 1870, and 1880 (manuscript censuses). For accounts of woolen processing, see the December 1961, Spring 1962, and Summer 1963 issues of the *Casselman Chronicle* (pages 4, 4, and 1, respectively). Kantner's mill was built around 1832 at 30' × 40', then enlarged with a 25' × 30' addition in 1881 (*History of Bedford, Somerset, and Fulton Counties*, 467). Kantner had six employees in the 1880s and made mostly yarn and carpets.

28. *History of Bedford, Somerset, and Fulton Counties*, 402; *Casselman Chronicle* (December 1961), 5, 9.

29. Carole Shammas, "How Self-Sufficient Was Early America?" *Journal of Interdisciplinary History* 13 (1982): 247–72; Thomas Dublin, "Rural Putting-Out Work in Early Nineteenth-Century New England: Women and the Transition to Capitalism in the Countryside," *New England Quarterly* 64 (December 1991): 531–73. Daniel Wright account book, Somerset Historical Center; Cover and Hays account book, Somerset Historical Center; Somerset *Herald and Farmers and Mechanics Register*, 9 June 1846; Somerset *Democrat*, 15 April 1876.

30. "Here We Go," Somerset *Democrat*, 12 July 1876.

31. Manufactures Census, Somerset County, 1870 (manuscript census). The average production of wheat stayed at around 50–60 bushels per farm for most of the century, mostly intended for flour to supply the family.

32. Ware, "Spotza"; Somerset *Democrat*, 16 May 1900 and 24 October 1883.

33. Somerset *Democrat*, 24 October and 14 November 1883; Kamphoefner et al., eds., *News*, 77; Somerset *Democrat*, 4 July 1883.

34. Somerset *Democrat*, 12 September 1900 and 11 July, 29 July, and 14 November 1883.

35. Somerset *Democrat*, 24 October 1900.

36. For three excellent summaries of quilting history in America, see Laurel Horton et al., *Quiltmaking in America: Beyond the Myths* (Nashville: Rutledge Hill Press, 1994); Pat Ferrero, Elaine Hedges, and Julie

Silber, *Hearts and Hands: The Influence of Women and Quilts on American Society* (San Francisco: The Quilt Digest Press, 1987); and Jacqueline Marx Atkins, *Shared Threads: Quilting Together—Past and Present* (New York: Viking Studio Books, 1994).

37. *Casselman Chronicle* (Fall 1963); estate inventories for George Rayman (1834); Conrad Shalis (1838), dried apples; Peter F. Hay (1847), cabbage and "Cabige Nive," dough trays, apple butter; Jacob Keller and Isaac Hardin (1848), vinegar, turnip, turkeys, bacon, ham, eggs, candles, pickle tub; [given name illegible] Stull (1848), sausage machine; and Jacob Sipe (1860), cheese boxes; Cable diary, 2 December 1881.

38. Kamphoefner, ed., *News*, 217. On German women's work, see W. R. Lee, "The Impact of Agrarian Change on Women's Work and Child Care in Early Nineteenth-Century Prussia," in *German Women in the Nineteenth Century*, ed. John C. Fout (New York: Holmes and Meier, 1984), 234–55. For a detailed description of Pennsylvania German women's work in Lancaster County that closely parallels evidence from Somerset County, see Phebe Earl Gibbons, *"Pennsylvania Dutch," and Other Essays*, 3d ed. (Philadelphia: J. B. Lippincott, 1882).

39. The following inventories mentioned cookstoves: Peter F. Hay (1847), a cooking stove worth $30; George Pile (1848), a Hathaway stove, valued at $25; Jacob Sipe (1860). Typical manufacturers' advertisements can be found in the Somerset *Herald and Whig*, 27 January 1864, and in the *Herald and Farmers and Mechanics Register*, 17 February 1846. The Manufactures Census, Allegheny Township, 1860 (manuscript census), 6; Stoystown Borough, 1.

40. Ruth Schwartz Cowan, *More Work for Mother: The Ironies of Household Technology from the Open Hearth to the Microwave* (New York: Basic Books, 1983); Somerset *Democrat*, 25 October 1876, front page.

41. Somerset *Herald and Whig*, 27 January 1864, 24 August 1864, 22 December 1869.

42. George Tedrow account book, Somerset Historical Center, 28 May 1832; Daniel Wright account book, Somerset Historical Center. Though most states, by century's end, had laws protecting the rights of married women to property, their effectiveness has been questioned by historians. See Norma Basch, *In the Eyes of the Law: Women, Marriage, and Property in Nineteenth Century New York* (Ithaca: Cornell University Press, 1982).

43. Wright account book, Somerset Historical Center; *Casselman Chronicle* (Spring/Summer 1965); *History of Bedford, Somerset, and Fulton Counties*, 439.

44. Jensen, *Loosening the Bonds*; Dublin, "Rural Putting-Out Work"; Sally McMurry, *Transforming Rural Life: Dairying Families and Agricultural Change, 1820–1885* (Baltimore: Johns Hopkins University Press, 1995).

45. Stephanie McCurry, *Masters of Small Worlds*. Patriarchy and anticapitalism are not invariably associated. Deborah Fink argues in *Agrarian Women: Wives and Mothers in Rural Nebraska, 1880–1940* (Chapel Hill: University of North Carolina Press, 1992) that in the Midwest, capitalist agriculture and patriarchy actually reinforced each other in an exploitative pattern: the more capitalist the farm, the more oppressive the power of the household head.

46. Carolyn Merchant, *Ecological Revolutions*.

47. E. P. Thompson, "Time, Work-Discipline, and Industrial Capitalism," *Past and Present* 38 (1967): 56–97. For clocks in inventories, see: Christian Schrock (1847); Frederick Mahler (1847); [given name illegible] Stull (1848), an eight-day clock; John Ripple (1848); Martin Fichtner (1848). Information on local clockmakers from James B. Whisker, *Pennsylvania Clockmakers and Watchmakers, 1660–1900* (Lewistown, N.Y.: Edwin Mellon, 1996), 115, 126.

48. Von Löher's journal is excerpted and translated by Frederic Trautmann in "Western Pennsylvania Through a German's Eyes: The Travels of Franz von Löher, 1846," *Western Pennsylvania Historical Magazine* 65 (July 1982): 221–29; the citation here is from 227.

49. *Old Franklin Almanac*, 1835, 341–42; *History of Bedford, Somerset, and Fulton Counties*, 556; Welfley, *History*, 516; Somerset *Democrat*, 26 January and 9 February 1876.

50. Royall, *Mrs. Royall's Pennsylvania*, 6.

51. Somerset *Herald*, 25 January 1871; map, Pennsylvania State Archives, Record Group 12, no. w212.

52. *History of Bedford, Somerset, and Fulton Counties*, 440; Welfley, *History*, 395.

53. *History of Bedford, Somerset, and Fulton Counties*, 467–70, 477–79, 491, 502, 509; U.S. Bureau of the Census, *Mortality, Property etc.*, vol. 4 of the 1860 census, 454–58; U.S. Bureau of the Census, *Report on Statistics of Churches*, vol. 16 of the 1890 census, 78.

54. Somerset County Landownership map, 1860, The Pennsylvania State University Libraries; Butler, *Awash in a Sea of Faith*, 271.

55. Ibid. The so-called rural cemetery has received a great deal of attention in landscape historiography. However, this term does not refer to cemeteries in rural areas; rather, it refers to the movement (dating to the Romantic era) to replace undifferentiated urban burial grounds with park-like urban cemeteries. Recently, scholars have added more complexity to the history of cemeteries, which, after all, reflect a great deal about our culture. Dell Upton, for example, characterizes the gridded above-ground cemetery of New Orleans as a "reform cemetery," a city of the dead that functioned as a counterpart to the world of the living, complete with social stratification. In both the rural cemetery and the urban "reform" cemetery, the landscape communicated the sentimentalization of death that was a hallmark of Victorian culture. See Upton, "The Urban Cemetery and the Urban Community: the Origin of the New Orleans Cemetery," in *Exploring Everyday Landscapes: Perspectives in Vernacular Architecture 7*, ed. Annmarie Adams and Sally McMurry (Knoxville: University of Tennessee Press, 1997), 131–49. The place held by the open-country cemeteries of rural America in this analysis is unclear. Aside from a few relatively uncritical surveys and massive amounts of genealogically inspired transcriptions of gravestone legends, little systematic research has been conducted to ask how these spaces functioned in relation to the rural community. It would be interesting to know, for example, whether the arrangement of gravestones reflected the social structure of the community in any way, or whether the appearance of cemeteries can be associated with locally specific theological shifts. See Ronald W. Gerbers, "The Country Cemetery as Cultural Epitaph: The Case of Penns and Nittany Valleys, Pennsylvania" (master's thesis, The Pennsylvania State University, 1979).

56. Trautmann, "Western Pennsylvania Through a German's Eyes," 227, 225.

57. Pennsylvania State Board of Agriculture *Annual Report* (Harrisburg, 1877); G. F. Johnson, "Agriculture in Pennsylvania: A Study of Trends, County and State, Since 1840," Pennsylvania Department of Agriculture *Bulletin* 12, no. 15 (1 November 1929): 9, 47. Somerset's proportion of improved land is calculated from data on 49, combined with figures in Chen and Pasto, "Facts on a Century of Agriculture," 42, table C3. Figures on woodland and forest are from U.S. Bureau of the Census, *Statistics of Agriculture* for the census of 1880, 31. Statewide, 39 percent of the land area was in forest in 1877, and 68 percent of farmland was improved in 1880.

58. Somerset *Herald*, 4 November 1845; Somerset *Democrat*, 24 January 1883.

59. Somerset *Democrat*, 4 July 1883.

60. For examples of real estate ads mentioning meadow acreage, see the Somerset *Herald*, 4 January, 25 January, and 1 March 1871. The manuscript Census of Agriculture confirms the pattern.

61. See the farm views for field configuration and size, especially the farms of Norman D. and Agnes Hay; S. S. and Annie Flickinger; William G. and Rebecca Schrock; S. F. and Rebecca Rieman; Jacob and Mary Musser; William H. and Isabella Miller; Michael and Katherine Zimmerman; and George Dumbauld. *Casselman Chronicle*, Fall 1962, Fall 1963, and Winter 1962.

62. Somerset *Democrat*, 16 May and 14 April 1883. The local Historic Resource Survey files confirm this.

63. Note, for example, a steam planing mill at Friedline Mills, Jenner Township; a waterpower planing mill at Hooversville, Quemahoning Township; and a steam sawmill at Mineral Point, Milford Township. In the business directory, E. Durst and Co. advertised a mill producing doors, sashes, blinds, etc., and custom work done to order in Elk Lick. Beers, *County Atlas*, 110, 19.

64. Somerset *Herald*, 17 February and 8 September 1846, weatherboarding; ad for "Buck's Cottage Colors," 4 January 1871. Richard Bushman's *The Refinement of America: Persons, Houses, Cities* (New York: Knopf, 1992) outlines the spread of gentility to the country.

65. Dell Upton, *Holy Things and Profane: Anglican Parish Churches in Colonial Virginia* (New York and Cambridge, Md.: Architectural History Foundation, 1986), 102–3.

66. See Henry Glassie, *Folk Housing in Middle Virginia* (Knoxville: University of Tennessee Press, 1975); James Deetz, *In Small Things Forgotten* (Garden City, N.Y.: Anchor Books, 1977); Bushman, *Refinement*.

67. Westmoreland County estate inventories, Abraham Overholt (1870).

68. Somerset *Democrat*, 12 December 1883.

69. See Bushman, *Refinement*, 260.

70. Somerset Historical Center oral history interviews, conducted in 1992.

71. Somerset *Herald*, 10 February 1846; 28 October 1845; 30 December 1845.

72. Somerset *Whig*, 23 October 1817; see also Somerset *Herald and Farmers and Mechanics Register*, 21 October 1845, 19 January 1846 ("with water running through"), 13 April, 15 June, and 15 September 1846; Somerset *Herald and Whig*, 4 September 1867, 30 August 1865, 4 December 1867, 15 December, 6 October, and 4 May 1869 (three stories). For ads for springhouses and wash houses, see Somerset *Whig*, 23 October 1817; Somerset *Democrat*, 15 March 1876, 20 December 1876, 7 January 1880, and 31 March 1880. Jensen, *Loosening the Bonds*, 97–98.

73. For stables, see Somerset *Whig*, 23 October 1817, 15 January 1818, 17 December 1818; Somerset *Herald*, 6 January 1829, 26 January 1830 (several); Somerset *Herald and Farmers and Mechanics Register*, 21 October 1845, 8 December 1846, 27 October 1846, 15 September 1846, 21 July 1846, 10 February 1846, 17 February 1846; Somerset *Herald*, 30 September 1828; Somerset *Herald and Whig*, 6 March 1867 (with threshing floor), 2 June 1869, 14 July 1869; and many in the 1880 Somerset *Democrat*.

74. For granaries, see Somerset *Herald and Farmers and Mechanics Register*, 21 October 1845; Somerset *Herald and Whig*, 30 August 1865; Somerset *Democrat*, 16 February 1876. For stillhouses, see Somerset *Whig*, 8 October 1818; Somerset *Herald and Whig*, 4 May 1869 (two stories). For wash house, see Somerset *Herald and Whig*, 4 September 1867, and Somerset *Herald and Farmers and Mechanics Register*, 27 October 1846; Somerset *Democrat*, 20 September 1876. For smokehouse, Somerset *Herald and Whig*, 6 January 1869; Somerset *Democrat*, 16 February 1876. For a tanyard, Somerset *Whig*, 30 September 1819. For a hog pen, see Somerset *Democrat*, 12 January 1880.

75. Somerset *Democrat*, 13 December 1876; Ware, "Spotza," 50–52.

76. For the following, the Somerset *Democrat* carried ads: wagon sheds: 21 January 1880, 16 February 1876; carriage house and buggy house: 16 February 1876 and 7 January 1880, respectively; ice house: 16 February 1876; tool houses: 16 February 1876; corncrib: 7 January and 21 January 1880; sheep stable: 21 January 1880; wood house: 31 March 1880; chicken houses: 16 February 1876.

77. See the following advertisements: Somerset *Herald and Whig*, 11 January, 30 August, 6 December, and 13 December 1865, 6 October and 15 December 1869; Somerset *Democrat*, 8 September 1876 and 31 March and 13 October 1880.

78. Somerset *Herald*, 30 September 1828; Somerset *Herald and Whig*, 6 November 1867.

79. *Pennsylvania Farm Journal* (August 1851), 145–46.

80. Cable diary, 4 September and 20 November 1884; 7 January, 12 January, 17 January, and 9–11 February 1885.

81. One local resident recalled that the cows "were in the barn in winter and were milked in the 'cow platform' in the summer. This enclosure had only a trough for chop to keep the cows contented, but no roof." *Casselman Chronicle* (Winter 1962), 5.

82. See also 2 October 1878; 25 April and 6 June 1880; 6 November 1883.

83. Sarah Garee Armstrong diary, Somerset Historical Center collection, typescript (original with Indiana County Historical Society).

CHAPTER 3

1. For general surveys of American agriculture during the period, see Fred Shannon, *The Farmer's Last Frontier: Agriculture, 1860–1897* (New York: Holt, Rinehart, and Winston, 1945); Gilbert Fite, *American Farmers, The New Minority* (Bloomington: Indiana University Press, 1981); Willard W. Cochrane, *The Development of American Agriculture: A Historical Analysis* (Minneapolis: University of Minnesota Press, 1979); John L. Shover, *First Majority, Last Minority: The Transforming of Rural Life in America* (De Kalb: Northern Illinois Press, 1976); David Danbom, *Born in the Country: A History of Rural America* (Baltimore: Johns Hopkins University Press, 1995).

2. David Danbom, *The Resisted Revolution: Urban America and the Industrialization of Agriculture, 1900–1930* (Ames: Iowa State University Press, 1979); Alan I. Marcus, *Agricultural Science and the Quest for Legitimacy* (Ames: Iowa State University Press, 1985); Charles Rosenberg, "Rationalization and Reality in the Shaping of American Agricultural Research, 1875–1914," *Social Studies of Science* 7 (1977): 401–22; Margaret Rossiter, "The Organization of the Agricultural Sciences," in *The Organization of Knowledge in Modern America, 1860–1920*, ed. A. Oleson and J. Voss (Baltimore: Johns Hopkins University Press, 1979).

3. Charles Brill, "A Strike for Unionism: Somerset County, Pennsylvania, 1922–1923" (master's thesis, The Pennsylvania State University, 1955), 2, 4, 5.

4. *Report of the Department of Mines of Pennsylvania*, Part II—Bituminous (Harrisburg: n.p., 1919–20). The census bureau defined "rural" places as those with fewer than twenty-five hundred people. The figures here are for the total population, not just for employed people; they are from the published federal census summaries for 1910, 1920, and 1930.

5. Welfley, *History*, 523–27. Margaret Mulrooney, *A Legacy of Coal: The Coal Company Towns of Southwestern Pennsylvania* (Washington, D.C.: National Park Service, 1989); Mildred Allen Beik, *The Miners of Windber: The Struggles of New Immigrants for Unionization, 1890s–1930s* (University Park: The Pennsylvania State University Press, 1996); Galen Novotny, "Seeking the Public as an Ally in the Somerset County, Pennsylvania Coal Strike of 1922" (honors thesis, The Pennsylvania State University, 1996); Brill, "A Strike for Unionism"; Heber Blankenhorn, *The Strike for Union* (New York: H. W. Wilson, 1924); Hapgood, *In Non-Union Mines: Diary of a Coal-Digger, August-September 1921* (New York: Bureau of Industrial Research, n.d.); Robert Bussel, *From Harvard to the Ranks of Labor: Powers Hapgood and the American Working Class* (University Park: The Pennsylvania State University Press, 1999). Figures on mine employment and fatalities are from *Report of the Department of Mines*, 28, 47.

6. For example, by 1924, 86 percent of county farmers purchased fertilizer, spending an average of $76 each. (This does not include lime.) See *Pennsylvania's Farms, Crops, and Livestock, 1926* (summary of 1924 census), Pennsylvania Department of Agriculture *General Bulletin*, no. 445 (1 May 1927).

7. Chen and Pasto, "Facts on a Century of Agriculture," 56. All farm-level 1924 figures in this chapter are from the manuscript state agricultural census.

8. See *Pennsylvania's Farms*. For an entertaining account of the auto's impact on rural life, see Reynold Wik, *Henry Ford and Grass-Roots America* (Ann Arbor: University of Michigan Press, 1982). See also Michael Berger, *The Devil Wagon in God's Country: The Automobile and Social Change in Rural America, 1893–1929* (Hamden, Conn.: Archon Books, 1979).
The local Granges passed resolutions opposing road bond issues on the grounds that they feared public indebtedness. See local Grange records, Somerset Historical Center.

9. Joseph Interrante, "'You Can't Go to Town in a Bathtub' : Automobile Movement and the Reorganization of American Rural Space, 1900–1930," *Radical History Review* (Fall 1979), 156. See also Berger, *Devil Wagon*.

10. *Pennsylvania's Farms*; Somerset *Standard*, 27 April 1905, 3 December 1917, and 17 March 1919; Emanuel Varner diary, 19 March 1890; Meyersdale *Commercial*, ads for Walter A. Wood mowing machines, 1 August 1884.

11. Somerset *Standard*, 17 May 1889; Somerset *Democrat*, 23 March 1899; Meyersdale *Commercial*, 10 March 1887; Somerset *Standard*, 1 December 1907.

12. *Pennsylvania's Farms*. Sixty-six percent of farmers grew wheat in 1880, 40 percent in 1924; 40 percent grew rye in 1880, 11 percent in 1920; 66 percent raised beef cattle in 1880, versus 30 percent in 1924; 66 percent of farms made maple sugar in 1880 and only 400 farms (out of 3,896) produced any in 1924.

13. Pennsylvania State University Extension records, Pennsylvania State University Archives, The Pennsylvania State University Libraries.

14. Ralph L. Watts, *Rural Pennsylvania* (New York: Macmillan Co., 1925), 310, 140; U.S. Bureau of the Census, summary for 1910.

15. Oral histories, Somerset Historical Center collections; home economics extension report (1934), 6. The Pennsylvania State University Archives, Extension Reports for Somerset County, Box 85.

16. The drop was from about a million pounds to a bit over three hundred thousand pounds. This was offset only slightly by a rise in syrup production (from fifteen thousand to sixty-five thousand gallons).

17. Fletcher, *Pennsylvania Agriculture and Country Life*, vol. 2, 163.

18. U.S. Bureau of the Census, 1940; see also Ware, "Spotza."

19. George Fiske Johnson, "Agriculture in Pennsylvania, A Study of Trends, County and State, Since 1840," Pennsylvania Department of Agriculture *General Bulletin*, no. 484 (1 November 1929), 31.

20. Somerset *Democrat*, 8 December 1880. These figures were calculated from census data using conversion factors from T. E. Lamont, "Agricultural Production in New York, 1866 to 1937," New York State Agricultural Experiment Station *Bulletin*, no. 693 (April 1938), 33. The equivalents are: 1 gallon of milk = 8.6 pounds; 1 gallon of cream = 8.25 pounds; it takes 10 pounds of milk to make 1 pound of cream. It takes 21 pounds of milk to make 1 pound of butter; 25.6 pounds of milk to make 1 pound of butterfat; and 10 pounds of milk to make 1 pound of cheese.

21. There is no survey of the dairy industry except for John Schlebecker's pamphlet, "A History of American Dairying" (Chicago: Rand McNally, 1967), and Ralph Selitzer's industry-sponsored *The Dairy Industry in America* (New York: Dairy and Ice Cream Field and Books for Industry, 1976). The best to date is Eric Lampard, *The Rise of the Dairy Industry in Wisconsin* (Madison: State Historical Society of Wisconsin, 1963). See also my *Transforming Rural Life*.

22. Patrick Nunnally, "From Churns to Butter Factories: The Industrialization of Iowa's Dairying, 1860–1900," *Annals of Iowa* (Winter 1989), 555–69; Nancy Grey Osterud, *Bonds of Community: The Lives of Farm Women in Nineteenth-Century New York* (Ithaca: Cornell University Press, 1991); Deborah Fink, *Open Country Iowa, Rural Women, Tradition, and Change* (Albany: State University of New York Press, 1986); Marjorie Griffin Cohen, *Women's Work: Markets and Economic Development in Nineteenth-Century Ontario* (Toronto: University of Toronto Press, 1988); McMurry, *Transforming Rural Life*.

23. The Somerset *Standard*, 12 July 1882, reported that only smaller farm operations joined.

24. By 1939, only about 13 percent of milk was churned into butter on farms, closer to the state level of about 5 percent.

25. It still is not clear what role was played by gender in this phenomenon. Women were still the main buttermakers, but we do not know much about their motivations or reactions during this period.

26. Somerset *Standard*, 1 November 1918; Emanuel Varner diary, 23 and 27 February 1885; 6 March 1885. More men churned in late-nineteenth-century New York State too. See McMurry, *Transforming Rural Life*. On the negotiation of work, see Osterud, *Bonds of Community*.

27. Fred Bateman, "Improvement in American Dairy Farming, 1850–1910: A Quantitative Analysis," *Journal of Economic History* (June 1968), 255–73.

28. Somerset *Standard*, 5 December 1907; Somerset Historical Center oral history collection.

29. The Somerset Historical Center oral history information is contained in a summary labeled "Chickens/Eggs summary," no date. Somerset *Standard*, 21 January 1897 and 14 February 1907. See also 31 October, 4 April, and 7 December 1907; *Casselman Chronicle* (Spring/Summer 1971); Pennsylvania State University Extension Records, Somerset County, 1920s and 1930s. See also Fink, *Open Country Iowa*.

30. Armstrong diary, 26 January 1880; Lehman diary, 16–17 July 1900, 1 October 1900.

31. *Casselman Chronicle* (Fall/Winter 1968); Armstrong diary; Lehman diary, 16–17 July 1900.

32. Pennsylvania State College Extension Records, Somerset County.

33. Lehman diary, 22 June and 7 July 1900; Varner diary, 2 October and 21 December 1885; Armstrong diary, 28 October and 25 November 1879; Cable diary, September 1882; F. Casebeer, "Somerset Fertilizer Production," *Laurel Messenger* 24 (August 1983): 85–87.

34. Somerset *Standard*, 6 September 1895.

35. See, for example, Pennsylvania State University Extension Reports, Somerset County, 1935, 20; a Rural Women's meeting at Edgewood Grove; and in 1932, the 4-H Club picnic (three hundred children and parents attended). Pennsylvania State University Archives, Extension Reports, Box 85.

36. McMurry, *Transforming Rural Life*, 225; James Mickel Williams, *An American Town* (New York: James Kempster, 1906).

37. Society of Farm Women Papers, Somerset Historical Center. Philip Jenkins, "The Ku Klux Klan in Pennsylvania, 1920–1940," *Western Pennsylvania Historical Magazine* 69 (1986): 121–37.

38. Brill, "A Strike for Unionism," 65.

39. Pennsylvania Department of Agriculture *Annual Report*, pt. 2, Forestry Division (Harrisburg, 1897), 189; Pennsylvania Department of Agriculture *Annual Report*, pt. 2, Forestry Division (Harrisburg, 1895), 331; *Forest Areas in Pennsylvania* (Harrisburg: Department of Forests and Waters, 1948). From 1877 to 1948, estimates of the county's forest cover stayed at around 50 percent.

40. Somerset *Democrat*, 25 April 1900. See, for example, notices in the Somerset *Democrat* for 25 April 1900 ($500,000 has been paid to local farmers); 3 January 1900 (a Rockwood farmer has sold the coal under his premises for $3,000); 13 June 1900 (A. A. Stutzman was paying farmers for coal rights). Estimates of total acreage from Welfley, *History*, 525–30.

41. John C. Cassady, *The Somerset County Outline* (Scottdale, Pa.: Mennonite Publishing House, 1932 and 1955), 213.

42. Hapgood, *In Non-Union Mines*, 19.

43. Lehman diary, 30 September and 12 December 1895. Weaver, "The Pennsylvania German House."

44. Home Economics Extension Report for 1931, 19; Pennsylvania State University Archives, Extension Records for Somerset County.

45. Varner diary, Somerset Historical Center; Somerset *Standard*, 10 May and 8 November 1889; 1 July and 28 September 1897.

46. Amos Long, "Pennsylvania Summer-Houses and Summer-Kitchens," *Pennsylvania Folklife* (Autumn 1965), 12. Oral history information gleaned from the section on kitchens in the narrative report. Dates are uncertain in many cases.

47. Interrante, "'You Can't Go to Town,'" 151–68; Katherine Jellison, *Entitled to Power: Farm Women and Technology 1913–1963* (Chapel Hill: University of North Carolina Press, 1993); Susan Ware, *Holding Their Own: American Women in the 1930s* (Boston: Twayne, 1982); Somerset County Extension Records, Pennsylvania State University Archives, Box 85. Home Economics Reports: 1940, p. 17; 1932, p. 8; 1935, p. 10.

48. This barn was erected with money from the sale of another family farm to the mining concern that built Jerome.

49. Though dairy legislation forced enclosures, these laws did not really take effect until the 1930s. Fletcher, *Pennsylvania Agriculture*, vol. 2, 217ff. The decline in herd size was from 15,151 to 13,500.

50. Somerset Historical Center oral histories, summary labeled "Dairy History," n. d.

51. Somerset *Standard*, 27 August 1908.

EPILOGUE

1. These data come from E. Willard Miller, ed., *A Geography of Pennsylvania* (University Park: The Pennsylvania State University Press, 1995), 79.

2. *1995 Somerset County Data Book* (Harrisburg: Pennsylvania State Data Center, 1995), 1.

3. Pennsylvania Agricultural Statistics Service, "Somerset County Crop and Livestock Data," *County Profiles: Somerset County* <http://www.nass.usda.gov/pa/cntymap/county.htm> (11 December 2000).

4. Green Mountain Energy Company, "New Wind Turbines Are Spinning in Pennsylvania" <http://www.greenmountain.com/electricity/choose/electricity_windfarm.asp> (11 December 2000).

5. U.S. Bureau of the Census, "U.S.A. Counties—Somerset County, Pennsylvania" <http://govinfo.library.orst.edu> (17 May 2000).

★ *index*

Numbers in italic type refer to pages with illustrations.